DEALING WITH AN
AMBIGUOUS WORLD

IPS–NATHAN LECTURES

DEALING WITH AN AMBIGUOUS WORLD

BILAHARI KAUSIKAN

Published by

World Scientific Publishing Co. Pte. Ltd.
5 Toh Tuck Link, Singapore 596224
USA office: 27 Warren Street, Suite 401-402, Hackensack, NJ 07601
UK office: 57 Shelton Street, Covent Garden, London WC2H 9HE

British Library Cataloguing-in-Publication Data
A catalogue record for this book is available from the British Library.

DEALING WITH AN AMBIGUOUS WORLD

ISBN 978-981-3201-99-6
ISBN 978-981-3202-00-9 (pbk)

Desk Editor: Sandhya Venkatesh

Typeset by Stallion Press
Email: enquiries@stallionpress.com

THE S R NATHAN FELLOWSHIP FOR THE STUDY OF SINGAPORE AND THE IPS-NATHAN LECTURES

The late S R Nathan, Singapore's sixth and longest-serving President, gave a lifetime of service to Singapore. To recognise Mr Nathan's unique contributions, the Institute of Policy Studies (IPS) began the process of setting up the S R Nathan Fellowship for the Study of Singapore in 2012, to fund further research into public policy and governance issues. With generous support from individual and corporate donors, IPS successfully raised around S$5.9 million (including the matching government grant) in 2013 to endow the Fellowship.

The IPS-Nathan Lectures series was launched in 2014 as part of the S R Nathan Fellowship. The lectures are delivered at the National University of Singapore so as to be as accessible as possible to undergraduates and the wider community. They aim to enrich the already-vibrant intellectual and cultural life on campus, by advancing public understanding and discussion of issues of critical national interest.

More information on the S R Nathan Fellowship for the Study of Singapore is available on the IPS website.

Other books in the IPS-Nathan Lectures series:

The Ocean in a Drop — Singapore: The Next Fifty Years
by Ho Kwon Ping

CONTENTS

Videos of the five lectures are available on the IPS website. Visit http://lkyspp.nus.edu.sg/ips/events/
ips-nathan-lectures

FOREWORD

These lectures deal with some international and regional issues that I believe are of importance to Singapore. It does not matter very much to me whether my compatriots agree or disagree with the substance of what I have to say. I hope of course that my arguments will not be dismissed as the mere ramblings of a pensioner. I would like them to at least provoke Singaporeans to think about these issues and form their own judgements about them.

The issues I discussed in my lectures, among others, will affect our future. If Singaporeans do not understand what is and is not possible for a city-state in Southeast Asia and make their own judgments about what is happening around us, they could be too easily swayed by external and internal influences whose foremost consideration is *not* Singapore's well-being. I fear that this may already be happening.

I am not confident that most Singaporeans do in fact think sufficiently about foreign affairs, even though the information that would enable them to do so is widely available. Singapore leaders regularly speak about external developments. Singaporeans have access to an array of international publications, and our local newspapers provide comprehensive coverage of foreign affairs. Their regular coverage of Southeast Asia is superior to most international publications.

Social media is supplanting the "mainstream media" everywhere as the preferred source of information. The latter term has even taken on a vaguely negative connotation. Social media can be useful when the source of the news is credible and the information provided is factual. But social media too often conflates facts with opinion and both with entertainment. Everyone may be entitled to an opinion, but not all opinions are born equal. It takes informed judgement to sift valid opinion from nonsense.

Our education system is admired internationally, and rightly so. But it does not adequately prepare Singaporeans to think about foreign affairs. We have de-emphasised the study of history, including our own history, in our schools. National education in schools and elsewhere is ritualised to the extent that it often evokes cynicism rather than understanding and it is to my mind an open question how much good it really does. We should rethink how we do national education and improve it.

The universities have an even more serious problem, although in their case it is not a failing peculiar to Singapore. Academics everywhere and in all disciplines are today speaking mainly to each other and about narrower and narrower slices of what they study. They too often scorn being "popular" and too often write in jargon impenetrable to all but fellow illuminati. It may not matter very much in the hard sciences; it matters a great deal in the social sciences and humanities. But I cannot really blame the academics. They get little credit for writing comprehensibly and for a wide audience: what counts for their careers and for the rankings of their universities is publication in refereed journals. I recently read that the average article in refereed journals has two or three readers.

I studied international relations. After three decades of practice, I have come to the conclusion that any resemblance between what I studied and what I did for a living is almost coincidental. International relations theory is generally too mechanical, gives insufficient weight to human agency, and is often based on premises that are irrelevant to Singapore's specific circumstances. It seems to me that the study of history, literature and philosophy is better preparation for understanding international affairs: history because we can be minimally certain only about what has already occurred; literature to deepen our understanding of human nature; philosophy to give us a broad view of issues.

Some years before I retired, I became aware of and increasingly uneasy about a tendency in our civil service to overly hedge assessments, sometimes to the point where it was difficult to grasp the point being made. I am not primarily referring to the Ministry of Foreign Affairs (MFA) or the other Ministries and agencies whose professional duty is to form judgements about international affairs. Those Ministries and agencies don't do too badly, although they too are not entirely free of this unfortunate tendency. But as I argued in the last of my lectures, it is today difficult, if not impossible, to neatly separate the foreign policy domain from other policy domains. I think that the propensity to overly hedge judgements has its roots in the way our civil service is structured. It is one example of the propensity to take a narrowly transactional and overly silo-ed approach and the risk aversion that is among its consequences. I may well be wrong about the cause, but I don't think I am wrong about the consequences which can be dangerous.

At a time when the international environment is, for all the reasons these lectures try to explain, becoming increasingly ambiguous and unpredictable, clarity of judgment becomes all the more crucial. A clear judgement can be as wrong as a fudged judgement. What I have said in these lectures may soon be exposed by events as wrong. Judgements about international affairs are intrinsically unstable: events are in constant flux and unpredictable; information is usually incomplete and sometimes deceptive. Consequently, assessments are as often wrong as right, and even when not wrong are usually only partially, situationally and contingently right. However, a clear judgement, clearly expressed, allows us to quickly recognise error and make adjustments. An overly hedged judgement conceals error.

These lectures are not just intended to argue a case; they are intended to illustrate, however imperfectly, a mode of thought that is contrary to what I fear may become the norm. And only to the extent that they succeed in this will these lectures have anything but ephemeral value.

I belong to a generation of Singapore Foreign Service officers who were privileged and fortunate enough to serve the late Mr Lee Kuan Yew, Mr S. Rajaratnam, and our other founding fathers. We served them in very humble capacities, making arrangements for their travels and taking notes at their meetings and only very much later in our careers, occasionally being asked to add our mite to their discussions. But we absorbed, almost by osmosis, something of how they thought.

Mr Lee and his comrades wielded Occam's razor with great intellectual ruthlessness. They had an almost uncanny ability to see through the pious platitudes that often obfuscate international issues and cut to the heart of even the most complex problem. It was, I think, a characteristic of a generation shaped by historical experiences more complicated, and certainly far more dangerous, than our own; woolly thinkers did not survive. The cast of thought that they developed was one of the key reasons for Singapore's success.

Mr S R Nathan, for whom this lecture series is named, is of that generation. Mr Nathan was my first Permanent Secretary. His constant admonition was to cut out the palaver and get to the point. He demanded loyalty: to friends and family, to MFA, and above all, loyalty to Singapore. Mr Nathan valued character as much as intelligence because without character, intelligence is directionless and turns selfish. He left an indelible imprint on MFA. If MFA has enjoyed any success, it rests on the foundations he laid. He was tough — he had to be to whip us into shape — but he always took responsibility for us. He gave us what he demanded from us. That is why to those of us who worked for him, Mr Nathan will forever be "The Boss".

My late father, Mr P.S. Raman, was also of that generation. It was my father who first sparked my interest in international affairs and it was from his example that I first learnt how to think about foreign affairs and diplomacy. And so when I wrote these lectures, I had my children in mind, my daughter Catherine Kamala Wei Sin P.S. Kausikan, and my son, David Raman Wei Siong P.S. Kausikan: these are some of the things I wanted to tell you.

Bilahari Kausikan
Singapore, August 13, 2016

ABOUT THE MODERATORS

Janadas Devan is the Director of the Institute of Policy Studies. He is concurrently the government's Chief of Communications at the Ministry of Communications and Information, and is also Deputy Secretary at the Prime Minister's Office.

Chan Heng Chee is an Ambassador-at-Large in the Singapore Foreign Ministry and Chairman of the Lee Kuan Yew Centre for Innovative Cities in the Singapore University of Technology and Design. She is Chairman of the National Arts Council, a Member of the Presidential Council for Minority Rights, a Member of the Constitutional Commission 2016, and Deputy Chairman of the Social Science Research Council.

Ong Keng Yong is Executive Deputy Chairman of the S. Rajaratnam School of International Studies at the Nanyang Technological University in Singapore. Concurrently, he is an Ambassador-at-Large in the Singapore Foreign Ministry, non-resident High Commissioner to Pakistan and non-resident Ambassador to Iran.

Gopinath Pillai is the Chairman of the Management Board of the Institute of South Asian Studies, National University of Singapore and an Ambassador-at-Large in the Singapore Foreign Ministry. He is also Chairman of the Indian Heritage Centre in Singapore.

Lecture I

AN AGE WITHOUT DEFINITION

Singapore is a unique country in many ways. One of our less discussed peculiarities is that although there can be few countries more exposed to and dependent on the international environment than we are, the level of public interest in and understanding of foreign policy is not high. Indeed I sometimes think of us as rather parochial. I must confess that for much of my career as a Foreign Service Officer I found it convenient to practise my trade without the distractions and complications of public attention that bedevil the diplomats of other countries. But I have since come to the conclusion — and not just because I am now safely retired with no executive responsibilities — that this is not only unsustainable, but undesirable.

Our domestic politics are becoming more complex. A more educated electorate is demanding a greater voice in policy. It is inevitable that sooner or later this will include foreign policy. This is not necessarily a bad thing since successful foreign policy must ultimately rest on a firm domestic consensus of shared assumptions. Such a foundation does not yet exist in Singapore. In its absence, foreign policy is being drawn into the arena of partisan politics in ways that could be kindly called naïve, but I think is more accurately described as irresponsible. We will increasingly need the ballast of an informed and realistic public understanding of foreign policy to keep us on a safe course.

At present, debates over domestic policies more often than not take place devoid of context, as if what we do on this tiny island can be entirely insulated from what is happening around us or as if we have an entirely free hand to do as we please. This can be dangerous. At the very least it leads to the loss of a sense of proportion when discussing domestic policies. Singapore is in a paradoxical situation: too many of our compatriots, particularly of the scribbling and chattering classes, that is to say our intelligentsia, sometimes seem almost ashamed of being Singaporean, whereas we are the object of admiration and emulation by foreigners.

This does not mean that our policies are beyond criticism. Far from it. Without criticism we cannot improve. And of course we should take the praises of foreigners, even when sincere, with a large dose of salt. But criticism must be informed by what is and is not possible for a small country situated in a complicated and often dangerous region. In a globalised world, there is no domestic policy that is not to some degree influenced by the external environment. It is unfortunate that too often foreigners seem more aware of the constraints under which Singapore labours, and hence can better appreciate what we have been able to do despite our constraints.

Singapore improbably survived and prospered over the last 50 years in no small part because of the ability of our founding generation of leaders to understand the world in which we found ourselves unexpectedly independent, and to devise policies that enabled us to navigate its dangers. I will, in this and subsequent lectures, sketch in broad strokes the changes in the external environment that we will face going forward, the strategic challenges that this will pose, and consider the extent to which we are prepared to meet them.

But first, a word or two about an aspect of foreign policy that I believe is not sufficiently understood. Its relationship to my subject may not be immediately obvious, but bear with me because I hope to make its relevance clear to those of you hardy enough to stay the course to the end of this series of lectures.

A successful foreign policy must take the world as it is and not mistake hopes for reality. This requires a clinical and indeed a cold-blooded assessment of our external environment. This is not easy. Information is almost always incomplete; obfuscation, if not downright deception, is a given and humans are unique in their innate propensity to deceive themselves. In my experience, the poorer sort of diplomat is somewhat more prone to self-deception than other members of the human species. Being called "Excellency" all the time doesn't make you excellent.

But there is also a more fundamental problem. Foreign policy deals with sentient beings that act and react with one another. The very effort to understand our environment changes what we are trying to understand. This makes the human world, which includes the realm of foreign policy, different from the material world that conforms to the laws of physics. A rock is a rock and will forever be only a rock. But human relations, including international relations, are a constantly shifting kaleidoscope of unpredictable patterns of possibilities. The result is complexity that, if not entirely unfathomable, is at least difficult for the human mind to grasp in a holistic way.

We cannot live in a state of perpetual perplexity or doubt; foreign policy cannot be made by Hamlets.

To deal with complexity we, whether consciously or not, resort to mental frameworks to simplify reality in order to comprehend it, in order to act. Simplification must result in some degree of distortion. And since we do not all choose to use the same frameworks, we do not all see or experience anything in exactly the same way. Moreover, all these frameworks — international law, international organisation, international community, all the concepts we use to try to make sense of international relations, indeed the very notion of "international relations" itself — are essentially human constructs that have little autonomous existence beyond what we invest in them by choosing to believe in their utility. And since we do not all share the same beliefs and what we believe changes, they are all at best always only partially and contingently true.

I do not want to exaggerate the point. We cannot just live happily in our own private worlds. In practice, there is usually a great deal of consensus among states on the basic premises and frameworks of international relations. And there are physical realities that prescribe the range of mental frameworks that we can rationally choose to believe in, for example, that Singapore is a small country and not a continent, located in Southeast Asia not the South Pacific. The human world does not have quite the same status as the material world but nevertheless has its own insistent reality that we ignore only at our peril.

There is nevertheless always some measure of choice, not always conscious, involved in the selection of what frameworks to use. Thereby arises the possibility of error; human nature being as it is, it is seductively easy to believe that *our* choices, *our* ideas, must be immutable facts that brook no alternatives. The highly educated and highly intelligent are more prone to this sort of error. Adam Smith is credited with the observation that "the learned give up the evidence of their senses to preserve the coherence of the ideas of their imagination." When this occurs — when the gap between our mental frameworks and reality grows too wide — the results are not pretty.

After the 2008–2009 global financial crisis, Alan Greenspan, the former Chairman of the US Federal Reserve confessed that his intellectual assumptions of a lifetime had been shaken and he was still trying to understand what had happened. He has since written a book to explain why economic forecasters failed so miserably. I haven't read it so I do not know his conclusions. But it is not my impression that the market fundamentalism and the political dysfunctionalities that were clearly among the factors responsible for the financial crisis have gone away. It is a cliché but nevertheless true that the hardest thing to change is a mind.

I believe the world is now at greater risk of this kind of error. We are in a phase of greater than usual international uncertainty.

The proximate cause was the end of the Cold War. President Putin of Russia is notorious in the West for describing the collapse of the Soviet Union as "the major geopolitical disaster of the century". In human terms for former Soviet citizens — particularly ethnic Russians, whose psychological bearings were cast adrift overnight, many of whom found themselves trapped in the often hostile environments of newly independent former Soviet republics — this was no more than a statement of fact. But one need not be infected with nostalgia for the glories, real or imagined, of the Soviet past or sentimental about the Cold War, to appreciate Mr Putin's comment on other grounds.

For almost half a century after the end of the Second World War, our fundamental understanding of the world — the basic mental framework that all states held in common — was the Cold War. It established the essential processes of international relations for us all. Irrespective of which side of the ideological divide we stood, and even if we tried to steer clear of either side by a policy of Non-Alignment — which was always for the majority of the Movement more pretence than real — the Cold War prescribed the parameters of the possible for us all with a stark and brutal clarity.

Despite its dangers, and they were great, the Cold War had one virtue — a clearly defined structure. The very danger gave the structure sharp resolution. Clarity and danger created order. The early Cold War saw several US-Soviet crises in the Caribbean, Berlin and the Middle East. But direct superpower confrontation soon proved too dangerous, and by the mid-1960s their competition largely manifested itself through proxies in peripheral regions where defeat or victory engaged no vital interests of the superpowers.

The result was what one scholar has called "The Long Peace". This was of course peace between the superpowers. It was not very peaceful for those careless, reckless, foolish or unfortunate enough to become proxies. But for prudent or lucky states on the periphery — and prudence creates its own luck — there was never very much doubt about how to position ourselves within the Cold War structure to avoid getting entangled in superpower proxy wars and perhaps even obtain some modest advantage from their rivalry. Singapore was among them.

That clarity of choice is gone and will not be recreated. We now have danger — although of a lesser magnitude — without clearly defined structure. No one really knows what will, or can, replace the Cold War structure. It has been a quarter of a century since the Berlin Wall came down and the Soviet Union imploded, yet we can still only define our times by reference to the age that preceded it: we still call this "the post-Cold War". We live in an age without definition.

There was a brief post-Cold War moment when one country seemed to hold all the levers of the world in its hands. The western side of the Cold War structure was entirely an American creation. The US and the Soviet Union both claimed to embody universal values. Once the latter was discredited and Moscow's Cold War structure dissolved, there seemed no alternative to American-led institutions, American power, American values and American ideas. History had ended. The economic analogue was "The Great Moderation" whereby the genius of American economists had reduced the complexity of economic systems and human behaviour to neat mathematical formulas, and harnessed the market to once and for all tame the business cycle.

By the end of the first decade of the 21st century, these delusions were dispelled by the failed wars in Iraq and Afghanistan and the near meltdown of Wall Street. Barack Obama rode the backlash into the White House. The general view regards his election as the vindication of American values. Perhaps. But I take the contrarian view that the very improbability of Mr Obama's election reflects disillusionment with the post-Cold War definition of American values and a groping after a different and more authentic definition. This at least in part explains the resonance of Obama's campaign slogan of "change". But expectations were so high that he was almost bound to disappoint. The unseemly and bewildering spectacle of the current primary campaigns — Republican and Democrat — suggests that the search for a new definition is still on-going, with an undercurrent of something akin to hysteria.

Without global structure, global leadership is diffused. Without global leadership many urgent international issues — take your pick, anything from climate change to nuclear proliferation to refugees to pandemics and more — will be left unresolved or dealt with only sub-optimally, enhancing the uncertainties. By the time of the 2008–2009 financial crisis it was clear that the brave new post-Cold War world order had not turned out quite as orderly as President George H.W. Bush, who had confidently proclaimed it, had expected, and that existing international institutions were inadequate to cope with such new types of crises.

Enter the G-20. At the Pittsburgh G-20 Summit in 2009, President Obama announced that the G-20 would replace the G-8 as the "premier forum" for international economic cooperation. The significance of his statement went beyond finance and economics. In effect, he was acknowledging that the American-led Cold War structure could not be the sole basis of a post-Cold War global structure.

The G-20 was thus heralded by some as a sign that the brief post-Cold War unipolar moment had been replaced by multipolarity. The term is imprecise but insofar as multipolarity implies a rough symmetry of power between different "poles" this is not a multipolar world and it is far from clear that it will become multipolar in the foreseeable future. Despite its manifold problems, the US is still at the pinnacle of the international hierarchy in almost every dimension of power and is likely to remain there. If there is multipolarity, it exists only at the regional level. The US is still the only truly global power. But it is also a power whose limits are now evident.

Ian Bremmer of the Eurasia Group has described the contemporary global order as G-Zero. It is a striking metaphor. But insofar as this conveys the image of a formless world, it overstates the case. The American order may be fraying at its edges and inadequate, but it has not disappeared. The G-20 has proved useful, but only within narrow and specialised parameters. The G-20 coexists in a not entirely coordinated fashion with the United Nations (UN) system and the Bretton Woods institutions. The UN, the World Bank, the International Monetary Fund (IMF) and other such institutions all still have their uses. But all are also to some degree dysfunctional; sometimes by design, sometimes because their original design was conceived under very different historical conditions after the Second World War. None is likely to be significantly reformed. We do not face a blank slate to write thereon whatever we please. This poses a different kind of challenge.

As the only truly global power, US leadership is irreplaceable. But it clearly cannot now exercise leadership alone. This is not new. The US did not exercise leadership alone during the Cold War. But without the strategic imperatives of the Cold War, there is no compelling reason for other major powers — US allies included — to accept US leadership except on an ad hoc and partial basis, which adds to the uncertainties of our time. There is also no compelling reason for the American people to continue shouldering the burdens and sacrifices of leadership. But which country or group of countries has the capacity to, or is inclined to, provide sustained help to the US?

Europe? The Transatlantic Alliance was the major pillar of the Western Cold War structure. But the end of the Cold War has deconstructed the idea of the "West" and made explicit what were once implicit nuances between European values and American values. The most liberal American — I use the term in its American sense of willingness to use state power to shape domestic economic and social outcomes — is less interventionist than the most conservative European, and I again use the term in its American sense of being for a minimal state. These differences could conceivably be managed. But Europe is now also tangled in knots of its own making and has neither the energy nor the appetite to take on global responsibilities, although for reasons of *amour propre* it occasionally pretends to do so, not always with happy results.

At the very heart of the post-Cold War European idea is a fundamental contradiction. The EU was conceived of as a post-nationalist construct. Ironically it was inspired by nationalist fears of a superior nationalism. Germany is larger than any other European state. After Bismarck united Germany in the 19th century, the "German Question" led to two world wars. It resurfaced in 1989 after the respite of Cold War division. A reunited Germany was to be tamed by the "pooling of sovereignties", the centrepieces of which were the common currency and the Schengen Agreement.

But the ambition, once launched, soared beyond Germany. Europe as a community of values was intended to be a new kind of global power. There was to be a new and superior pan-European identity based on an ideal of universal rights and a generous social model. This was as much a delusion as the communist dream of creating a "new socialist man". Nationalism cannot be wished away. The instinct to define oneself by distinguishing like from the "other" is an intrinsic and primordial part of human nature. Any political project undertaken in defiance of human nature is bound to eventually fail. In this respect the EU stands as a prime example of the futility and danger of letting mental frameworks, however appealing or noble, outrun reality.

European elites deeply believe in their utopian vision of Europe and the elite answer to any obstacle to the realisation of this vision has generally been "more Europe". But the man-in-the-street, *rue, strasse* or *calle* clearly does not agree with his enlightened betters and we are now witnessing the *denouement* of the internal contradictions of the post-Cold War European idea. The rise of extreme right-wing, neo-fascist anti-EU movements is one manifestation. The Eurozone crisis is another. Was it ever realistic to expect Greeks to behave with the fiscal discipline of Germans? Cultural differences, the social norms they generate and ultimately the differing conceptions of the "good life" do matter. But these are not the worst consequences of the divergence between ideal and reality.

I have never made a secret of my scepticism about the wilder boundaries of the European idea. In response, a European friend — and contrary to the belief of some, I do have several European friends — urged patience. It may take another generation or more, he said, but we will get there. Already young Europeans have embraced the idea of Europe far more enthusiastically than their parents or grandparents, he argued. Who are these young Europeans,

I asked. Are they all middle-class, white, employed, at least nominally Christian or secular? He changed the subject. Too many non-white, Muslim Europeans face discrimination, ghettoisation and disproportionately high levels of unemployment, making them in effect a class of *untermensch*. Is it too fanciful to think that the divergence between the lofty European ideal and the grim reality they experience makes them susceptible to radicalisation? The Paris attacks, and those in London before that, were carried out by such second-generation "Europeans". The flood of Middle-Eastern refugees and illegal immigrants can only exacerbate the situation.

I take no joy in Europe's travails. In our own interests we must hope that Europe sorts itself out as soon as possible. But this requires a scaling down of ambition to close the gap between ideal and reality. Among other things this must entail acceptance of a more sustainable social model, some form of fiscal regime policed by Berlin and above all, a painfully wrenching redefinition of European values and the meaning of being European. It will not be easy. Things will probably have to get worse and there will be many a futile gyration to evade reality before the inevitability of change is accepted.

The result will be a different and hopefully a more humble Europe. But certainly not one that can offer an alternative global vision. A "common security and foreign policy" if not abandoned entirely, is unlikely to remain more than a pious aspiration. Europe bungled in the Balkans, bungled in North Africa, and its fecklessness was a major cause of the crisis in Ukraine. Rather than Europe helping the US, it was the US that pulled Europe's chestnuts out of all these fires on Europe's own borders. From 1989 to 2014, the defence budgets of all EU members except Estonia stagnated or declined. Terrorist threats and a resurgent Russia notwithstanding, I do not expect significant increases in European defence budgets. Soft power is no substitute for hard power; you cannot have the former if you do not have the latter and contemporary Europe simply cannot afford to be a global geopolitical force.

America's East Asian allies — Japan, the Republic of Korea, Australia and New Zealand — can at best help mainly in their own region and only sporadically elsewhere. And even in East Asia, as I will explain in a subsequent lecture, they are being subjected to powerful new forces that threaten to circumscribe what they can do.

Can the BRICS — Brazil, Russia, India, China and South Africa — help? I doubt it, at least not in any significant way. Let us not forget that the term was first coined by a fund manager as a marketing slogan designed to part the unwary from their money and not as a geopolitical concept. Since then much of the lustre has worn off these emerging markets and while the BRICS now hold regular Summits and other meetings, have established a secretariat of sorts, and there is even a BRICS Bank, it is still not a self-evidently viable geopolitical concept.

Not much unites the BRICS except the desire for greater recognition of their status. Their ambitions are contradictory or I think will eventually prove contradictory: does China support India's aspiration to become a Permanent Member of the UN Security Council? Moscow and Beijing now insistently profess partnership, perhaps too insistently, but can Chinese and Russian ambitions in Central Asia really be reconciled? What coherence the BRICS have as a group is provided by their economic links with China, which trades and invests more with each of the others than the rest do with one another, and China's central role in the group is not regarded by the others without ambivalence. In any case, Brazil and South Africa play only relatively limited regional roles which are not uncontested by others in their regions.

Russia is a dissatisfied power, still smouldering with resentment at the loss of superpower status. Its main motivation is to prove that it still matters, particularly in its "near abroad". The story of American and European relations with Russia in the 1990s was one of squandered opportunity. In the immediate post-Cold War period, the US and Europe made a serious strategic mistake by treating post-Soviet Russia condescendingly as a defeated country, and Moscow believes, not without justification, that promises made at the end of the Cold War were not honoured because it was weak. In economic and demographic terms Russia is on a long-term downward trajectory. Still for now it has the political will and sufficient muscle to demonstrate that its core interests, as in Ukraine and Syria, cannot be disregarded with impunity. Russia is not irrational and will cooperate with the West when its interests dictate it should. But it has no viable new global vision and is not in a position to exercise a global geopolitical role except in a formal diplomatic sense as a Permanent Member of the UN Security Council.

Unlike Russia, India is not a dissatisfied power. Independent India has always had a global vision of itself. But that very vision has made it wary of playing any other major power's game. Acutely conscious of its ancient civilisation, it certainly will not play deputy to the US sheriff but seek an independent role. Does India's capability match its vision? Not yet. India is reforming. Its long-term prospects are good. Prime Minister Modi clearly wants to change India, but change does not come quickly to a subcontinental-sized country where each constituent state is practically a country unto itself. And notwithstanding its global vision, governing a vast, bewilderingly complicated democracy will always absorb most of any Indian government's energies. India more naturally looks inwards than outwards.

In practice, India's main external preoccupation is Pakistan, perhaps too much so, but understandably given their history and Pakistan's longstanding ties with China. India fought and lost a brief but traumatic war with China in 1962. Its illusions of Chinese-Indian brotherhood shattered, India then spent decades trying its best to ignore China, interacting only at the margins. It no longer has that luxury, but still does not quite know how to deal with China and so eyes it warily, while flirting with China's other Asian rival, Japan. But despite the apparent coincidence of strategic interests — promoted, or at any rate hyped, by their current Prime Ministers — I cannot think of two more mutually incomprehensible Asian cultures than India and Japan. This is not a partnership whose closer evolution as part of a new global structure is to be taken as a given.

Any new global order must have US-China relations as a central pillar. But we are still far from a G-2 world and it is not a forgone conclusion that it will ever be a G-2 world. I will deal with US-China relations in detail in a subsequent lecture. For now, it suffices to note only a few points.

First, US-China relations defy simple characterisation. China and the US are clearly not enemies. Neither can they be clearly said to be friends or natural partners. In this respect, US-China relations exemplify one of the most salient characteristics of post-Cold War major power relations: ambiguity. Profound interdependence of a new type coexists with equally profound strategic mistrust. The same is true of EU-Russia relations, Sino-Indian relations and Sino-Japanese relations.

Second, the main beneficiary of the end of the Cold War was not the "West" but China. Freed of the constraints imposed by its de facto membership of the US-led anti-Soviet alliance which it accepted out of necessity, but still largely a free-rider globally and so without onerous international responsibilities, China has since the 1990s been free to single-mindedly pursue its own interests. It plugged itself more successfully than any other major developing country into the opportunities afforded by post-Cold War globalisation and thus rose with the results we all know.

Third, what will China do with its new status and power? That is not so clear, perhaps not even to China's own leaders. As the main beneficiary of the existing order, China has no strong incentive to kick over the table. Neither has it any deep attachment to a system that is heir to the order it holds responsible for "a hundred years of humiliation". Deng Xiaoping advised: "Hide your strength, bide your time". Has that time now come? I would not rush to any conclusion one way or the other. President Xi Jinping has been more ambitious than any of his predecessors since Mao Zedong in articulating an international vision for China. But it is primarily an East Asian and Eurasian and not a global vision, and the vision lacks detailed resolution; still more a "China Dream" than a China plan. Nor has China been consistent in either the articulation of its interests or its actions. Even in East Asia where Chinese and US interests most directly intersect, I do not believe that either China or the US yet precisely knows what they want from each other, even as they seek a new accommodation with each other.

The world now finds itself in an indeterminate situation. There is no satisfied country powerful enough to maintain the existing global order by itself; nor is there any satisfied country that can offer consistent help to maintain the existing global order. There is no country that is simultaneously dissatisfied enough and powerful enough to change the existing global order. The uncertain interregnum that we now find ourselves in is likely to last a long time, perhaps decades and not just a few years.

Why was the promise of a new post-Cold War world order not fulfilled? One key factor was the US attitude in the immediate post-Cold War period, which proved self-defeating and made it more difficult than necessary for other major powers to swallow American leadership. The fundamental error was to misinterpret the meaning of the end of the Cold War and the collapse of the Soviet Union, and to conflate these related but distinct events.

The Soviet Union undoubtedly failed. But did America or the "West" unambiguously win? What does "winning" in this context mean anyway? What is the "West" that allegedly won? In the rush of events these questions, among others, were insufficiently probed.

Almost two years separate the fall of the Berlin Wall and the collapse of the Soviet Union. And the US or the "West" generally was not necessarily the key actor. Would the Cold War have ended in the way it did had Mikhail Gorbachev not been inclined to make the decisions he did with regard to the reunification of Germany and Soviet forces in East Europe? He could have resisted. But arguably Gorbachev had already concluded that his attempts to reform the Soviet system required the end of Cold War tensions, and the Soviet Union collapsed not because of the end of the Cold War but despite the end of the Cold War. Could Gorbachev's reforms have succeeded, as reforms did in China's essentially similar Leninist system, had Gorbachev's vanity not caused him to foolishly confuse Western flattery for domestic support and pursue *glasnost* ahead of *perestroika*, fatally loosening the Communist Party of the Soviet Union's control at a crucial time? Would the Soviet Union have collapsed so suddenly if not for the personal antagonism and rivalry between Boris Yeltsin and Gorbachev and the ambitions of the leaders of the constituent republics of the Soviet Union, particularly the Ukraine?

There is of course no way of answering these questions definitively just as there is no way of dismissing them entirely, and that is the point. History is replete with contingencies and the consequences of human agency are intrinsically unpredictable and often more limited than the actors may have thought. The memoirs President George H.W. Bush co-authored with his National Security Advisor Brent Scowcroft, as well as other studies of the end of the Cold War, make clear that the decision to accept German reunification was not easy and Chancellor Kohl in effect forced the hands of America and his European partners. From other sources, we now know that the Berlin Wall was breached because a nervous German Democratic Republic spokesman bungled an answer at a press conference and in the resulting confusion no one knew what to do when hordes of East Germans rushed the Wall. In his memoirs, President Bush explicitly said that he was reluctant to force the break-up of the Soviet Union because of concern about control of the Soviet nuclear arsenal. In the end Scowcroft recalled: "We could actually do very little one way or the other to influence the outcome…."

That modest judgement was of course *ex post facto*. The memoirs were written when passions had cooled and published eight years after the Soviet Union collapsed. The attitude at the time was very different. In his 1992 State of the Union Address, President George H.W. Bush declared: "By the grace of God, America won the Cold War". He went on to describe a US-centric view of the future: "A world once divided into two armed camps now recognises one sole and pre-eminent power, the United States of America. And this they regard with no dread. For the world trusts us with power, and the world is right."

Naked American triumphalism was given a superficial intellectual gloss by Francis Fukuyama's infamous article in the neoconservative journal *The National Interest*, arguing that with America's victory, "History" had ended. History took no notice of Professor Fukuyama's theories and went rolling bloodily along, manifesting itself among other ways, through genocide in Rwanda and vicious wars of ethnic cleansing in the former Yugoslavia. Undeterred, the good Professor then wrote an entire book insisting that history had indeed ended in the special philosophical sense he meant, but the rest of us were insufficiently erudite to understand or notice. It was not until the wars in Iraq and Afghanistan — at least in part inspired by universalist theories such as those he propounded — proved unwinnable, that Professor Fukuyama thought it prudent to write yet another book denying that he had ever been a neoconservative. He has since occupied himself writing hefty tomes on other subjects and, I believe, occasionally lecturing at the Lee Kuan Yew School of Public Policy.

Making fun of the learned is akin to shooting fish in a barrel; not very sporting perhaps, but too tempting to resist. In any case, I can seldom resist the temptation. My purpose this time is however a serious one: to illustrate the stubborn persistence of mental frameworks, irrespective of their appropriateness and in defiance of empirical evidence. And despite the accumulated weight of evidence, the universalist impulse still lingers in more invidious ways and continues to have real effects on policy.

I have already alluded to the way it was used to justify an ill-considered war to effect regime change in Iraq. The 2003 war shook confidence in American leadership from which America has yet to fully recover. It precipitated a split in the Transatlantic Alliance and the EU. France and Germany led defiance of America; Blair's Britain enthusiastically embraced the war. Yet the same universalist impulse, lurking under the guise of humanitarian intervention, later led France and some other EU members of NATO into equally ill-considered bombing campaigns to try to change regimes, successfully in Libya, unsuccessfully in Syria.

If American allies were disquieted, what impact would it have had on countries like China, Russia, India and in the Middle-East and Southeast Asia?

Inappropriate mental frameworks may not matter very much when the international order is settled. They matter a great deal in times of international uncertainty when basic assumptions are shaken and the global order lacks clear definition. It is precisely in those times when the human mind, discombobulated by too much uncertainty, most desperately and thus uncritically seeks out frameworks that will give the comfort of familiarity and comprehension in the midst of disorienting flux. Oftentimes the comfort is illusionary. Contemporary examples are slogans like "A New Cold War" or "Asia Rising" as well as theories like the so-called "Thucydides Trap" or "A Clash of Civilizations" or analogies with pre-First World War Europe. I believe they are all at best over-simplifications; at worse, dangerous nonsense.

The basic strategic challenge facing all of us in times of international uncertainty is: how do we position ourselves to preserve the widest range of options and avoid being forced into invidious choices? This is more difficult than the basic Cold War challenge of choosing wisely. When the international structure lacks clear definition, when major power relationships defy simple characterisation and the major powers are themselves groping towards new accommodations with each other, we have no firm landmarks from which to take bearings and we can only navigate with reference to our own assessments. And if our assessments are based on false frameworks, we might well mistake rocks and shoals for safe passage.

Questions and Answers
Moderator: Janadas Devan

Janadas Devan: I would like to say a few words about this year's S R Nathan Fellow. There is nobody better than Bilahari Kausikan to talk about Singapore's foreign policy. His won't be an academic view — his view is from the foxhole. His views arise from the crucible of experience. He marshals his thought, his thinking on our foreign policy, to do battle for Singapore, and he has done it over his lifetime. He has served every foreign minister since Mr S. Rajaratnam, and he has worked with all three of Singapore's prime ministers. And indeed, if you want to know how the founding fathers, the first formulators of Singapore's foreign policy, how, not what they thought; if you want to eavesdrop on the conversation between Dr Goh Keng Swee and Mr Rajaratnam and Mr Lee Kuan Yew about our foreign policy, there is nobody better to listen to than Bilahari Kausikan. We now have around 30 minutes for questions.

Question: Can I invite you to be more self-critical about our own region? Is it completely illusory that we try and aim towards an ASEAN Economic Community (AEC)? What were the false assumptions that people made, or is there clear strategic value to the AEC?

Bilahari Kausikan (BK): The essential and enduring purpose of ASEAN is to enable the small states of Southeast Asia — the biggest of us is small; all of us combined are small compared to the major powers — to retain some measure of autonomy in the midst of great power competition, initially in a Cold War context and now in a post-Cold War context which, as I've tried to explain, is more complicated than the Cold War context. In a sense, everything ASEAN does, including all our community-building efforts, are means towards that end. They are as important as means as they are as ends in themselves.

"Community" is probably too loaded a term to describe what we are doing because we adopted the term from the EU at a time when the EU's feet of clay were not so evident. Community implies supra-nationality, and that's not on anybody's agenda in any of our community pillars except in a very limited way in the dispute settlement mechanism of the AEC. That mechanism has never been tested and I suspect may never be tested.

We have now reached the end of one phase of the economic integration project. We have not done badly so we could declare victory for this phase with some credibility. The problem is what we do next. We have done all the easy things, so what we do next is going to be more difficult. And some of the complexities that I have described are going to play into this as well as complexities in the domestic politics of individual ASEAN member states.

Question: Professor Kishore Mahbubani wrote a book titled *The New Asian Hemisphere*, which emphasises a shift in power towards the East. With regards to that, is it evident that something is happening with the reclamation works in the South China Sea?

BK: It is very clear that China is rising. You have to be blind, deaf, dumb and living in a different dimension not to see that. It is the latest phase of a process of change in East Asia that began with the Meiji Restoration in Japan.

Question: From your lecture earlier, I got the sense that we did quite well in the last 50 years in terms of foreign policy. Can you give more context to this? We were relatively weaker then and we are stronger and hopefully better now. And actually, the environment has changed so much that if we are not careful, we may do worse than what we used to.

BK: I entirely agree with you. When we became unexpectedly independent, we didn't even have a foreign ministry. We had no idea of foreign policy. We had some experience in other aspects of governance, but not foreign policy because we never expected to be independent. In fact, even when I joined the foreign ministry in 1981, the entire political division of the foreign ministry was about maybe 20 people. That's about the size of our divisions that deal with Southeast Asia today. There's a story about Mr Rajaratnam — perhaps apocryphal, but which captures those times just after we were kicked out of Malaysia. There was a press conference that he had to give as the new Foreign Minister. He asked Mr Lee Kuan Yew, "What shall I say?", and back came the answer "Just wear a tie, Raja, you'll think of something!"

Obviously, we are much better prepared now — we can't be worse prepared! But as you yourself pointed out, and I entirely agree, the nature of the challenges have changed, the nature of Singapore has changed, and while I am not pessimistic, I think we have to be aware of the changes and the challenges in order to deal with them.

Question: Is there something that you used to worry about, that you're not worried about anymore? If not, is there something that you think worries everyone right now except you?

BK: What I worry about is people not worrying — and there have been signs of that, of people taking things for granted. For instance, some people have, under the guise of academic research, tried to plant the idea into our political debate that we are not vulnerable after all, or that we did not start from such a small base and that we were quite developed in 1965. Yes, we were more developed in 1965 than many other countries, but there were many other countries that were more developed than us in 1965 and look at them now. So that worries me a lot. What other people are worried about that I am not worried about I don't know because I am not clairvoyant — I cannot read other people's minds.

Question: It is quite legendary, your discomfort with academics, but now you're a thought leader by sitting on that stage. I would like to challenge you — what would be some of the fundamental tenets of a Bilahari School of International Relations?

BK: My fundamental tenet is not to have any school because once you have a school of thought, you are trapped in one framework and you are going to be in deep trouble. By the way I am not against academics in general — I once almost became one which is probably a close shave for both the university and for me — I am against silly academics. I am against stupidity.

Question: After the 1989 fall of the Berlin Wall, was the Ministry of Foreign Affairs (MFA) scared shitless? Or did the Ministry see this as an opportunity?

BK: We, like everybody else, were caught by surprise. We had no idea what would happen next. It was clear that one worry — a constant worry — during the Cold War was over. It was clear that one manifestation of the Cold War that preoccupied my generation of Foreign Service officers and from which we learnt our trade (the Vietnamese invasion and occupation of Cambodia) was coming to an end. But we had no clue about what would happen next, and I don't think we were alone in that. In retrospect, it was better to be clueless than to be overconfident.

For a small country, foreign policy is always very largely a series of improvisations. Actually this is also true for big countries but they take more convincing that it is so. I have never understood why some people are fixated on the idea of grand strategy. Grand strategy is to my mind a very abstract concept that really has very little relationship to what you need to do on a day-to-day basis. You cannot predict the future with any great certainty. For small countries, you don't even have the illusion that some big countries have, that they can control events to the nth degree. So all you can do is improvise — that's what we did before, and that's what we did after the fall of the Berlin Wall, and that's what we do right now and we will continue to do. Of course, improvise with an idea of where you want or need to go, but still improvising how to get there. My worry, to go back to an earlier question, is that complacency and certain other factors which I will deal with in the last lecture, may, if we are not careful, erode the nimbleness of mind and policy that is needed to improvise in a rapidly-changing world.

Question: What role would water and energy play in shaping foreign policy in the future?

BK: These are fundamental issues. The fact that the US is no longer totally dependent on Middle East oil is a big factor. It doesn't mean the US can now ignore the Middle East because many of America's friends and allies are still dependent on its oil — but this is certainly going to shape events in a certain way. Obviously the universalist ideologies were one factor in the way the US and the West perceived the Arab Spring and responded to it. The hesitation over supporting [former Egyptian President Hosni] Mubarak or not, was due to many factors. But I often wonder would the US have dithered that much and finally abandoned him if the energy factor had not already carried less weight in its calculations by that time. The Middle East is still the primary source of China's energy. China now relies on the 5th Fleet and 7th Fleet to protect its energy supply routes. Now this is unsustainable — for a major power to rely on another major power to protect something as vital as energy — so China is going to develop a blue water navy. Will that be a factor of cooperation because, in principle, the US and China have the same interests, or will it be a factor of competition? How it will affect other powers like Japan and India, I don't know, but it will certainly affect them in some way.

Water is obviously a very vital thing. It is now no longer secret because the former head of the Malaysian Armed Forces spoke about it in an interview and I have quoted him on several occasions. He said that Lee Kuan Yew had once told him that if anybody tried to interfere with our water supply from Johor, he would move the Singapore Armed Forces in. That kept the Malaysians honest, as far as water is concerned. It is maybe not such a vital factor anymore because we have it within our means to become self-sufficient in water, although it is certainly still very important. But it is certainly going to be a factor in other parts of the world. China has plans to build many dams in the upper reaches of the Mekong. This gives them, at least potentially, a hold on five ASEAN countries that rely on the Mekong.

Now I'm not saying that China is going to use this to squeeze them, I don't know that; the Chinese themselves probably don't know too at this point of time. Laos is also building dams, and the Chinese built a dam for Ethiopia in the upper reaches of the Nile, which is causing immense problems and angst among the downstream states. Water is a scarce resource. How this will play out, I can't tell you right now. But energy and water are going to be major factors.

Question: What do you think of the current calibre of the Foreign Service officers in the MFA to advance Singapore's interests compared to those of your time?

BK: The quality of young Foreign Service Officers is generally much better than us. Frankly, with the selection process in place now, I am not sure I would get in if I applied today. Our independence was unexpected. MFA had to recruit people in a great hurry and those recruited had little if anything by way of training to prepare them for the job. We now have a very elaborate selection process and systematic training. As a result, the younger officers are better.

There is one difference though, which is very hard to make up for. Since we were so small then, we all had to do everything, and we had to do it at a very young age without too much preparation, and you either learnt to swim or you sank. We now have a better formal preparation process for our young officers, but we are a much larger organisation so they see and deal with smaller slices of our foreign policy than I did. When I joined I was desk officer for North America but I also did Europe and much of my time was spent on Cambodia and, four months after I joined, I was sent out with a senior officer to do something in the region on the Cambodian issue because there was an emergency that suddenly cropped up and there was nobody else to deal with it. That could not happen today. We can't manufacture crises for training purposes. So while the quality is much better, the formal training is much more methodical, the preparation is better, but they don't get as much hands-on experience because we are now a bigger organisation. But I think they will cope. I have always made it a point to meet as many of the young officers as possible. They are very good.

Question: Can or should Singapore forever remain a sovereign independent country? I assume that for your series of lectures, the assumption is that every morning we take our national pledge and that Singapore is independent and sovereign. Is there the possibility that this may not be the case? If there is that possibility, what do you think could contribute to the country losing its sovereignty?

BK: That is a good question. Certainly, the purpose of all our policies, not just foreign policy, should be to keep us a sovereign and independent nation. But that is not to be taken for granted. I don't think our formal sovereignty will be compromised in the sense that somebody will invade and occupy us. That sort of thing is not very likely and we can deal with that. That's why we keep a very strong Singapore Armed Forces (SAF) to deter and prevent such evil thoughts from ever arising in anybody's mind. But that is not the only story. You can remain formally sovereign but your sovereignty can be severely compromised. There are now 193 members of the UN. They are all sovereign states, they have a seat in the UN, they have a vote in the UN, they have a flag. But for some of them, far too many of them, that's where it ends. Their sovereignty is compromised because they do not have the wherewithal to maintain it, because they are pulled hither and thither by internal conflicts, sometimes supported by external parties, and there are many other scenarios. We have to be conscious that sovereignty is not something to be taken for granted. To me the most serious threat to our sovereignty is loss of our social cohesion. Then different parts of your population are going to be pulled in different directions or become beholden to different countries outside Singapore.

Question: What do you think of the legitimacy of the Malaysian government and also, following this train of thought, how the legitimacy of a government affects foreign policy conducted with other governments?

BK: The legitimacy of the Malaysian government is something for Malaysians to decide. We will deal with any government that is in power in any country. We are not the moral police.

Question: We are living in Asia, and we hear a lot about the China Dream. So my question is if the China Dream is something for China and we wish them a good dream, or has the rest of Asia to do with the China Dream?

BK: You really have to ask the Chinese, not me, because I am not sure what it means. The China Dream is such a broad dream that there is room in it for sweet dreams, for nightmares, for anything.

Question: What is your personal opinion on young Singaporeans who want to maintain a dual passport, a dual nationality with another country? In an increasingly ambiguous world, could Singapore's policy on not allowing joint or dual nationalities be outdated?

BK: No, I don't think so. If you are not allowed dual nationality, you have to choose; you have to make some commitment one way or the other. I don't think very much of people who want to hedge.

Lecture II

US-CHINA RELATIONS: GROPING TOWARDS A NEW *MODUS VIVENDI*

U S-China relations set the tone for East Asia: when they are stable, the region is calm; when they are roiled, the region is uneasy. In time the same will hold true, I believe, for other regions as well. US-China relations will certainly be a, if not *the*, central pillar of any new post-Cold War international order.

US-China relations are mature: it has been 44 years since President Nixon's visit to Beijing transformed the global strategic landscape. US-China relations are intricately interdependent across a broad spectrum of domains. And US-China relations are infused with deep strategic distrust. The US and China are currently groping towards a new *modus vivendi* with each other and the rest of East Asia. The complexity of US-China relations, and hence the complexity of the adjustments between them that are underway, are a large part of the uncertainties of our times.

I am not clairvoyant. The purpose of this lecture is not to predict the timing, shape or nature of the future accommodation between the US and China or even if there will be one. My purpose is more modest: it is to sketch in very wide strokes some of the issues that will have to be confronted in this process. In particular, I want to deal with the roots of the strategic distrust that exists between them. Unless that is understood and dealt with, no matter how well the US and China may work together on climate change or terrorism or finance or Afghanistan or any other specific issue, a stable new equilibrium will be difficult — if not impossible — to achieve. And even if some sort of equilibrium is reached, it will be difficult to maintain.

Despite or perhaps because of their long experience of each other, US-China relations have been rife with misunderstanding. The most persistent of these misunderstandings in recent times is the notion that economic reform will lead to political reform. American attitudes towards China have oscillated between hopes and fears that perhaps say more about America than China. In the 19th century, many Americans believed that trade with China was, as John K. Fairbank, the great American historian of China, described it, "our manifest destiny under the invisible hand of divine providence". One could conclude that the illusion has persisted ever since. At any rate, when the notion of destiny, divine or otherwise, intrudes into the analysis of international affairs, trouble usually follows. Looking back, what is surprising is that despite persistent misunderstanding — usually masquerading as profound insight — there has been so little trouble, although when trouble ensues it has been spectacular, as during the Korean War.

Today the dominant attitude seems to be drifting towards regarding China as a threat, at least in the American media and political discourse. Perhaps it is, although I prefer the word "challenge". But it is in any case important to understand the nature of the challenge accurately and exaggerating the so-called "China threat" is as bad as wishful thinking. So let me state my bottom-line upfront.

Competition and rivalry are intrinsic parts of relations between all major powers. As China gains strength and confidence, it is bound to pursue its interests more assertively and acquire the instruments to do so. Former President Hu Jintao said as much in 2009 when he announced China should pursue "Four Strengths", one of which was greater influence in international politics. Since then, the People's Liberation Army (PLA) has assumed a higher profile in China's external relations, particularly in East Asia but also as far afield as the Horn of Africa. Military modernisation was one of the "Four Modernisations" announced as early as 1978, and we should not profess shock or surprise that China has now begun to acquire the military capability befitting a major power. We may consider China's military modernisation as in our interests or see it as against our interests, but China acquiring a modern military is not in itself unusual. Competition is not necessarily conflict. The important question is what use China makes of its growing military strength.

This is not a question that should lend itself to facile answers. So let me clear away some of the theoretical debris that has accumulated around it. In my first lecture I described these theories as mental frameworks that some cling to in order to comfort themselves with a false familiarity in a situation that is in fact intrinsically unfamiliar and uncertain. Clearing the debris will go some way to defining realistic parameters within which the US and China must seek a new accommodation.

In my first lecture, I described US-China relations as defying simple characterisation. But we can at least say what the relationship is not. It is certainly not a "Clash of Civilizations". For the last 200 years or so, the fundamental challenge confronting the non-western world is how to adapt to a western defined modernity. The very concept of the modern is western. All non-western countries have, in different degrees, had to change themselves. But only a handful of countries, almost all in East Asia beginning with Meiji Japan, have successfully met the challenge. China is the most important example. Communism is a western ideology. The Chinese Communist Party (CCP) is the latest and most successful iteration of a series of political experiments in search of "wealth and power" to deal with western predations that began in the late Qing Dynasty and which continue to this day.

Those East Asian countries that have most successfully adapted to the western definition of modernity, China included, have in a sense achieved the ambition of Fukuzawa Yukichi, the Meiji era reformer, of "leaving Asia and joining the West". This does not mean that we have all somehow become or will become "good westerners". What does that mean anyway?

By changing itself, China is changing the very concept of the political "West" which has now been compelled to adapt its definition of self to new realities. The changes are most pronounced in Europe. Among other things, the price Norway had to pay for giving Liu Xiaobo the Nobel Peace Prize in 2010, the cringingly obsequious welcome that President Xi Jinping received in London last year — Lord Macartney must have spun in his grave — and the spectacle of European leaders trooping to Beijing cap in hand after the

Eurozone crisis began, are visible symbols of the evolving political definition of the "West".

The US has always been a more robust and self-confident country than a tired Europe now confused and unsure about the sustainability of its own post-Cold War identity. China could not have succeeded without the US. China's success is in a very fundamental way also an American success, albeit a not entirely comfortable one for America. This perhaps makes adaptation more difficult for the US than Europe and adds in no small part to the complexity of the strategic adjustments that are underway between the US and China.

But whether it admits it or not, the US too has begun to adapt. There can be no "Clash of Civilizations" because we are now all hybrids and will become even more so. There are no "pure" traditional civilisations anywhere. If there is indeed a "Clash of Civilizations", it is not with the West as represented by the US, but between a part of the Islamic world and all else who have to whatever degree adapted to the western definition of modernity, including most Muslims.

The most objective measure of adaptation is economic development. As its economy matures and it restructures its economy, China's growth is bound to moderate. Still, according to a recent study by the East Asian Institute of this university, even at a lower rate of growth of 6.5%, China generates additional GDP that is equivalent to 80% of Indonesia's current GDP or a third of India's current GDP. China faces many challenges. I do not assume that China will continue to grow in a smooth upward trajectory. No country has ever done so. Why should we expect China to be an exception? But it would be imprudent to assume that China will fail. The CCP has a record of adaptability. It has survived many traumas that would have wrecked a less robust creature, never mind that many of those traumas were self-inflicted.

The inevitably irregular rhythms of economic growth ought to make us cautious about accepting simplistic characterisations of US-China relations as some variant of a contrast between a rising China and a declining US. This posits a false dichotomy. China is certainly rising but the US is not in decline, although if we confine our view of the US only to the political shenanigans in its capital we could be forgiven for coming to such a conclusion. But the most significant developments in America do not necessarily take place in the political arena or in Washington DC. They occur in the 50 states, in American corporations, on Wall Street and in its universities and research laboratories. All who have underestimated American creativity and resilience have come to regret it. The changes in the distribution of power are relative and not absolute. As I pointed out in my first lecture, the US is still preeminent in most indices of power and is likely to remain so for the foreseeable future.

This is most obvious in the military realm. China has carefully studied the experience of the former Soviet Union, and while it will continue to improve its military capabilities, it is not likely to make the Soviet mistake of bankrupting itself by trying to match or surpass the US in every military system or in every theatre of operations. It does not have to do so. Before too long, China will reach a more symmetrical military equation with the US in East Asia. This will have very important implications for the maritime disputes in the South China Sea (SCS) which have become something of a proxy for the strategic adjustments underway between the US and China. I will deal with the SCS in my next lecture on ASEAN and Southeast Asia. For now, suffice to say that while military planners cannot ignore any contingency, and in a system of sovereign states the possibility of war can never be entirely discounted, war is not a very probable scenario. I think war is highly improbable.

Neither the US nor China is looking for trouble or spoiling for a fight. The essential priorities of both are internal not external. Of course, neither is going to roll over and let the other tickle its tummy. That is not how great powers behave. Both will not relent in the pursuit of their own interests which sometimes will be incompatible. There will be friction and tensions. But the most vital of all Chinese interests is the preservation of CCP rule. Beijing knows that win, lose or draw — and the most likely outcome of any military conflict with the US is a loss — the CCP's grip on power will be placed in grave jeopardy.

Chinese leaders sometimes talk tough as the leaders of all great powers are wont to do. But they are not reckless. They have studied the rise of other great powers and do not want to repeat their mistakes. China has repeatedly stressed that its "rise" will be "peaceful" and has even modified the original slogan of "peaceful rise" to "peaceful development" as a less threatening formulation. President Xi Jinping has articulated an ambitious "China Dream" and he has been more assertive than his predecessor. But President Xi Jinping is a "princeling" who must regard CCP rule as his patrimony to be preserved. I doubt he will be adventurist even as he asserts China's new status externally, while grappling with the many complicated challenges that confront the CCP internally. He will not gamble with his patrimony.

There has been a historical tendency for America to look inwards after periods of intense external engagement. The wars that the US chose to fight but lost — or at least did not win — in the Middle East after 2003 were the longest in American history, longer than the Korean and Vietnam wars, longer even than the Second World War. President Obama was elected on the backlash. As the sole global power, the US cannot retreat into complete isolationism. Like it or not, the world will intrude and in East Asia specifically there has been a fundamental consistency in US policy over the last 40 years or more that I expect will be maintained. But the political mood that has sustained Donald Trump and Bernie Sanders in their unlikely Presidential campaigns is disillusionment with globalisation and working and middle class insecurity about their future in an increasingly unfamiliar and uncertain world.

There is an impression across East Asia, shared even by some American Asia specialists of both political parties, that the second Obama administration has been less engaged and weaker than the first Obama administration. This is not entirely accurate but what matters is perception. Whoever next occupies the White House will therefore probably talk and even act tougher. But no American President can ignore the national mood which is not for more wars of choice.

With both sides inclined towards prudence, I have little regard for mechanistic theories of US-China relations such as the so-called "Thucydides Trap". It is true that historically, strategic adjustments of the magnitude that are underway between the US and China have either been the result of war or ended in war. But to treat someone as an enemy is to make an enemy and the theory of the "Thucydides Trap" does not place sufficient emphasis on human agency: to recognise that there may be a trap is to go a long way towards avoiding it. In any case, China will soon acquire a credible second strike capability if it does not already have one. The prospect of Mutually

Assured Destruction has the effect of freezing the international order as it substantially did during the Cold War when, except in the Middle East, most geopolitical changes were due to internal rather than external developments. It impels caution. The primary military risk in US-China relations is conflict by accident, not war by design.

If war between the US and China is highly improbable, is there or will there be a "New Cold War" between the US and China? There will almost certainly be tense episodes. But I do not think this is an appropriate metaphor to understand the US-China dynamic.

Unlike in US-Soviet relations during the Cold War there is no fundamentally irreconcilable ideological divide between the US and a China that has now enthusiastically embraced the market. During the Cold War both the US and the Soviet Union legitimated themselves through the claim of universality for their respective systems. This made their competition a zero-sum game and the Soviet Union a revisionist power by definition even if its actual policies were often conservative. We think of the US as custodian of the status quo, but the US is also a revisionist power. Don't take my word for it: ask the Iraqis or Syrians. Every great power is selectively and simultaneously revisionist when it suits its purposes, and a staunch upholder of the status quo when it does not.

As I argued in my first lecture, while China may not be an entirely satisfied power, neither is it clearly a revisionist power. The SCS is an exception. But globally, China is still largely a free-rider. China wants its new status acknowledged, and it was never very realistic to expect China to meekly accept the role of "responsible stakeholder" — which is a polite way of describing a junior partner — in an order it had little say in shaping. But China has by and large worked within institutions such as the United Nations (UN), World Trade Organization (WTO), World Bank and International Monetary Fund (IMF) and abided by their decisions. Chinese initiatives such as the Asian Infrastructure Investment Bank (AIIB) complement existing insititutions. China has never claimed universality, except for a brief Maoist period which was but a blip in the long sweep of Chinese history. Instead China regarded itself as *the* Universe and demanded acknowledgment of that status. Something — too much, in my view — of that attitude still lingers in Chinese policies in East Asia and complicates China's relations with the US and other countries in the region. But that is a different matter from claiming universality or being revisionist.

The Soviet Union was containable because it largely contained itself by pursuing autarky. The US and the Soviet Union were linked primarily by the need to avoid mutual destruction. But China is so vital a node in the world economy and the interdependence between the US and China so deep and wide that the US might as well try to contain itself as try to contain China. This would be an exercise in futility. The US and China both know that they cannot achieve their basic national goals without working with the other. I do not think that either necessarily likes the situation they find themselves in, but both are pragmatic and accept it.

The very complexity of US-China relations — the enormous range of issues that the relationship now encompasses — generates a certain self-correcting dynamic. Whether you begin from the inclination to view the relationship through the distorting prism of democracy and human rights promotion as did the first Clinton administration in 1993, or you start from the equally distorting premise of regarding China primarily as a strategic competitor as did the neo-conservatives at the beginning of the George W. Bush administration in 2001, the very effort to balance and reconcile interests across a broad range of issues that cannot be ignored eventually drives policy to the centre. Lest you think that this is an overly sanguine conclusion, the key word is "eventually". There can be a whole lot of damage both to the relationship and collaterally to third parties before the centre is reached.

I am aware of the argument, based on what I consider a false historical analogy with Europe before the First World War, that interdependence did not then prevent Imperial Germany and the country formerly known as Great Britain from blundering into war. The classic description of European interdependence of that period was by John Maynard Keynes when he wrote of an inhabitant of London being able to "order by telephone, sipping his morning tea in bed, the various products of the whole earth". Is there a fundamental difference between the situation in Europe then and between the US and China now?

I think so and let me venture a hypothesis that I am too slothful to research and will leave to others more energetic and knowledgeable to prove or disprove if they are so inclined. The key difference is I think in Keynes' use of the word "products". The classical theory of comparative advantage holds that if I have an advantage in, say, producing beef and you have an advantage in, say, producing wine, we should each stick to producing what we have an advantage in producing and if we exchange beef for wine, we will both live happily ever after replete and drunk. But is this how the most economically significant part of international trade is today conducted?

I doubt that the concept of a production chain existed before the First World War, or if it existed, it was only in a very rudimentary form. I suspect that the most economically significant parts of contemporary world trade are not in natural resources or manufactured finished products, but in gizmos of one sort or another as part of transnational production chains by multinational corporations. This I think raises the costs of disrupting interdependence to qualitatively new levels and creates a kind of economic mutually assured, if not exactly destruction, at least impoverishment. I do not claim that interdependence, whether of this new type or the common-or-garden-variety, makes war between the US and China impossible, only that it enhances the other factors that make war highly improbable.

So where does all this leave us? I do not think it makes the strategic adjustments any easier. But it does imply that the parameters within which the US and China must seek a new accommodation are narrower than what we might have been led to expect by the media or the more sensationalist sort of academic analysis.

I earlier argued that it would be futile for the US to try and contain China. It would be equally futile for Beijing to try to exclude the US from East Asia. Both the US and China will remain essential parts of the East Asian strategic equation. China has proposed a "new type of major power relations" to the US. It is not entirely clear what China means by this, but by any definition it implies some sort of role for the US in East Asia, even though the specifics of that role are yet to be determined. The delineation of their respective roles is in fact what the groping after a new US-China *modus vivendi* is all about.

At the 4th Summit of the Conference on Interaction and Confidence Building Measures in Asia (CICA) in Shanghai in May 2014, President Xi Jinping resurrected the notion that "it is for the peoples of Asia to run the affairs of Asia, solve the problems of Asia and uphold the security of Asia". Although the idea has a venerable if unhappy history — the ghost of the

Greater East Asia Co-Prosperity Sphere haunts the idea — and bears a generic resemblance to China's ritualistic argument that outside powers should not interfere in the SCS disputes, I am not inclined to read too much into it.

Who or what is "Asian"? Is it a geographic, cultural or political identity? Russia is a member of CICA. So is Israel. Are they "Asian"? The US is an observer in CICA. So are Belarus and Ukraine. What in a globalised world is an "outside power" or a "region"? CICA is not obviously an "Asian" forum. Nor are any of the other regional organisations and forums in which China participates, including the Shanghai Cooperation Organisation (SCO), a Chinese initiative which has Russia as a member and Belarus as an observer. Any inconsistency between the idea President Xi floated at CICA and the proposed "new type of major power relations" is perhaps an indication that China is still uncertain about what geopolitical concept would be in its best interests in a post-Cold War world and hence reluctant to foreclose any option. In any case, the idea that Asian issues should be managed only by Asians now seems to have been displaced by President Xi's grand vision of "One Belt, One Road". This is primarily an economic framework but has geopolitical implications as an ambitious vision of a Sinocentric *Eurasian* — and not just "Asian" — order.

Japan is undoubtedly "Asian". The impossibility of displacing Japan from East Asia is the strongest argument against any Chinese design to entirely exclude the US from the region. Sino-Japanese relations are complicated and will remain so even as tensions wax and wane. Without the US or even if the US-Japan alliance is significantly weakened, Japan may well decide to go nuclear and it has the ability to do so very quickly. If Japan goes nuclear, South Korea has the capability to follow suit. It was the US that quashed such thoughts in Seoul (and Taiwan) during the 1970s, but they have never entirely disappeared and have recently resurfaced.

China can do without these serious potential complications to an already complicated East Asian strategic equation. China is modernising its nuclear forces. Once China acquires a credible second strike capability, an East Asian version of the question attributed to Charles de Gaulle must arise: will San Francisco be sacrificed to save Tokyo? It may well already be whispered in the *Kantei*.[1] It is not in China's interest to encourage such questions to surface

---

[1] The *Kantei* is the main office and residence of the Japanese Prime Minister.

prematurely let alone be answered because the most probable answers will not be the answers Beijing wants to hear. I am sure that China would like to reclaim something of its central historical role in East Asia from the US. But how much to reclaim and how to do so without provoking a response from Japan and South Korea is a matter of very fine judgement and the cost of mistakes would be extremely high. I think the Chinese leadership knows this.

I chose the word "groping" to describe the process of the US and China trying to reach a new *modus vivendi* with some care. The outcome of the strategic adjustments underway will not be determined by a deliberate process of negotiation, by American and Chinese leaders sitting around a table as Stalin, Roosevelt and Churchill did at Yalta as the Second World War drew to a close. That can only happen if there is some climactic *denouement* to the process and that is precisely what both sides are trying to avoid. I think that the outcome will instead be determined by the accumulation of a slew of big and small diplomatic, political, military and economic decisions taken at all levels over a long period, probably decades. Many of these decisions will be ad hoc responses to situations or issues as they crop up and each decision may bear little or no obvious relationship to the overall strategic outcomes American and Chinese leaders seek, assuming that they know precisely what they want from each other, which is not to be taken for granted. It is not even to be taken for granted that there will ever be a definitive outcome.

I stated at the beginning of this lecture that US-China relations are infused with strategic distrust. Such uncertainties are one cause of distrust. Interdependence may also enhance strategic distrust by exposing mutual vulnerabilities. All the more so because China's rise has been psychologically disquieting to many in the West because in China, capitalism flourishes without democracy. This is regarded as somehow unnatural and illegitimate because it punctures the western myth of the universality of its political values and of the inevitability of the development of political forms similar to its own. Unlike the former Soviet Union, China cannot be dismissed as an economic failure. China thus challenges in a very fundamental way the western sense of self which assumes its political and moral superiority as a key element.

Of course in these politically correct times the western sense of its superiority is rarely, if ever, admitted and would be vehemently denied. But the attitudes and modes of thought ingrained during the two hundred years or so when first Europe and subsequently America shaped the basic structures, processes and concepts of international relations are not easily shaken off. They linger in invidious perhaps even unconscious ways, camouflaged by talk of universality, the promotion of human rights and democracy and good governance. It is the basic mental framework within which the US views itself and the world, the foundation of which is the idea of America as moral exemplar and Shining City on the Hill. As I argued in my first lecture, the Western assumption of superiority may have been reinforced by misinterpretation of the meaning of the end of the Cold War.

I will deal with the Myth of Universality in my fourth lecture. For now, let me just note that this is not just an abstract intellectual matter. The claim that certain political forms and values are universal was used to justify military interventions to change regimes in North Africa and the Middle East. All these interventions turned out very badly. They have resulted in greater instability in the region which have had global consequences and added to the general uncertainties of our times. But I do not think that there has been any fundamental change to the cast of mind that led to these disasters, even if some of the more extreme variants of the idea of universality such as the notion that History had ended are now smothered in an embarrassed silence.

Attempts to change regimes in the Middle East and the bloody messes that resulted were closely watched by China and others in East Asia. Prudence has dictated that military intervention in the name of universality has been deployed only against the weak. This has tempered but not erased the doubts and anxieties that this approach has aroused in many countries, including China. Of course, no one is mad enough to subject China to kinetic intervention. But that is beside the point. Not all interventions are military and East Asia, Singapore included, has experienced more than our fair share of Western attempts to interfere in our domestic affairs. It seems very hard for the white man to lay down his burden and forswear the habit of whipping the heathen along the path of righteousness, even when the effort is utterly ineffectual.

I laughed when I read about Lord Patten and British parliamentarians pontificating about democracy in Hong Kong during the "Occupy Central" demonstrations. That only made the British look more hypocritical than usual. But when 20 American Senators wrote to President Obama on the same subject and when the President felt obliged to pronounce, however gingerly, on Hong Kong, that was no laughing matter.

The US and China have had a number of senior level discussions on the "new type of major power relations" that China has suggested. It has three broad elements. Both sides readily agree that they should try to minimise disagreements. They also readily agree that they should try to foster habits of cooperation. But the US has been unable to give clear endorsement to the third element that is perhaps the most important element to the Chinese: mutual respect for core interests. Why? There are indeed aspects of the concept of "core interest" that need clarification. Is it for instance an invitation to create spheres of influence? But I think the US knows that preservation of CCP rule is the most vital of Chinese core interests and is reluctant to endorse this explicitly. The US deals with the CCP pragmatically; it has no choice. But to explicitly invest CCP rule with legitimacy requires a redefinition of American values, including a de facto abandonment of the idea of universality that is apparently too painful to bear.

American leaders and officials often speak more to be heard domestically than internationally. There is often a large element of ritual in their invocations of the universality of democracy and human rights. But this idea is so essential a part of the American psyche that I do not think their words are always just posturing. I think Chinese leaders suspect that this is so too. The words of great powers reverberate more loudly and widely than may be intended and American politicians do not sufficiently understand how their pronouncements may grate on foreign ears and have strategic consequences. Americans sometimes forget that domestic politics is not an American monopoly. The days when even the most powerful of Chinese leaders can entirely disregard the opinions of their own people or insulate them from inconvenient foreign pronouncements are long gone.

This is a particularly delicate phase of China's development. Beijing is now embarking on a second and more difficult stage of reform that in essence requires loosening the centre's grip on crucial sectors of the economy while preserving CCP rule. Can it be done? One should certainly hope so because all the alternatives are worse. But no one really knows, including, I think, China's leaders. China's external confidence masks a deep internal insecurity.

Social and labour protests are widespread, their impact potentially magnified through the Internet and social media. China has about 700 million Internet users. The CCP has so far been able to prevent local protests from escalating into national threats. Still, at a time when the CCP is grappling with existential questions, it is understandable that Chinese leaders should regard American attitudes towards universality and incautious words on Hong Kong or Tibet or Xinjiang or Taiwan or other sensitive issues, with grave suspicion: as ultimately intended to destabilise and delegitimise the CCP; a complication to their already complex problems. But there seems to be great reluctance by the US to confront this core issue.

On their part, Chinese leaders and officials too do not seem to understand that their own attitudes can evoke distrust. If a new *modus vivendi* requires the US to acknowledge that different political systems can have their own legitimacy, it requires China to resist the temptations of triumphalist nationalism.

With communism discredited as an ideology, the CCP is increasingly relying on nationalism to legitimate its rule. Chinese nationalism is often unsettling, but the issue is not nationalism per se. The US is also a highly nationalistic country. The essential source of American and Chinese nationalism is a sense of exceptionalism; the US and China both consider themselves exceptional countries. But the conclusions they draw are different. America is an inclusive culture that wants everyone to become like it and believes that the world would be a better place if this were so. China has an exclusive culture that rejects the notion that anyone could become like China as impossibly pretentious. To China, the best others can do is humbly acknowledge China's superiority and the sooner we do so the better for everyone.

This is a very ancient and deeply ingrained feature of China's approach to international relations. Throughout its history, China took great pains to preserve the forms of its centrality, at least in its own mind, even when the facts were otherwise. It never lost its sense of superiority even when powerless before the West and Japan. Now that China has re-emerged as a major power, this sense of superiority has become the underlying cause of the difficulties in China's relations with many countries. The attitude that China is *entitled* to have its superiority acknowledged and that failure to do so can only be due to recalcitrance or ill-intention, is why I think China will always suffer a deficit in "soft power" and evoke resentment. It is most pronounced in the case of Sino-Japanese relations. In June last year at a World Peace Forum organised by Tsinghua University, Foreign Minister Wang Yi bluntly told the audience that the key to improvement in Sino-Japanese relations was for Japan to accept China's rise and change its "mentality", by which he clearly meant accept a subordinate status.

I do not think there is any country, Japan included, that would deny China's rise as a geopolitical fact. You would have to be living on another planet to do so. But the Chinese assumption that acknowledgment of this fact this should be accompanied by normative acceptance of subordination within a natural hierarchy with China at its apex is an entirely different matter. No country will readily accept this and it is perhaps more difficult for Japan than most countries. Seldom if ever in their long history of interactions have Japan and China had to deal with each other on the basis of equality and both find it very difficult to do so. Many public opinion surveys in Japan have shown that in the space of a relatively short time, China has gone from being one of the most popular countries to being the most unpopular country, surpassing even Russia in this respect, which is a remarkable failure of Chinese diplomacy.

This Chinese attitude is not confined to Japan. Singapore has a very good relationship with China. But Chinese leaders and officials, despite our repeatedly correcting them, persistently refer to Singapore as a "Chinese country" and say that we should therefore "understand" them better, meaning of course that we more than other countries should know our position in life and show deference even at the cost of our own interests. It is not even confined to the Chinese attitude towards small countries — and almost every country is smaller than China — or to a country which just happens to have a majority Chinese ethnic population like ourselves. A few weeks ago I asked a visiting Chinese scholar if he thought that the current state of China's relations with Russia could be maintained. His immediate, almost Pavlovian, response was that it could, provided Russia accepted its status. He obviously did not mean Russia as China's equal. I thought this did not augur well for Sino-Russia relations. I think it is also a factor in Sino-India relations.

Does this attitude contaminate US-China relations as well? Perhaps not at present. Some vague notion of equality seems implicit in the concept of a "new type of major power relations". China has cautioned the US not to "embolden small countries" and Chinese diplomats have on occasion warned that if China's interests in the SCS are not recognised by ASEAN it will settle matters with the US without ASEAN. This also implies, if not equality, at least that China regards the US as being on a different level than other countries. But if and when China overtakes the US as the world's largest economy, the psychological framework within which China now approaches the US might change. I do not think it makes much substantive difference if an economy is ranked first or second as both will still be hugely influential. But Chinese confidence will certainly get a boost. The line between confidence and over-confidence is a thin one. It is always dangerous to believe one's own propaganda because that is when miscalculations often occur.

In East Asia, the assumption of Chinese centrality and superiority is particularly difficult to accept because it seems to encompass a strong element of Revanchism. This is not the same thing as revisionism but still causes anxiety. Almost exactly two years ago, President Xi Jinping met Lien Chan, the former Taiwanese Vice-President in China. In a speech that *The People's Daily* published on its front page under the title "The Chinese Dream to Fulfil the Great Rejuvenation of the Chinese People Together", President Xi placed the "Great Rejuvenation" — a phrase he also used in his opening speech when he met Ma Ying-jeou in Singapore last year — in the historical context of how Taiwan had been occupied by foreign powers when the Chinese nation was weak.

Reconciliation between China and Taiwan is of course to be welcomed. Every country in East Asia recognises the People's Republic of China as "One China". But by casting the "Chinese Dream" of reconciliation with Taiwan as an instance of the rectification of historical injustices inflicted upon a weak China, it suggested and left open broader questions. There is no doubt that China suffered many injustices in the 19th century and first half of the 20th century. Does a rising China intend to rectify all these historical injustices? If not, how will it choose which injustices to rectify? By what means does China intend to rectify historical injustices?

The anxieties are accentuated because China seems to be increasingly relying on history to justify its claims of sovereignty in the SCS and elsewhere. China has such a long history that it can be used to justify almost anything and China also has a tradition of manipulating history as a tool of statecraft. Japan again provides the most vivid recent example of this aspect of Chinese nationalism, although the US and the West in general have not been spared. The CCP has described itself as, to quote former President Jiang Zemin, the "finest and most thoroughgoing patriot" which had redeemed China after "a hundred years of humiliation". The Chinese public has been subjected to a steady drumbeat of various reminders of Japanese atrocities in China to fan and keep alive bitter memories of the Second World War and the CCP's role in defeating Japan, particularly during last year's celebration of the 70th anniversary of the end of the war.

But it was not always so. Consider, for example, this statement: "As you have formally apologised for the debts you incurred in the past, it is not reasonable to ask you for payments of those debts. You cannot be asked to apologise every day, can you? It is not good for a nation to feel constantly guilty..."

This is not some right-wing Japanese politician trying to justify Japan's wartime record. It is a statement by Chairman Mao himself to a delegation of the Japanese Diet only a decade after the end of World War Two. And when Mao Zedong met former Japanese Prime Minister Kakuei Tanaka in 1972, he brushed aside Tanaka's attempts to apologise, saying that he was grateful to Japan because without the war the CCP would not been able to seize power. Under Mao, the CCP's primary claim to legitimacy was class struggle. The CCP then emphasised its defeat of the Kuomintang (KMT) as representative of the old order it overthrew. But once China began to embrace the market economy and particularly after 2002 when businessmen working in private enterprises — in other words, "capitalists" — were allowed to join the CCP, class struggle lost credibility as a means of legitimating CCP rule and the emphasis shifted to the CCP's defeat of Japan, even though it was the KMT not the CCP that bore the brunt of the fighting against Japan.

Such manipulations of history and the narrative of China as a victim are not costless to China and carry risks. A great power cannot forever portray itself as a victim without calling its intentions into question. Chinese diplomacy is characterised by a passive-aggressiveness which is the corollary of the portrayal of China as victim. The classic, indeed clichéd but alas still used, illustration of this tactic is the accusation that for one reason or another someone has "hurt the feelings of 1.3 billion people". This aims to simultaneously make you feel bad — you must be a truly obnoxious human being to hurt the feelings of so many people — and is a not-so-subtle warning about getting on the wrong side of a big country. Chinese diplomats also whine about ASEAN "bullying" China or "ganging up" against China. All 10 members of ASEAN combined are smaller than China. This absurd complaint is in effect a threat. It sets up a false dilemma as if ASEAN's only choice is to agree with China or be against China and the obvious insinuation is that this would be unwise. Such tactics raise doubts about the kind of partnership China really wants with ASEAN and are not in China's own interest. But Chinese diplomats do not seem to care, perhaps because some ASEAN members do fall for this tactic.

What China cannot ignore is how the narrative of the CCP as the champion and redeemer of a victimised China could dangerously narrow China's options if an accident with the US or Japan should occur. War is not in China's interest, and Beijing may for all the reasons I have earlier set out, want to contain the incident. But Beijing could be trapped by its own historical narrative, and the highly nationalistic public opinion that the CCP both cultivates and fears may force China down paths it does not really want to travel. I think Chinese leaders are aware of this danger but cannot abandon or tone down the narrative they have chosen to legitimate their right to rule because they have no convincing replacement.

Let me conclude this evening's lecture with a final point on US-China relations. After news broke a few days ago of China's deployment of surface-to-air missiles on a disputed island in the Paracels, President Obama criticised the action as "…China resorting to the old style of might makes right, as opposed to working through international law and international norms to establish claims, and to resolve disputes." I entirely agree. But the use of the phrase "old style" also brought to mind Secretary of State Kerry's characterisation almost two years ago of Russian actions in Ukraine as "…19th century behaviour in the 21st century".

Both statements seemed to me to miss a fundamental point. A century is not merely a unit of time but also a political construct. It is pointless merely to complain about a competitor operating on the basis of a different political construct. Why assume that everyone necessarily operates within the same frame as oneself? That could lead to being ambushed by events. One of the basic functions of diplomacy is to see the world through your competitors' eyes in order to understand the frame of reference he is operating within, and thereafter one of the basic purposes of statecraft to use what means are available and appropriate to manoeuvre him into your preferred frame of reference or, if this is not possible, to operate within the same frame in order to achieve your purposes.

A stable *modus vivendi* can only be reached if all parties are operating within the same frame of reference. Are the US and China operating within the same frame of reference? I think they do substantially, but not entirely. And therefrom springs the complexity and risks of the relationship. Can they be brought within a common framework? That is not yet clear. Time will tell. But I do sometimes wonder whether the eventual answer, if there is an answer, may not prove more challenging than the question.

I do not think any of the broad parameters of US-China relations and the basic issues that I have sketched will be resolved anytime soon, if ever. But I am not pessimistic about US-China relations because, as I have stressed, both countries are pragmatic and prudent. They want and need a stable relationship with each other. Neither is looking for trouble and the issues between them, while difficult and complicated, can be managed and are being managed. What it does mean is that while the US and China grope towards a new *modus vivendi*, East Asia and particularly Southeast Asia, will have to navigate a prolonged period of more than usual uncertainty and stress.

Questions and Answers

Chan Heng Chee (CHC): Let me begin by saying to Bilahari that he really gave an excellent lecture which was thoughtful and, I think, insightful. And I particularly like the way that he dealt with the value impulses of the United States and China in their foreign policy and in dealing with each other. Because I think that the nub of the problem for the US-China relationship is indeed that strategic mistrust, which arises from the fact that the Chinese suspect that the United States and Americans want to change their system and they cannot accept the way the Chinese are, and so there's this constant pushing back and forth.

This has been a rich lecture but there is so much more to cover because the US-China relationship is indeed vast and covers many areas. Let me just very briefly summarise the key points that Bilahari touched on — that it is difficult to characterise the US-China relationship; that this is not a clash of civilisations because the Chinese, in fact, do adopt many aspects of modernisation and the Western system; this is not a cold war because there is so much interrelationship and activities, in fact, economically, the relationship is almost symbiotic. And the US is going to be the leading power for the next decade and beyond. And to be quite honest, I think the Chinese admit this. I have heard Chinese officials in Beijing say that for the next decade — they say decade, I say beyond — the US will be the leading superpower so they don't see themselves taking over them. War is unlikely, I agree, and that's the point he's made, and that it will be competition and rivalry that will mark the relationship. And China in fact is not a revisionist country, it has done very well in this particular system. The first question I would ask Bilahari is: you have not really touched very much on the strategic ambitions of China. You have discussed the footprint that China has tried to lay out through the different groupings it sets out: SCO, CICA, "One Belt, One Road". And they talk of a new model for the major power relations, and there are different footprints, different models for different relationships. I can see that they are trying to do that and they are not sure what will actually work and what will be the final one. How would you characterise China's strategic ambition for the Asia Pacific? Do you see China pushing out the US eventually? Or wanting the US to be out of the Asia Pacific eventually?

Bilahari Kausikan (BK): I have no doubt that the Chinese would like to reclaim something of their historical central role in at least East Asia from the US. But how to do it? They don't have the capability to push the US out entirely and I'm not sure that they believe it is in their interest to push the US out entirely, because as I tried to explain, if they do that, one possible consequence would be Japan and possibly South Korea going nuclear. And I don't think they want that because it would be a terrible complication to their lives that I think they will try to avoid. But the ambition is there. Whether it can be achieved, I don't think the Chinese themselves know. That is perhaps why one interpretation of a new type of great power relations is an invitation — which the US has so far declined — to form spheres of predominant influence. Not exclusive influence, for the US is never going to exit East Asia and I think the Chinese are not going to say, "I'm never going to the other side of the Pacific Ocean". But I think that the fundamental problem of finding a new accommodation, a new *modus vivendi*, is that both the US and the Chinese do not yet really know what they want from the other. The US knows it needs some kind of new accommodation, a new *modus vivendi*: what is the shape of it? How much must it give up? What price must it pay? It doesn't know. The Chinese want what I told you they want. But how to get it? How to do it without provoking other kinds of consequences? They don't know. It is not as if they've got a plan and the

US has a plan and you sit down across from each other at a table and say, let's see how we can reconcile our plans. It's not going to work that way. It's going to work by this groping process, through cumulative, maybe unconscious, small decisions. And that makes it more difficult for the rest of us.

CHC: Thank you. I agree. Now, you concluded your lecture by saying that, in fact, the countries may be operating with different frames of references and you talked of cooperation between the US and China in several areas. Do you think North Korea is one area where they are able to cooperate with more or less a common, or similar, frame of reference?

BK: I said that I think they are substantially, but not entirely, within the same frame and that's the difficulty. North Korea is one example of the misalignment of their frames of reference. There is no love lost between the North Koreans and the Chinese. I have been to North Korea and if you hear them talk about the Chinese, your hair will stand on end. Similarly, I have heard Chinese officials talk about North Koreans and it is not with great fondness and affection either.

I know that the Chinese do not like the North Korean nuclear programme. To that extent, they have a common concern with the US. But common concerns are not the same thing as common interests. There is a persistent belief in the US across many administrations that they can work with China on North Korea. What is China's basic interest in North Korea? There are five Communist systems left in the world — four are in Asia. North Korea is one of them. No matter how much the Chinese may dislike the North Korean nuclear programme, to expect the Chinese to take robust actions against North Korea is a pipe dream. They may go along with UN sanctions, but what counts is how they implement them. Because if China is seen to be complicit in undermining the rule of one Communist party, that has immediate domestic implications for the CCP's own rule. China cannot undermine another Communist system. To me, this is obvious. So while the Chinese are not enamoured with the North Koreans and are upset with their nuclear programme, what they can do about it must always fall short of de-stabilising the regime to the extent that another Communist party falls. The North Koreans have one weapon that the Chinese have no answer to — that weapon is to threaten to die.

Why the Americans cannot understand this defeats me. It shows that while both are substantially within the same frame, they are not entirely within the same frame.

CHC: Do you think China's concern is also with refugees coming across to the mainland?

BK: That is one concern but this is a much more fundamental concern. Refugees can be dealt with; *in extremis*, you shoot them or you push them back and the Chinese are quite capable of doing that. But to undermine another Communist regime will give evil thoughts to your own people.

CHC: So what are the US and China working on when they work on North Korea?

BK: I think the Chinese are playing the US for all it's worth. So the UN Security Council imposes a few more sanctions, so what? North Korea is already so sanctioned that the effect is marginal. Anyway, the Chinese will always be very selective in implementing any kind of sanction. That is a fact of life and there is nothing much you can do. Anyway, I don't think North Korea is such a big problem.

North Korea just wants a nuclear weapon so that its regime can survive. Now, if you are willing to swallow Iran, which is at least a threshold nuclear weapon state and — God only knows what is the limit to Iran's ambitions — why can't you just swallow what the North Koreans want? What the North Koreans want is American love and affection. They have a very peculiar way of going about seeking love and affection but that's what they want. They want a peace treaty with the US. That's all. I know the US can't give this to them. Politically, it is impossible for any administration to do it. But what they want is intrinsically not a very big thing.

CHC: One last question and I'll leave the others to have a shot at you. This one is about China and Japan. I think you gave Japan an easy ride actually. You talk of China having to get over it. Forget the war and the atrocities and stop harping on it. But don't you think that Japan should also get over it and stop going to the [Yasukuni] Shrine all the time, provoking every other country in the region?

BK: I think this is a good question, but it's a much more complex question than you may think. The essential point I made about Sino-Japanese relations is that China manipulates history for political purposes. At one time, Mao Zedong said that the Second World War is not important — no need to apologise. Many Japanese prime ministers have gone to the shrine. In fact, even the Showa emperor, Emperor Hirohito, had gone to the shrine — there was no problem. That was before the souls of Class A war criminals were interred in the shrine. And that is also a complicated problem.

Most people don't know what a Class A war criminal is. A Class A war crime was defined something like this — to wage aggressive war and commit crimes against the peace. Now, that is a very problematic statement. War is a legitimate instrument of state policy. And what is an aggressive war? If you lose, then your war is aggressive. If you win, then your war is justified. And the specific charge against those Class A war criminals is that they waged aggressive war over quite a long period — I think it was 15 or 18 years, or maybe even longer. Not one of those hanged as Class A war criminals was in power throughout that entire period of time. The only person who was in power throughout that time was Emperor Hirohito, in whose name the war was waged. And once the decision to spare Hirohito was made, executing the others became a little problematic because none of them was in power throughout the whole period. And what is aggressive war against the peace anyway? I'm not saying that those people did not richly deserve to be hanged, maybe they deserved it, but not for the charge for which they were actually hanged. Class B and Class C war criminals are the common or garden variety type of war criminals, mistreating prisoners of war, killing civilians and so on. Some of those Class A war criminals may have been complicit in that too. But to hang them for crimes against the peace over a period of time when none of them was in power for the entire period — that is a bit problematic.

Where the Japanese can be faulted is not the Yasukuni Shrine issue per se. I think they have not sufficiently educated their people in their own history, with various Japanese governments — the Abe government included — not stopping some of the more their extreme right wing supporters such as the chairman of NHK, from saying stupid things, and for allowing some of the more right-wing of Japanese academics to quibble over things like exactly how many people were killed at Nanjing. The apology that Abe gave last year was quite a comprehensive one and I think that is about as good as it gets. And it is pointless to constantly tell the Japanese that they must be sincere. It's not a question of sincerity. It's whether it is in the interest of China and South Korea to consider the apology sincere.

Question: My question to you is — has China, or Xi Jinping, acted too soon? Because in the days of Deng Xiaoping, they would have quietly built up their strength and then waited for glory another day. But it seems to me that China has not fully developed their strength and they have begun to assert themselves. I'm not arguing that they should go into direct confrontation or competition, but I'm arguing on the basis that this is probably an issue of arrogance right? Because America wants to be dominant and so does China.

BK: Has China acted too soon? I'm not sure. I think a lot of the statements that come out of China, just like a lot of statements that come out of America, are meant primarily for domestic consumption. And there are good reasons why they do that. If you look at Chinese behaviour in the world, with the exceptions of the maritime disputes in the SCS and the East China Sea, they have actually been quite prudent. As I said, China has been more or less a free-rider on the existing system; they are not revisionists. In the SCS and the East China Sea, I think they are revanchists, which is not quite the same as revisionists. Revanchism is reclaiming what you think was yours; revisionism is creating a new order. But if you look at what Xi Jinping says, the huge visions he's put out, "One Belt, One Road" and so on, I think the answer must be yes, it's a bit premature. Still a vision is not a plan and what he has done in implementing that vision is actually still quite limited and I'm not even sure that the Belt is going to succeed. I think the Road, the southern part will probably substantially, if not totally, succeed, but the Belt is very problematic for a whole lot of reasons. So should he have said all these things? If you're talking about capability to implement or scaring people maybe it was premature. But he had good domestic reasons to do so. So from that point of view, it's not premature because domestic politics is *now* — you cannot wait. But you look at their behaviour apart from the SCS, East China Sea, they have not done all that much in the rest of the world.

CHC: But Bilahari, would you agree that actually great powers tend to want to have visions? I think every American president comes forth and tries to set up a vision also. And I think China is trying to play that game now.

BK: There's nothing very unusual about it.

CHC: And Xi Jinping is much more articulate, and much more ready to articulate these visions.

BK: His visions have been bolder and he has been more assertive about China's interests than his immediate predecessors.

CHC: Right. Shanghai Cooperation Organisation was not in Xi Jinping's time, it was in Hu Jintao's time.

BK: So I think it depends on where you want to slice it. From a domestic point of view, probably it is not premature because he needed it. From an international point of view, is it premature to have a vision? I'm not sure. As Heng Chee said, all major powers have visions — Xi Jinping has not really done all that much to implement it. A bit in the Belt, quite a lot in the Road, certainly in the South and East China Seas quite a lot, but globally not that much. Don't listen to what great powers say, watch what they do.

Question: Earlier you were explaining how the US and Chinese flavours of exceptionalism were fundamentally different. Can you please shed some light as to why that may be and how those different forms developed?

BK: In a word, history. They have different histories; they have different experiences of history; they have different conceptions of themselves in history. America is basically founded by people who ran away from Europe and wanted to have a new country based on different principles. China has always been there and it believes it's reclaiming its rightful place in the world. But they both believe that they are exceptional. Both are wrong by the way. They are not as exceptional as they think, at least in my view. But that's their self-image.

Question: I wanted to know what you think about the US presidential elections. How will a Republican or Democrat President affect the US-China relationship? And how would the dynamics of this relationship differ depending on whether it's a Republican or Democrat administration?

BK: I told you during the lecture that I'm not clairvoyant, but I will venture a guess anyway. I think rightly or wrongly, fairly or unfairly, there is a perception that the second administration of President Obama has been less engaged in East Asia, and weak. So whether it is a Republican or a Democrat that next sits in the White House, I think American policy is bound to get more assertive towards China. Now, that does not mean it's going to be reckless, it does not mean it's going to be imprudent, but it's going to be more assertive. How exactly more assertive? God only knows.

Question: I was just curious about a point you made earlier about the possibility of South Korea, or Japan going nuclear in the event that America disengages from East Asia. What I'm curious about is that, won't they face the risk of a backlash from the international community in the same way that North Korea is now facing, and Iran used to face, especially from China, Russia and the UN in such a way that it would come at a great cost to themselves and in a very perverse way bring international isolation upon them and change the balance of power in China's favour?

BK: Who is the "international community" and how do I get in touch with it?

Question: The UN? The Security Council?

BK: The UN? No. If that kind of situation arises where Japan believes it must go nuclear, it will mean that Japan has completely lost faith in the US alliance, or because China has been overly successful in displacing the US from East Asia. In such a situation, I think Japan and South Korea will see this as an existential question. And therefore the good regard of the international community will not be a major consideration. Don't be naïve about the UN. In that situation, if the US is unable to maintain the nuclear shield, I can envisage the US playing the role that China now plays *vis-à-vis* North Korea in the Security Council on behalf of Japan. If China puts forward a resolution to sanction Japan for going nuclear there will be a good chance that the US will veto it. There is no such thing as "the international community".

CHC: And it's never all fair.

BK: "International community" is a construct that we use to sound good. It's something we use when we want to make somebody else feel bad.

CHC: My sense is that you will have some rhetoric against Japan and South Korea for acquiring nuclear weapons but that's all.

BK: They have the capability. Japan, at least, already has the means to go nuclear. They already have the fissionable material. Not a very efficient sort of fissionable material but they have it already. They already have the technology to create the device; they already have the means of delivery. Nobody is making a big fuss about it.

Question: My question is with regard to the different roles the military plays in China and the US. In the US, the military is subordinate to the government. In China, the Central Military Commission is, if not the key organ, then one of the key organs by which the state is run. One of the things that we talked about in this lecture is how any framework is going to be arrived at not by countries sitting down and discussing but getting to it piece by piece — you said small decisions accruing, perhaps unconsciously. So when you have military influence in China, doesn't that up the risk of small decisions being made in a way that escalates rather than de-escalates?

BK: I don't think so. The military is subordinate to civilian rule in both the US and China: in China to the Party, in the US to the state.

CHC: And the commander-in-chief is the President.

BK: Things may well get out of hand, but I doubt for the reason that you suggest. I have read arguments that the PLA is out of control in China. I think it's rubbish. The PLA is an instrument of the Party. And Xi Jinping, much more than his predecessors, has got it in his hands. It may slip from his grasp, but for now at least, I don't think that will be the factor if things get out of hand.

Question: I'm a full-time national serviceman. My question is related to what you said about China and the US being unlikely to engage in a war by design. Now, China and the US have friction over specific issues such as intellectual property rights and cyber security. China has, in the past, worked through proxies. An example, and correct me if I'm wrong, is where China supports Maoism in the Northeastern states of India in response to India's support for an independent Tibet. Do you foresee — I know that you're not clairvoyant — but do you foresee China and the US, keeping in mind that elections are coming up, engaging in similar ways to achieve ad hoc measures of leverage over each other?

BK: That is how great powers behave. They are not going to confront each other directly if they can help it. They will go and poke each other indirectly, through other people, through proxies, on the sides. So of course they will do this. This is normal behaviour. It does not mean war is going to break out the day after tomorrow, so you can serve your national service in peace. If you have to be mobilised, it will not be because of either the US or China.

Question: I'd like to ask your opinion on the possibility of a more independent Japan emerging because as much as the US and Japan are aligned when it comes to questions about China, Japan is increasingly fed up with the American presence in Okinawa and is trying to emerge as its own more separate economy and get rid of US influence over its economy.

BK: I don't think you're right in the first place. The Okinawans are fed up with the American presence in Okinawa — that is quite a different thing from saying that Japan is fed up with the American presence in Japan.

Question: But also there is a traditional Japanese sense of exceptionalism as much as there is for the US and China.

BK: I think the Japanese do value the US alliance. They do not want to go back to the early Showa period [when they were in competition with the US]; they do not want to have to lose faith in the Americans if they can possibly help it. And actually, I see no sign of it at present. The US and Japan have issues but they are mainly economic issues and these are issues within an alliance, at least for now. So I think while there are a whole host of things in the world to worry about, the weakening of the US and Japan alliance is not among those things to immediately worry about.

Question: The US Senate recently voted to rename the road that the Chinese embassy is on, 1 Liu Xiaobo Plaza. My question is twofold. What do you think the US Senate hopes to achieve by this? And to what extent will internal factions in both US and China undermine the US-China relationship?

BK: I don't know what the US Senate hopes to achieve. I thought it was a particularly stupid move. It will achieve nothing except make some senators feel better about themselves for a little while. Anyway, President Obama already said he will veto it. So it's not going to happen. It's just one of those futile gestures that complicates US-China relations. But by raising this issue, you have made a very good point. I think the key factors that are going to determine the relationship are not international factors, but the domestic factors. It will be domestic factors which may bring them into conflict or which complicates things. For example this stupid little gesture by the Senate is completely meaningless: irritates without achieving anything. I asked a friend — a very right wing American friend — through e-mail, "All right, you have named the street that the Chinese embassy is on after a Chinese dissident, but the Singapore embassy is next to the Chinese embassy. Are you going to name our little stretch of road after Lee Kuan Yew?" There was no answer.

CHC: I would like to just elaborate on the point that Bilahari made, that really it is the domestic politics that will drive foreign policy and we have to take note of that. The one thing that we have to remember is that the ground in the US is changing. Just as in the 1960s and 1970s, the Vietnam War and the counter-culture revolution in the US had drastically transformed American society. I think today, something is again happening in the US. And the change that is taking place in the population, with the long recession, the two wars in Iraq and Afghanistan, and with immigration, globalisation, jobs being lost and jobs being displaced, and the great inequality that has arisen in the US, people are unhappy and there is a great disconnect taking place between the people and the government. And you see outsiders, anti-establishment figures like Bernie Sanders, Donald Trump and Ted Cruz gaining the votes, which surprises everyone. In fact, America today is much less interested in putting boots on the ground, taking up wars of choice and being interventionist. What will this do to American foreign policy? These social trends would be something that would be very interesting and I think we should bear that in mind.

BK: I do not believe that Xi Jinping wakes up every day and the first thing he thinks about is what to do about America. And I don't think Obama wakes up and thinks first about what to do about China either. These big countries are difficult enough to govern by themselves and, as I said in passing during the lecture, their essential preoccupations are internal.

Lecture III

ASEAN & US-CHINA COMPETITION IN SOUTHEAST ASIA

n my last lecture I argued that the chief priorities of both the US and China are internal and both therefore want to avoid war or serious conflict as they seek a new *modus vivendi* with each other. At the same time neither will cease to pursue their interests. On a global scale, China is not a clearly revisionist power. But Beijing clearly wants to reclaim something of its historical centrality in East Asia. The US has emphasised that it intends to remain an East Asian power. The strategic challenge for China is therefore how to shift the US from the very centre of the East Asian strategic equation and occupy that space, but without provoking responses from the US and Japan that could jeopardise Chinese Communist Party (CCP) rule. For the US the strategic challenge is how to accommodate China, while reassuring friends and allies that it intends to hold its position without stumbling into conflict. In Southeast Asia, US-China competition in the South China Sea (SCS) has emerged as a proxy for the broader strategic adjustments that are underway.

The SCS is not the only issue in US-China relations; it is perhaps not even the most important issue in their relationship. But the SCS is today the issue where the parameters of US–China competition and their interests are most clearly defined. Like it or not, the region will draw conclusions about

American resolve and Chinese intentions from the SCS issue which will also shape perceptions of ASEAN.

Continental Asia shades into mainland Southeast Asia which in turn dribbles into archipelagic Southeast Asia, the islands of which are strung along crucial sea-routes linking the Pacific and Indian Oceans. India and China have both profoundly influenced Southeast Asia, but in recent history, the latter more than the former. The notion of China as a nation-state with defined borders is relatively new. Throughout its long history, "China" has meant different things at different times. What is now Yunnan in Southwest China was perhaps only firmly considered Chinese in the late Qing dynasty. More often than not, power and control ebbed and flowed without consideration for what are now national boundaries. China's border with Myanmar was not definitively demarcated until 1960; its land borders with Laos and Vietnam not until 1991 and 1999 respectively; and the tri-junction between Laos, China and Vietnam not until 2006.

Borderlands and strategic sea-routes are always contested, and US-China competition is only the most recent manifestation. The interests of major powers have always intersected in Southeast Asia which was once dubbed "the Balkans of Asia". In the 19th century, failure to manage the resulting pressures led to colonial rule. Thailand remained independent as much due to luck and the need of the colonial powers for a buffer state as it was due to Thai diplomatic adroitness. In Indochina, nationalist independence struggles became entangled with Cold War rivalries which in Southeast Asia were far from cold. In 1967, this historical backdrop was vivid in the strategic consciousness of the newly independent states of Southeast Asia. A major factor leading to the formation of ASEAN was the common interest of the non-communist states of Southeast Asia, all of whom faced threats from externally supported communist insurgencies, in preserving maximum autonomy in the midst of major power competition. Whatever our other differences, and they were great, we realised if we did not hang together we would hang separately.

ASEAN is a mechanism for managing external pressures and preserving the autonomy of its members by ensuring at least a modicum of cohesion, order and civility in our relationships in a region where none of this was to be taken for granted. The Cold War is of course long over. But this remains

ASEAN's fundamental and enduring purpose. ASEAN's declared goal of establishing a "Community" across the three pillars of political and security cooperation, economic integration and socio-cultural cooperation are in a sense as important as means towards this fundamental end as they are ends in themselves.

Southeast Asia is an extremely diverse region. Diversity simultaneously makes regional cooperation both very necessary and very difficult to achieve. ASEAN is an inter-state organisation which must work by reconciling national interests. The diversities of Southeast Asia are moreover not just of political systems or levels of economic development. Such differences could, at least in principle, converge. The key diversities of Southeast Asia are visceral differences of race, language and religion which define core identities and shape the domestic politics of ASEAN member states. They inevitably colour their calculations of national interest and inter-state relations. It is not easy to imagine such primordial factors ever being erased. The potential nexus between the domestic politics of ASEAN member states, intra-ASEAN relations and the interests of external powers in ASEAN is thus a possibility that can never be discounted and must be continually managed. The dangers of such a nexus were underscored by the 1963–1966 *Konfrontasi*, an undeclared war waged by Sukarno's Indonesia against Malaysia and Singapore. *Konfrontasi* was driven by Indonesian domestic politics, the dynamics of which led Sukarno to toy with a Beijing–Jakarta "Axis" as a counter to the West in the context of the Cold War. This was averted by a failed communist coup in Indonesia, the bloody aftermath of which quickly took on anti-Chinese overtones. Of course the region today presents a very different environment, thanks in no small part to ASEAN. But the general challenge of managing diversity has not gone away. I doubt it ever will.[1]

---

[1] The first lecture pointed out that the EU was based on a fundamental contradiction: a post-nationalist construct inspired by nationalist fears of a superior, German, nationalism. There is a superficial but misleading parallel with Europe insofar as ASEAN's origins lie in Southeast Asia's need for a regional order to deal with the nationalism of its largest country, Indonesia. But unlike the EU, ASEAN did not deny the reality of competing nationalisms or try to supplant it with some delusional higher purpose. In a region whose geopolitical location at the intersection of major power interests puts the autonomy and sovereignty of small states at continual risk, ASEAN harnessed the nationalisms of its members to a mechanism that could enhance their capacity to retain autonomy and sovereignty. Despite differences on many other issues, these were and remain objectives we all can share.

ASEAN is an inter-state organisation which therefore must, and can only, work by trying to reconcile sovereign interests through consensus and, despite the Charter that came into force in 2008, largely informally. Any other mode of decision-making risks rupture with unpredictable consequences because any other mode of decision-making risks small differences escalating into major splits. The basic consensus on which ASEAN rests is a consensus on always having a consensus: even if it is only a consensus on goals that we know full well cannot be realised or can only be partially realised. Its corollary is the principle of non-interference in the internal affairs of other members. Better to agree only on a form of words or set aside areas where consensus cannot be reached or avert our eyes from the disagreeable, than disagree openly because who knows where disagreement may lead us? The downside of working by consensus — the unavoidable price we pay for having any sort of regional mechanism — is an unfortunate tendency to privilege form over substance which all too often morphs into self-delusion and wishful thinking.

Nowhere is this clearer than in ASEAN's approach towards regional security. Since 1971, ASEAN has been formally committed to establishing a Zone of Peace, Freedom and Neutrality (ZOPFAN) in Southeast Asia. ZOPFAN was based on the superficially attractive but entirely delusionary notion that regional security could best be secured by excluding the major powers from the affairs of Southeast Asia. Inconvenient questions such as how the major powers could be persuaded to show such forbearance and what to do if they refused were ignored. Curiously, ZOPFAN enthusiasts apparently failed to notice that at least one major power, China, is geographically contiguous to Southeast Asia, cannot therefore be excluded from the region, and in 1971 was still actively supporting communist insurgencies in Southeast Asia as well as the war in Vietnam.

ZOPFAN sat uneasily with the demands of the Cold War which made simplistic notions of neutrality or non-alignment dangerous, as Norodom Sihanouk's Cambodia and Souvanna Phouma's Laos discovered at grievous cost. The Cold War instead impelled a search for balance. Not "balance" necessarily directed against one major power or another, but balance conceived of as a state of major power equilibrium that would enable ASEAN members to positively engage all major powers without getting embroiled in their quarrels. Neutrality or non-alignment could be safely pursued only within such equilibrium. Conditions that facilitate equilibrium cannot be established by simply lying low and hoping for the best. An ostrich thinks it is safe; but head in ground and rear in air is a posture that only invites trouble. Facilitating equilibrium requires taking a positive stand on sometimes sensitive issues. This is true for formal US treaty allies like the Philippines and Thailand, as it is for Singapore which was and remains formally non-aligned but maintains close defence and security ties with the US and, prior to its withdrawal east of Suez, with the UK which maintained military bases in Singapore as part of the American-led global security system. So vital were these ties that Singapore's first Foreign Minister, the late S. Rajaratnam, almost walked out of the 1967 Bangkok meeting discussing the establishment of ASEAN before an eleventh hour compromise was reached by declaring that foreign bases in Southeast Asia were "temporary".

The ASEAN members who supported ZOPFAN either found some obscure satisfaction in striking virtuous postures while hitching a free ride, or had other reasons for doing so. For Singapore the most crucial "balance" was not against communism or any major power, but the balance which supplements our own national efforts to maintain deterrence in our immediate neighbourhood and keeps our neighbours honest. ZOPFAN was in line with Indonesia's preference for conditions that would facilitate "regional solutions to regional problems" which is to be understood as Indonesian solutions. Indonesia seems to believe that its size entitles it to a privileged position in major power calculations. To some extent this may be true, but only to a far lesser extent than Jakarta fondly believes. The major powers are happy, for their own reasons, to nurture the illusion.

The formation of the ASEAN Regional Forum (ARF) in 1994 marked a significant, if ill-understood, shift of security concept away from ZOPFAN. The ARF has often been derided as a talk-shop. The criticism is not unjustified, but also beside the point. ZOPFAN regarded the major powers as illegitimate intrusions into Southeast Asia, at best tolerated as a necessary evil but not encouraged. This sometimes placed Singapore in an awkward position. So long as ZOPFAN with its implicit premise that regional problems should be dealt with only by regional states remained the only official ASEAN security concept, it gave our neighbours a political lever to use if they wished to pressure us for whatever reason. This was manageable but a distraction and an unnecessary irritant in already complicated bilateral relationships.

The ARF is a forum explicitly dedicated to discussions on regional security, created by the sovereign choice of all ASEAN members who have, again by their sovereign choice, invited all the major powers to discuss regional security and other issues affecting Southeast Asia. Whether anyone realised it or not, this was a shift from ZOPFAN. The fundamental purpose of the ARF is to entrench this shift in how regional security is conceptualised and to encourage and legitimise the interest of major powers in Southeast Asian security. After ARF, who can now reasonably or credibly argue that the major powers have no legitimate interest in the security of Southeast Asia?

It has had some effect. In 1990, when Singapore concluded a Memorandum of Understanding (MOU) with the US for very limited use of our facilities by a small logistics unit of the 7ᵗʰ Fleet, our neighbours reacted with an outrage worthy of nuns who have discovered a pimp in their cloister. That the outrage was hypocritical — our neighbours too had their own quiet defence ties with the US — did not make it any less of a nuisance. But in 2005, when Singapore and the US signed a Strategic Framework Agreement that was far wider in scope than the 1990 MOU, there was nary a whimper. The same was true of the enhanced bilateral Defence Cooperation Agreement with the US announced in 2015. The broadening of ASEAN's concept of regional security also opened the way for the participation of major powers in other ASEAN-led forums such as the East Asia Summit (EAS) as well as the ASEAN Defence Ministers Meeting Plus (ADMM-Plus).

I do not want to claim too much for the ARF. Clearly there were other and perhaps more important reasons for the change of attitude, Chinese behaviour and internal political changes in our neighbours among them. In any case, the shift towards a more realistic concept of regional security is incomplete. ASEAN wasted an inordinate amount of time negotiating the 1995 treaty establishing a Southeast Asian Nuclear Weapon Free Zone (SEANWFZ). SEANWFZ is supposed to be a component of ZOPFAN. It came into force in 1997.

All NWFZs provide only false comfort: the security assurances they provide are useless because under any circumstance when the use of nuclear weapons becomes probable, any treaty will be just a piece of paper. These make-believe games of arms control give those inclined to play them only the sensation of being involved in grave matters of war and peace. They are harmless so long as they are not taken too seriously and nothing vital is compromised. The SEANWFZ Treaty was concluded only after difficult and protracted negotiations reached agreement on Article 7 of the treaty, which allows visits to and transits through Southeast Asia by foreign naval vessels and military aircraft. The understanding is that we will not ask if any are carrying nuclear weapons and will not be told if we are foolish enough to ask.

Three Nuclear Weapons States (NWS) — the UK, France and Russia — have made acceptance of reservations a condition for their accession to SEANWFZ even though the Treaty explicitly forbids reservations. This was entirely predictable. If the US and China have as yet made no reservations, it is undoubtedly because the other three NWS have done their dirty work for them. One Russian reservation gives Moscow the right to unilaterally determine if any ASEAN member is in breach of SEANWFZ. This effectively abrogates Article 7 and sets a very undesirable precedent. If ASEAN accepts the reservation, it could one day be used to pressure us to object to the US presence. Indonesia and a few other ASEAN members are keen to have the NWS sign on, seemingly believing that the accession of the NWS even with reservations that could undermine the regional balance, somehow demonstrates ASEAN's "centrality". Was this an attempt to keep alive the essential idea behind ZOPFAN? Perhaps. But the penchant to privilege form and to treat ASEAN diplomacy as a type of psychotherapy designed to promote self-esteem rather than advance interests was clearly also at play.[2]

---

[2] Shockingly, the Obama administration was prepared to go along with the Russian reservation and has pressured Singapore, which it identified, not incorrectly, as the most resistant of ASEAN members, to accept it. The Obama administration said that it had submitted the Russian reservation to its legal experts who concluded that it posed no legal impediment to America's ability to deploy its forces into and through Southeast Asia. This disingenuous argument was completely beside the point. All NWFZs are primarily political and the central issue is political, not legal. If another NWS, possibly China, should in future object to the US military presence citing the Russian precedent, it would have to be dealt with politically and not legally. At the very least, acceptance of the Russian reservation could be used to confuse public opinion and undermine political support for the hosting of US military assets. Why did the Obama administration adopt such an attitude? Perhaps because American officials were loath to contradict their President who had received the Nobel Peace Prize apparently for doing nothing more than advocate a world free of nuclear weapons. These officials perhaps wanted to ingratiate themselves with the President and his staff by showing that they had facilitated acceptance of SEANWFZ by the NWS as a step in that direction. At any rate, the Obama administration's attitude towards SEANWFZ seems to have been driven more by bureaucratic and careerist impulses than strategic calculations, demonstrating that fecklessness is not an ASEAN monopoly. Recently the Obama administration

I have emphasised these hard truths about ASEAN because 49 years after its formation, they are still not sufficiently understood. I do not mean to suggest that ASEAN is useless. Far from it. There has been no war between its members. We have so far leveraged on our relationships with major powers to our advantage, while avoiding becoming embroiled in their conflicts. These are not insignificant achievements. They are the foundation of the region's growth and development. None of this was to be taken for granted given the parlous state of Southeast Asia in 1967.

ASEAN strengths and weaknesses are two sides of a single coin. Suharto's Indonesia, in contrast to Sukarno's Indonesia, accepted decision-making by consensus. This was a crucial factor that enabled ASEAN to survive where earlier attempts at regional organisation failed. The weaknesses did not matter too much as long as the international structure was clear. There was never much doubt about how the original five non-communist ASEAN members, joined by Brunei after 1984, should position ourselves within the Cold War structure. During the Cold War, China was a de facto member of the US led anti-Soviet alliance and made common cause with ASEAN against the Soviet-backed Vietnamese occupation of Cambodia. In the SCS, China fought South Vietnam over the Paracels in 1974 and fought a unified Vietnam in the Spratlys in 1988, but neither incident really concerned ASEAN very much. Maintaining ASEAN unity and working with China to respond to Vietnam's invasion and occupation of Cambodia, which seemed the first step to realising Hanoi's boast that it intended to bring "genuine independence" to all of Southeast Asia, were more immediate concerns. Even if some eyebrows were quietly raised at China's actions in the SCS and over its 1979 "lesson" to Vietnam, differences could be set aside for another day.

But once the clarity of the Cold War structure began to blur in the late 1980s, ASEAN unity loosened. Indonesia regarded itself as a privileged interlocutor with Vietnam and opened direct negotiations with Hanoi on a Cambodia settlement, barely paying lip-service to the common ASEAN position. After the Cold War, ASEAN's limitations have become more salient. ASEAN's expansion to include all 10 states of Southeast Asia has made

seems to be toying with adopting a "No First Use" nuclear doctrine. If it does so, extended deterrence in East Asia will be undermined.

arriving at consensus more difficult. There was greater room for debate and disagreement over how to position an expanded ASEAN *vis-à-vis* China and the US; less incentive to reconcile national interests with regional interests. If ASEAN's resistance to the Vietnamese occupation of Cambodia was the apotheosis of ASEAN's regional security role, the unprecedented failure of the 45th ASEAN Foreign Minister's Meeting in 2012 to issue a Joint Statement — due to the stubborn refusal of the Cambodian Chair to consider any text on the SCS that might in the slightest way offend Cambodia's Chinese patron — was surely ASEAN's nadir. Prime Minister Hun Sen subsequently described Cambodia's support for China as a "strategic choice".

Since the fiasco in Cambodia, ASEAN has managed to cobble together statements of principle on the SCS. Statements are useful but only in a limited way. They prescribe norms that represent the lowest common denominator of consensus but do not erase substantive differences of interest, modify behaviour or change facts on the ground.

The SCS disputes place ASEAN in the midst of US-China competition. The US and China as well as other major powers acknowledge "ASEAN Centrality" and certainly give the appearance of courting ASEAN. I have lost count of the number of ASEAN-China Summits and other high level meetings with China. The US has held five Leaders-level meetings with ASEAN, of which the Sunnylands meeting in February 2016 is the latest and first standalone Summit. The US and China both now describe their relationship with ASEAN as "strategic"; the adjective lacks precise definition but is clearly intended to make us feel important. Since 2013, China's "2+7 Cooperation Framework" has served as an ambitious and very generous blueprint for developing relations with ASEAN. The US is more strapped for cash than China but has done what it can to pony up as well.

Before our heads are completely turned by the flowers and candy and public displays of affection, the reality of our situation will be clear if we remind ourselves that before "ASEAN Centrality" became our term of choice, we used to speak of "ASEAN being in the driver's seat". The person in the driver's seat is sometimes only the chauffeur. We should not allow the mantra of "ASEAN Centrality" to mesmerise us into believing that we are in full control. The US and China use ASEAN-led multilateral forums as a secondary means of engaging each other. Their most important interactions are always going to be bilateral. It is of course nevertheless in our interest to encourage the US and China to participate in ASEAN forums. This gives us at least a *soupcon* of influence where we would otherwise have none. But it would be prudent not to forget that ASEAN is as much an arena as an actor and that ASEAN-led forums work best only when they do not work too well. The major powers then find them occasionally useful to advance their interests but are assured that they cannot frustrate their most vital designs. If any ASEAN process looks like becoming inconveniently effective, the major powers will not hesitate to divide ASEAN as China did in 2012.[3]

The most important factor in ASEAN-China relations is the obvious disparity of size and power. Small countries destined by geography to live on the periphery of big countries are always going to experience a degree of anxiety. Big countries have a responsibility to reassure which China has only partially fulfilled. This is not for want of trying or lack of instruments. Trade and investments are not just mutually beneficial commercial transactions but also juicy diplomatic carrots that Chinese diplomats dangle before ASEAN. Aid is a diplomatic tool that China has lavishly deployed, particularly in mainland Southeast Asia. Several ASEAN countries have readily accepted Chinese largesse and naturally it would be foolish for any country to scorn the economic opportunities that China offers. Taken in totality, ASEAN-China relations are positive. But how a big country deals with small countries over sovereignty disputes will always cast the darkest shadows over relations because the possibility of securing sovereignty by superior force can never be discounted and China has not shied away from doing so.

It would be tedious to recount every instance of China's use of force or unilateral assertions of sovereignty backed by the threat of force in the SCS. In 2012, China established Sansha City under Hainan Province with jurisdiction over the disputed Paracels and Spratlys Islands as well as Macclesfield Bank. The following year it promulgated the Hainan Fishing Regulations which was an assertion of domestic law over contested areas. China has since become more aggressive in enforcing what it considers its domestic rights in the SCS. Since 2013 China has begun an ambitious programme of land reclamation in the SCS, has constructed various kinds of structures

---

[3] China did so again at the China-ASEAN Foreign Minister's Meeting held in Kunming in June 2016.

on the new artificial islands and deployed military assets on some of them. China has argued that it was not the first to reclaim land or deploy military assets in the SCS. This may be true but is irrelevant. The speed and scope of China's reclamation dwarfs anything any other claimant has done and the actions of a major power will always convey a different signature than that of small countries. China's argument that the infrastructure it has built is a common good for the benefit of all users of the SCS hardly seems intended to be believed.

China continues to engage ASEAN on a Code of Conduct (COC) for the SCS but in a barely convincing way. Progress has been glacial and Chinese diplomats often hold discussions on the COC hostage to ASEAN refraining from taking positions on the SCS that displease China.[4] On occasion, Chinese diplomats even seem to have perversely gone out of their way to accentuate rather than assuage anxieties. Once, after our Prime Minister spoke on the SCS at an ASEAN Summit, a senior Chinese diplomat told one of my younger colleagues that "silence is golden". If he meant to suggest that we were not entitled to a view on an important issue that affects our interests, he only undermined the credibility of China's claim to "peaceful development". This was not an isolated incident nor has Singapore been particularly singled out. China routinely attempts to pressure ASEAN members, with varying degrees of success, not to raise the SCS in ASEAN-led forums or not to support other countries who do so.

The general attitude that such attempts illustrate is not confined to the SCS issue but sometimes is on display even in seemingly trivial matters. Some years before I retired, one of my counterparts from an ASEAN country that was then holding the ASEAN Chair told me that the Chinese Ambassador to his country had forced him to shift an ASEAN leader attending a Summit out of a hotel that had already been allocated to that ASEAN delegation, so that then-Premier Wen Jiabao could stay there. The Ambassador insisted on this although the hotel allocated to Premier Wen was of equal quality. Did Premier Wen know where he was staying? Would he have cared if he had

---

[4] At the Vientiane ASEAN Ministerial Meeting held in July 2016, Foreign Minister Wang Yi said that negotiations on a COC should be fast-tracked and an agreement on a framework for a COC should be reached by 2017. We shall see if this has any effect on the negotiations.

known? But the episode certainly left a deep impression on my counterpart and no doubt on the ASEAN delegation that was forced to move as well.

I could go on recounting similar stories. Every ASEAN diplomat who has dealt with China has a fund of such anecdotes. But I think I have said enough to make the point. Chinese diplomats often profess bewilderment that China's generosity towards ASEAN has not evoked gratitude or assuaged mistrust and pretend to ascribe this to malignant external influences. I do not think that Chinese diplomats are more inept or disingenuous than the diplomats of other countries. Their behaviour is, I think, better understood as illustrating the passive-aggressive style and the positing of false dilemmas to force acceptance of China's inherent superiority as the natural normative order of East Asian international relations — or at least Southeast Asian international relations because I doubt that Japan will ever accept the Chinese notion of regional order — that I described as characteristic of Chinese diplomacy in my last lecture.

Chinese diplomacy constantly hammers home the idea that if bilateral ties or ASEAN-China relations suffer because ASEAN stubbornly insists on speaking up on the SCS even when our mouths are stuffed with delicious Chinese cake, or because the Chinese Premier has to stay in one hotel rather than another, or if some date they propose for a meeting cannot be agreed upon because it is inconvenient for ASEAN, it is *our* fault and ours alone. China does not merely want consideration of its interests. China expects deference to its interests to be internalised by ASEAN members as a mode of thought; it wants the relationship to be defined not just by a calculation of ASEAN interests *vis-à-vis* China but "correct thinking" which leads to "correct behaviour". Foreign policy calculations are subject to continual revision; correct thinking is a permanent part of the sub-conscious. This differentiates Chinese diplomacy from the diplomacy of other major powers and represents a melding of Westphalian diplomatic practice with ancient Chinese statecraft. The very triviality of the behaviour China sometimes tries to impose underscores the cast of mind it seeks to embed in ASEAN through an almost Pavlovian process of conditioning. It does not always work. It can be counterproductive. But it works often enough and well enough with enough ASEAN members for China to persist.

Edward Luttwak has written of what he termed China's "great power autism". This is probably true but not peculiar to China — all great powers are to some degree "autistic" where their interests are concerned — but this is an inadequate explanation if "autism" implies lack of awareness. China is certainly aware of the cost of its actions. Significantly the first "2" in the "2+7 Framework" China set up for ASEAN-China relations is "deepening strategic mutual trust" which acknowledges the existence of a trust deficit. President Xi Jinping himself has emphasised the need to "increase mutual trust" with Southeast Asia, among other occasions, in his speech at this university last year. This again suggests that he knows that the present level of trust is inadequate.

ASEAN has begun to push back against China's assertiveness. Some ASEAN claimants including Vietnam have moved closer to the US and Japan to balance China. At the Summit with ASEAN held in March 2016, two out of three of China's proposals — the cookies that China regularly doles out at such events — failed to gain acceptance and one was accepted only after delay. Indonesia, a non-claimant state, has expressed concern over the impact of China's claims on its Exclusive Economic Zone (EEZ) in the Natunas and signalled its intention to deploy some of its most advanced military assets there. But whatever their concerns, there is a limit to which an ASEAN member can tilt towards the US.

No one can ignore or shun China. Vietnam is the prime example. Quite apart from the SCS disputes, Vietnam has a long and troubled history with China, but a senior Vietnamese official once told me, "Every Vietnamese leader must be able to stand up to China and get along with China. If anyone thinks this cannot be done at the same time, he doesn't deserve to be a leader". That China and Vietnam are two out of only five remaining communist systems is an additional link. The current muddle in Malaysia over whether or not Chinese vessels had intruded into its waters — one Minister said yes but another contradicted him — perhaps illustrates the multiple and contradic- tory forces at play in ASEAN. In any case, whatever costs in relations with ASEAN that China may have to pay for its assertiveness in the SCS may not be considered unbearably high by Beijing as compared to the interests at stake.

What are those interests? I doubt that control over resources of any kind figures very prominently in China's calculations on the SCS. Resources could be shared without prejudice to claims of sovereignty as China has itself suggested, although its own actions do not make any such agreement likely in the immediate future.

We can dismiss too the possibility that China is trying to strengthen its legal case. China does not even acknowledge that many areas contested by ASEAN claimants are in dispute. In his Singapore lecture, President Xi categorically asserted that, "The South China Sea islands have been China's territory since ancient times." Uncertainty over what China's "9-dash line" signifies has added to regional and international concerns. But China has said that it will not recognise the decisions of the Arbitral Tribunal on the case the Philippines brought against it under the United Nations Convention on the Law of the Sea (UNCLOS) even though that would at least clarify the legal status of the "9-dash line". Chinese diplomats have on occasion even argued that it is not in ASEAN's interest that China should clarify its claims. I do not think that China considers the SCS disputes a legal matter, although it has on occasion employed the vocabulary of international law in support of its position. But that is not the same thing as recognising a legal dispute and it has not been consistent in doing so. As I pointed out in the last lecture, China has recently relied more on history to justify its claims.

Military planners must prepare for all contingencies but I doubt that China's actions in the SCS are primarily intended to gain military advantage *vis-à-vis* the US. In the event of a war with the US, the artificial islands and the military assets on them will be vapourised within minutes and will not affect the outcome in any significant way. In any case, as I argued in my last lecture, war between the US and China is highly improbable. Beijing has carefully kept each of its actions in the SCS below a threshold that would compel even the most reluctant of US administrations to respond kinetically. The US has made clear that its alliance with Japan covers disputed islands in the East China Sea; it has been ambiguous about and thus in effect made clear that the same does not apply to its alliance with the Philippines and disputed territories in the SCS. War in support of America's principal East Asian ally, Japan, is credible even if unlikely; war over tiny islands, reefs and atolls would be absurd.

Even in scenarios short of war, I doubt that China really considers the deployment of military assets on these artificial islands a serious deterrent to Freedom of Navigation (FON) operations of the kind the US conducted last year and earlier this year. The US may become a little more cautious — it has never been reckless — but it will not stop operating in the SCS. Military assets that are unlikely to be used are at best a weak deterrent. If for example the People's Liberation Army (PLA) sinks a US naval vessel or shoots down a US military aircraft, the US will certainly retaliate. This will confront the Chinese leadership with a very invidious choice: a token or ineffectual response will expose the hollowness of the CCP's legitimating narrative of having led the "Great Rejuvenation" of China which will at least complicate if not jeopardise the CCP's hold on power; but escalation risks being forced to follow the highly jingoistic Chinese public opinion the CCP has cultivated down a path that Beijing does not really want to travel because it leads to the same outcome as the first choice. The Chinese leadership will strenuously try to avoid being placed in such a situation.

China's use of history to legitimate CCP rule and justify sovereignty claims gets us, I think, to the crux of the matter. For the past century, the legitimacy of any Chinese government has depended on its ability to defend China's sovereignty and preserve its borders. But what are those borders? Can the CCP meekly accept the borders imposed on a weak China that has now, to use Mao Zedong's phrase, "stood up" under communist leadership? China is not reckless but the CCP must at least give the appearance of recovering lost territory. Revanchism is an intrinsic part of the story of China's "Great Rejuvenation".

The lands lost to a weak China include what are now parts of Siberia and the Russian Far East, Mongolia, Hong Kong and Macau, Taiwan as well as the Paracels and Spratlys in the SCS. Siberia and the Russian Far East and Mongolia are now beyond recovery. Hong Kong and Macau reverted to Beijing's rule almost 30 years ago. The US has made clear it will not support independence for Taiwan. Without US support, independence is impossible. With that core concern assuaged, Beijing can multiply the economic threads binding Taiwan to the mainland and bide its time, confident that irrespective of internal changes and how the people of Taiwan regard themselves, Taiwan's long-term trajectory cannot run counter to China's interest. Changing the status quo is not an immediate possibility but is no longer an urgent issue, although China still eyes Taiwan's Democratic Progressive Party distrustfully and will never entirely forgo the option of forceful reunification.

That leaves the SCS territories to put some credible shreds of meat on the bare bones of the CCP's version of history as it navigates a second and more difficult phase of reforms and tries to manage social and labour unrest at a time of moderating growth and a future when slower growth will be China's "new normal". The very insignificance of the territories in dispute in the SCS may well be part of their attraction to Beijing for this essentially domestic political purpose. The costs and consequences of chest-thumping and acting tough in the SCS are minimal. Deterrence or its lack works both ways. If the Chinese cannot deter the US from operating in the SCS because the risks of doing so are too high to be credible, by the same token neither can the US deter or reverse Chinese activities in the SCS. China is not going to dig up the artificial islands it has constructed and throw the sand back into the sea or give up what it says was Chinese territory since "ancient times". Critical statements by the US, Europe or other countries from around the world calling on China to respect international law can be brushed aside. On the SCS the only opinion that really matters to the CCP is that of its own people. In the SCS, the CCP can declare victory without taking unacceptable risks.[5]

It was also no accident that the deployment of surface-to-air missiles on Woody Island in the Paracels was revealed shortly after the conclusion of the US-ASEAN Sunnylands Summit. While the artificial islands are inconsequential in military terms, they are a potent reminder to ASEAN that China is a geographic fact whereas the US presence in the SCS is the

---

[5]The Arbitral Tribunal delivered its award on the case the Philippines had brought against China on 12 July 2016. As the date approached, the Chinese Ministry of Foreign Affairs (MFA), despite all its earlier bluster about ignoring the judgment, seemed nervous. It had repeatedly warned ASEAN not to "internationalise" the SCS issue, but it did precisely that by gathering so-called statements of support for China's position from about 70 countries. Many of these statements were ambiguous and fell short of unequivocal statements of support for China, some were withdrawn and many were from countries that have only the vaguest of notions about the issues, if any, and so lacked credibility. The Tribunal's decision changed nothing on the ground. But as the Tribunal ruled against China on the main issue — the legal status of its "9-dash line" — these statements are obviously intended to muddy the waters if the Chinese people start to question why a respected international body has ruled against China on something Beijing has claimed was Chinese since "ancient times". For the same reason the Chinese MFA impugned the integrity of the Tribunal. But China took precautions to protect the Philippine Embassy in Beijing from protests and tried to dampen online nationalist sentiments. So obviously they also want to contain nationalist anger at the Tribunal's decision.

consequence of a geopolitical calculation. This is an idea that China never tires of seeding in ways subtle or direct. The implications of this idea should not be exaggerated, nor can they be shrugged off as entirely invalid either. Until relatively recently, the US took a somewhat hands-off approach to disputes in the SCS. When China first clashed with ASEAN over Mischief Reef in 1995, it took some persuading to get the US to declare a position of principle. Moreover, it is, I think, a geopolitical calculation that, despite all the media hullabaloo and tough talk including by the President himself, engages no US interest that is fundamentally irreconcilable with Chinese interests.

American and Chinese interests are not symmetrical. The SCS is more important to China than to the US. If I am correct that the SCS issue is ultimately connected to the legitimacy of CCP rule, it is an existential issue for China; a "core interest" although China denies it has applied that term to the SCS, no doubt in order to avoid unduly exciting us natives.[6] The US takes no position on the merits of the various claims of sovereignty but defines its interests in terms of upholding international law and Freedom of Navigation (FON). These are important interests but not on the same level as the basic underlying Chinese interest. FON and the integrity of international law are certainly not existential interests threatening the survival of the American system. I doubt that they are even interests that the US must defend at all costs.

China argues that it has never and will never interfere with FON. China's position is not without credibility as far as merchant marine traffic is concerned because it too is a trading nation. The US riposte is that there is a fundamental difference between FON as a right enshrined in UNCLOS and FON granted by the leave and favour of a major power, and that China's disregard for international law with regard to its SCS claims casts doubt over its commitment to uphold FON. This is true. But what the US glosses over is that it is not party to UNCLOS and is not very likely to become party to UNCLOS in the foreseeable future. Instead, the US says it considers UNCLOS largely customary international law and abides by it on that basis.

---

[6] When this lecture was delivered, this was a conclusion derived by inference from known facts. However on 18 July 2016, Admiral Wu Shengli, Commander of the PLA Navy, has done us the favour of explicitly telling his American counterpart, Admiral John Richardson, that the SCS is China's "core interest" and concerns the "foundation of the Party's governance" (as reported by Xinhua News Agency).

One does not have to be an extreme sceptic to suspect that this may be an ingeniously plausible way of misdirecting attention from the possibility that the US too upholds FON by its leave and favour: as a choice the US has made on the basis of a particular calculation of American national interests and not an obligation it must honour irrespective of whether calculations of interests change. It seems to me, for example, that some of the operational activities for the Proliferation Security Initiative that the US suggested after 9/11 — which included intercepting and searching vessels on the high seas — were significant derogations of FON as generally understood, abandoned only when other countries found them too much to swallow. I do not want to press the point too far. But it does not seem unreasonable to conclude that ultimately there may be fewer differences between the Chinese and American positions on FON than immediately meets the eye. A country may have more trust in one major power than the other, but this is a matter of preference, not law.

In strategic terms, the US wants to be able to operate in and through Southeast Asia and deploy its navy from its west coast through the Pacific to the Indian Ocean and Persian Gulf and back without impediment. This is an important interest, but is it a vital interest? Possibly. In any case, who can stop the US from doing so? This is a contingency that military planners must think about for extreme scenarios but is not particularly useful for understanding day-to-day international relations. To try to stop the US could be a *casus belli* and China does not want to risk war. What remains are differences between the US and China over what military activities short of hostilities can legitimately be conducted outside territorial seas in a country's EEZ. I wonder whether the current differences on this issue are less the result of fundamentally opposed concepts than they are a reflection of disparities in capabilities that one day will be narrowed.

China has historically been primarily a land power but is now in the process of turning itself into a maritime power as well. The PLA Navy (PLAN) has begun to operate in distant waters, albeit still only sporadically. Of particular note for Southeast Asia were: China's deployment of a surveillance ship off the coast of Hawaii during the Rim of the Pacific Exercise (RIMPAC) in 2014 (PLAN had participated by invitation in RIMPAC but the surveillance ship was not part of the exercise); a PLAN exercise the same year in the eastern Indian Ocean between Australia's Christmas Island and Indonesia during which the Chinese Navy transited through the Sunda and Lombok Straits; and the transit of Chinese naval vessels through American territorial seas off Alaska in 2015.

These deployments were depicted by the media as China flexing its new naval muscles and that was probably part of China's intention. But what I think was more interesting was the Chinese Ministry of Defence's statement on its RIMPAC surveillance ship deployment. It said: "The People's Liberation Army naval ships' operation in waters outside the territorial seas of other countries is in line with international law and international practice". This could have been a statement by the spokesman of the US 7th Fleet about its operations in the SCS. And indeed the Commander of the United States Pacific Command at that time described the deployment of the surveillance ship as "an acceptance by the Chinese of what we've been saying to them for some time, [which] is that military operations and survey operations in another country's EEZs, where you have national — your own national security interest, are within international law and are acceptable…a fundamental right that nations have."

As capabilities converge so do concepts; as concepts converge so may interests. At present, the basic common interest of both the US and China in the SCS is to minimise the risk of conflict by accident while continuing to assert what each considers their rights. They have begun to elaborate codes of conduct for unplanned encounters at sea and in the air and implement them.[7] This is of course good news and to be welcomed, but in the long run not necessarily entirely unequivocal good news.

In my last lecture, I argued that China is unlikely to be foolish enough to try and match US military capabilities in every theatre of operations but that it is probably inevitable that a more equal naval equation will eventually

---

[7] Admiral Harry Harris, Commander of the US Pacific Command, is well known for his hawkish views on Chinese behaviour in the SCS. But on the sidelines of the Shangri-La Dialogue held in Singapore in June 2016, he told the press that "We have seen positive behaviour in the past several months from China…every now and then you'll see an incident in the air that we may judge to be unsafe, but those are really over the course of time rare." US-China competition in the SCS may be becoming ritualised as a relatively predictable pattern of patrol and protest develops and the US and China reach a de facto accommodation.

develop in the SCS. When this occurs we should not assume, given the fundamental asymmetry of US and Chinese interests in the SCS, that the *modus vivendi* they may then reach in Southeast Asia must necessarily be in ASEAN's interests. Dealing with US-China competition is difficult but at least leaves open the possibility of manoeuvre. Dealing with US-China agreement — an implicit de facto agreement if not an explicit *de jure* agreement — may be even more uncomfortable. There will be less room to move and when major powers strike a deal they generally try to make lesser beings pay the price.

Of course such an eventuality is still a long way off and indeed may never come to pass. But it would be prudent to look past the loud trading of accusations and counter-accusations by the two sides and the kind of analysis put out by the more excitable sort of media and academic commentator, and think about what may currently seem unthinkable. Before you dismiss the possibility of US-China collusion as a paranoid fantasy, understand that stranger things have happened. At the International Conference on what was then called Kampuchea held at the UN in 1981 the US took China's side against ASEAN on whether or not the Khmer Rouge should return to power when the Vietnamese withdrew. ASEAN wanted elections but China supported the return of the Khmer Rouge. Did any of you imagine that the US once had in effect supported the return of a genocidal regime? The Assistant Secretary of State for East Asia at that time saw the relationship with China as the paramount US interest and even threatened the Singapore Foreign Minister at that time, S. Dhanabalan, that there would be "blood on the floor" if we did not change our position.

I hope the US understands that such concerns lurk not very far beneath the surface in East Asia where memories are long. Since the "Nixon shock" of 1972, Japan has periodically worried about being "passed" by its principal ally. If China has a responsibility to constantly reassure the small countries on its periphery, the US as "offshore balancer" has a parallel responsibility and a more complex one. To the countries of Southeast Asia, the American porridge is always going to be too hot or too cold; countries will always fear the US entangling them in its quarrels with rivals or being left to deal with other major powers without adequate support. It will be difficult for the US to persuade us that the porridge is just right. Such are the burdens a Great Power must shoulder.

But of late the US has itself added to these burdens. One such occasion was when a red line was drawn with a swaggering flourish, but then faded to pink and finally disappeared in the chaos of Syria. It was immensely damaging and will not be easily forgotten, particularly since I think the episode betrayed a certain mood in the American body politic that is on display in the on-going primary campaigns and will outlast the current administration.

Modern Southeast Asian history can be understood as a quest for autonomy in which process the formation of ASEAN was a crucial step. But so can modern Chinese history also be understood as a search to restore the autonomy lost in the 19th century and early 20th century. ASEAN and China have no choice but to live with each other. We are not enemies but as I earlier argued, relations between big and small neighbours cannot but be uneasy. Where the balance of autonomies will be eventually struck between ASEAN and China is the central issue in the relationship that will in turn determine the extent to which the regional architecture remains open and inclusive. This is one aspect of the uncertainty and ambiguity that my first lecture argued are the most salient characteristics of the post-Cold War world. To reach and maintain an acceptable balance requires ASEAN to meet what I described in that lecture as the basic strategic challenge of our times: avoiding being forced into invidious choices and keeping open the maximum range of options.

Meeting the challenge is as much a matter of preserving a state of mind — an intellectual balance — as it is a political, economic or military balance. Not too long ago, the late Malcolm Fraser, a former Australian Prime Minister, wrote a book in which he argued that the alliance with the US had become a strategic liability for Australia. It is true that across East Asia, American friends and allies face something of a dichotomy between economic calculations of interest in which even a slower growing China looms large, and security calculations of interest in which the US will remain the key factor for the foreseeable future. But note that I used the word "dichotomy" not "dilemma". Trade and investment are not favours China bestows upon the region. China needs the region as much as the region needs China, and as my last lecture argued, the parameters of US-China competition are narrower and less stark than sometimes assumed. It is thus difficult but not impossible to balance the two sets of interests. We cannot do so if we concede that a dilemma exists. To recognise a dilemma is to accept the very mental framework that Chinese diplomacy seeks to impose on the region and foreclose options. This was Fraser's fundamental intellectual error that led to a fallacious conclusion.

If the former leader of a staunch US ally can fall into such a mental trap, how much more difficult will it be for a disparate group of countries to avoid doing so? But we should not adopt a fatalistic attitude because that is the essential trap. To recognise error is the first step in avoiding it. And we are not without some advantages.

The small countries of Southeast Asia have lived in the midst of competition by larger powers for many centuries even before they were states in the modern sense of the term. To promiscuously and simultaneously balance, hedge and bandwagon is embedded in our foreign policy DNA. Not only do we not see any contradiction in doing so, this is an instinctive response honed by centuries of hard experience. But this instinct is today at some risk of being dulled in at least some members of ASEAN in whom the struthious delusions of ZOPFAN and SEANWFZ seem alive and well or may serve as a convenient excuse for those who have succumbed to the allure of Chinese largesse. We must recognise that the SCS is today the principal arena where complex mind games to condition mental frameworks in ASEAN members are underway. To take positions necessarily entails some risk. But to merely lie low and keep silent or only use words that are intended to be devoid of meaning on an issue as important as the SCS compromises autonomy, surrenders options and hence only invites greater risks.

As I have earlier indicated, the most important of these mind-games relate to the US presence in the SCS. Unfortunately, China understands ASEAN better than the US and knows far better how to work with ASEAN, which is a polite way of saying manipulate our weaknesses: the proclivity to privilege form and woolly thinking on regional security. What the US knows or has learnt about ASEAN has to be largely relearnt every four years. Whatever its other virtues, the American political system is something of a liability in Southeast Asia where its eccentricities are not as well understood as some Americans may believe.

In this respect, the Obama administration's use of the metaphor of a "pivot" or "rebalance" to describe its approach towards the region was in my view inappropriate. A "pivot" swings in different directions; what "rebalances" one way could well move in another. The metaphor inadvertently supports the Chinese tactic of emphasising the potential discontinuity of US policy. The metaphor also raises expectations that are almost bound to be disappointed because as the only global power, the US is always going to have responsibilities in other regions that it cannot ignore. What should have been emphasised instead was the essential continuity of the US presence in East Asia over many administrations of both parties. But the political imperative of distinguishing one administration's policies from another even when the differences are minimal is in-built into the American political system and we will just have to live with it.

Some commentators seem to regard a US-led Trans-Pacific Partnership (TPP) as part of an American containment strategy and in competition with a China-led Regional Comprehensive Economic Partnership (RCEP) that is, presumably, a Chinese break-out response to the TPP. This is nonsense. All the East Asian members of the TPP are also in the RCEP and some have bilateral Free Trade Agreements (FTA) with both China and the US. I spent a considerable part of my last lecture describing US-China interdependence and why it is as impossible for the US to contain China as it is for China to completely displace the US from East Asia. What is at stake is not whether it will be an American Southeast Asia or a Chinese Southeast Asia but where the balance of relative influence will lie and whether the regional architecture will be relatively open or relatively exclusive, and I stress the word "relative".

Of course, even slight shifts in the balance of influence in the regional environment can make a major difference to small countries. The many projects planned or being implemented under the ASEAN-China "2+7 Cooperation Framework", China's investments in infrastructure such as railroads under President Xi Jinping's vision of "One Belt, One Road", as well as burgeoning trade and other economic ties are binding southwest China and Southeast Asia into one economic space. This is certainly a development opportunity that is not to be rejected. But as national boundaries become hazy, old historical patterns are being re-established in new ways and Westphalian concepts of inter-state relations may be modified. There surely will be political and strategic and not just economic implications. The framework within which we calculate our interests could narrow. This is the geopolitical significance of the ASEAN Economic Community (AEC). Economic integration is an imperative not just for economic reasons but to encourage calculations of national interests by ASEAN member states within our own frameworks rather than become overly dependent on Chinese frameworks.

Economic integration is always politically difficult and the next phase of ASEAN economic integration which aims at establishing a common market and production platform will be more complicated than the first. The easy things have already been done. The domestic politics of ASEAN members is becoming more uncertain. Thailand and Malaysia are poised on the cusp of systemic change. Indonesia has yet to reach a stable post-Suharto internal equilibrium and is still an incoherent system seized with a somewhat petulant economic nationalism. There is significant uncertainty about the policies of the new Myanmar government because it has no experience of governance and, the military apart, inherits weak institutions. The Philippines has presidential elections in a few months and is not renowned for policy continuity. I sense buyer's remorse in Laos and Cambodia over the present level of integration commitments. In Singapore, some opposition parties are trying to cast doubt over open economic policies particularly with regard to foreign labour. In any case, we should not deceive ourselves that even under ideal circumstances for integration — and our circumstances are far from ideal — ASEAN can adequately cope alone.

This is particularly true in mainland Southeast Asia. To give but one example, China has built seven dams in the upper reaches of the Mekong River and reportedly plans 21 more. This is a permanent new geopolitical fact, analogous to artificial islands in the SCS, which the five ASEAN members through which the Mekong flows cannot ignore. Recently, China announced that to relieve drought in Thailand, Laos and Cambodia, it would release more water from its dams on the Mekong. There is an old Chinese proverb, "When drinking water, think of the source". Balance at sea must be matched by balance on land. The US Lower Mekong Initiative is a useful political symbol of commitment but substantively paltry by comparison to what China has put on the table and symbols only take you so far. What Japan has initiated for infrastructure development in Southeast Asia is far more substantive and significant. But unlike balance at sea, to reach balance on land will take more than the efforts of one or two countries.

I believe there is a need for a broader and more coordinated effort for infrastructure development projects in mainland Southeast Asia. One possibility is public-private partnerships by multinational consortiums of companies from the US, Japan, Australia, South Korea and India. This would considerably broaden the range of options for mainland Southeast Asia, prevent the entrenchment of a fatalistic mindset and serve as a crucial complement to the maritime capability building programmes some of these countries have started for ASEAN. Chinese participation in such consortiums is not to be ruled out. As China's growth moderates and its population ages, there will be many demands on state coffers and the scale and ambition of what China has planned cannot be undertaken by China alone as Beijing itself realises. This was the rationale for the Asian Infrastructure Investment Bank (AIIB). It was a strategic mistake for the US and Japan to have stayed out of it. Fortunately it is not an irreversible mistake. Collaboration with China by the US and its allies in the AIIB for infrastructure development is desirable to take the starkest zero-sum edges off strategic competition in Southeast Asia and expose false dilemmas as false.

Questions and Answers

Question: Your narrative presupposes that there is continuity in US foreign policy. What happens if the Republican and Democratic Party have a situation whereby the presidential nominees are either Bernie Sanders or Donald Trump and they are in favour of rebalancing away from Asia and the Far East. What happens in that scenario?

Bilahari Kausikan (BK): There has been a basic continuity in US policy in East Asia for 40 years or so. But Trump and Bernie Sanders, as I have alluded to in this lecture, have been tapping on the same undercurrent in the body politic which is basically anti-globalisation, a sense of insecurity in America's engagement with the world which makes them uncertain about their future. I think you must have read the *New York Times* interview that Trump gave, where he said that he is for America First. He is going to take a far more transactional approach towards the rest of the world and he specifically mentioned Korea and Japan.

Trump could well get enough delegates to be the Republican Party's nominee but I think that the Republican establishment knows that it is in a fix; it has a terrible dilemma. You could have a brokered convention but you will have a grassroots rebellion. If you have a normal convention, you will have to endorse Trump. I think Sanders will fizzle out and he is not the concern. So it will be Hillary against Trump, if that happens. I would like to think that Hillary will be a certainty and she will win. And if she wins, the basic continuity that I have described will continue. But so many strange things have happened during this election season that I am hesitant to be very confident in my predictions. Since Hillary is a member of the establishment, can she tap into that mood that Sanders and Trump are tapping into? And if mainstream Republicans don't vote for Trump and don't vote for Hillary, will the undercurrent I referred to earlier swell in favour of Trump? I have no idea whether this will happen, but the prospect is not pretty. This is a long answer to your short question; the short answer is I don't know.

Question: I have three questions. First, you mentioned the role of China, the role of the US with regard to small states, but what about Russia and the EU? Russia is always looking out for a warm water port, would it take advantage of looking for a partner in Asia?

Second, many threats that China faced in the 19th and 20th century originated from the seas and US was part of the eight-nation alliance in the 1900s that invaded China after the Boxer rebellion. Could this memory in China's mind still be very fresh and they feel that if they don't capitalise on the sea, they will lose out?

Third, I understand the Responsibility to Protect (R2P) doctrine sometimes equals to the right to intervene based on humanitarian grounds. On the issue of the Rohingya refugees — the Rakhine state has over a million of these people and most of these people are not recognised as citizens and not given legal protection — what is ASEAN's stand on this?

BK: The EU is strategically irrelevant in East Asia although it has an important economic role in this region. But even then, I suspect it is not so much the EU as the EU, but just Germany, France, the UK, Netherlands and so on. Russia is on a trajectory that will make itself junior partner to China if it continues on this trajectory. The Soviet Union had a role in this region because of the Soviet Pacific fleet. No big Pacific fleet, no big role. Russia is a member of several East Asian forums, the Asia-Pacific Economic Cooperation, the EAS, the ARF, and it plays a role in them. Russia cannot be ignored because it is a Permanent Member of the UN Security Council, but it is not a major player in the region. The major players are first China and the US, and on the second tier are American allies like Japan, South Korea, Australia, maybe India occasionally.

Second question, why shouldn't China try to turn itself into a maritime power? No reason why China shouldn't be a maritime power; it is trying to become one and it will eventually succeed.

And your last question on the Rohingyas. R2P is one of those concepts that sound very good but does not really work very well in practice. It has only been deployed against very weak and insignificant countries. The Rohingyas are an issue ASEAN does not want to take any responsibility for because there is no solution. Sometimes you have to grow calluses on your heart, to quote Mr Lee Kuan Yew, or you will bleed to death. Nobody — not just ASEAN — wants to take responsibility. So don't expect anyone to do anything really useful about the Rohingyas. One thing you should learn about international relations: just because a problem exists doesn't mean that there will be a solution.

Question: You spoke about how domestic public opinion holds strong influence on foreign policy and we are seeing an increasingly vocal electorate across ASEAN, especially in Singapore. You mentioned in your previous lectures that politicising foreign policy might stifle one's ability to be nimble. My question is in two parts. The first part is on the misinformed intelligentsia, or in your own words, stupid people. You cited Malcom Fraser's fallacy. What is the biggest fallacy you have heard among the public intelligentsia in Singapore? And how can we better manage the politicising of foreign affairs in Singapore? The second part is for the people, the electorate, what is your recommended approach to explaining foreign policy so that even the man on the streets understands and rallies behind the government's position in foreign affairs?

BK: The answer to your question is the idea that Singapore is not vulnerable, which is perpetuated in various ways. The issue is not that there should not be political debates about foreign policy. The issue is that political debates about foreign policy should take place within broad, generally accepted parameters. There are parameters for every country that define what the country can and cannot do and the parameters are narrow for smaller countries. And the denial of that — which is represented by saying that we are not vulnerable — is I think the biggest and the stupidest idea with foreign policy implications that has been put forward. On what we can do about it, come for the last lecture.

Question: Could you comment briefly about India's interest and perspectives on the SCS dispute?

BK: India has occasionally sent some ships for exercises in the SCS and India has made some statements on the SCS. India is the other big power that is contiguous to Southeast Asia. We would like India to play a bigger role. Singapore, played — I think it is fair to say — the leading role in bringing India back into ASEAN circles after the estrangement over Cambodia's occupation by Vietnam in the 1980s. But the reality is that a big, complicated country like India will more naturally be inward looking than outward looking and insofar as India is outwardly directed, it is more directed westwards towards Pakistan and Afghanistan than eastwards. China is a complicated country. India is a far more complicated country. It has no choice but to look inward. It plays an occasional role but is not a major player in the SCS. It is potentially a major player on land if it can help in infrastructure development in conjunction with others. It has a plan to build a road from the eastern part of India eastwards across Myanmar, and it is a good plan. That will make a very big strategic difference.

Question: I'm a JC2 student. And I'm going to ask you a question related to the H2 syllabus in the 'A' Levels. You made a reference to how in the post-Cold War context, Indonesia actually paid lip service to the ASEAN way when resolving the Cambodian crisis and chose to engage with the relevant parties bilaterally. But what we studied in our textbooks is that it was ultimately ASEAN disunity that undermined the effectiveness of dealing with the Cambodian crisis to the point where Vietnam actually rejected the eight point proposal and any meetings with preconditions set by Thailand and Singapore. So it was portrayed as ASEAN being unable to resolve these problems because of the hard line stance by Singapore and Thailand, therefore they needed the bilateral method by Jakarta.

BK: Which textbook is this? No, it is a gross oversimplification. I have never read a good book about the Cambodian issue. Several of us in this room devoted one decade of our lives to various aspects of it but I have never read any book that does justice to what transpired.

Question: So it's not true?

BK: It is simultaneously true and not true. Please don't write this in your exam or you will be sure to fail.

Let me explain. First of all, it was never ever in ASEAN's power to resolve the Cambodian crisis. The Cambodian crisis was essentially a Sino-Soviet proxy fight. These are big powers. ASEAN's role — and ASEAN held together quite well until the end — was to prevent the rest of the world accepting Vietnam's invasion and occupation of Cambodia as *a fait accompli*. If that happened, it would have been the end of the story. To prevent this happening, we fought diplomatic battles for 10 years, and quite successfully. The proposal that ASEAN put forward was meant to be rejected by Vietnam so it made Vietnam look bad. So that ASEAN could go to the UN and tell them "look we made an eight point proposal, and they rejected it". This is diplomacy you know, my dear. And there were many such episodes throughout those 10 years.

A solution became possible towards the end of the 1980s after Mr Gorbachev came to power in what was then called the Soviet Union. And Mr Gorbachev decided he had to retrench some of the over-extensions of the Soviet Union in order to concentrate on internal reform. Now, he messed up the internal reform but that's another matter. So he decided to settle. The Chinese and the Soviets settled, then the other Permanent Members of the UN Security Council got into the act. ASEAN had very little role in the settlement. That is the harsh fact. Of course, Indonesia likes bustling around. There were a few meetings called the Jakarta Informal Meetings or JIM and, between the JIMs, there were working groups, but what they achieved was limited.

I knew these meetings were all futile. This was a big power game. The end game was a big power game. Preventing *a fait accompli* was an ASEAN game because ASEAN, made up of small countries, could lobby much more effectively in the UN and in the Non-Aligned Movement than the big countries. But once it got to the end, I knew this was a waste of time. I got fed up in one Jakarta working group meeting, so I left and went to the bar of the hotel where the meeting was held. I was having a beer. My Chinese counterpart, who later became the first Chinese Ambassador to Singapore, came to see me and said, "Don't worry, we have settled with the Vietnamese". I said, "Okay good, tell me what's the settlement" and then he told me some things which came to pass after a few months, so he wasn't making things up. I can't blame your textbooks or your teachers because textbooks only go by documents that ASEAN put out and your teachers only know what is in the textbooks. Many things were just tactical moves and not meant to be believed, not meant to be accepted. In fact, if the Vietnamese were cleverer, they would have accepted the eight points and then we would have been in a fix. So, understand that what is on the surface of international relations is not necessarily the most important thing.

Question: But you wouldn't reject the argument that ultimately the Cambodian crisis did give ASEAN a lot of legitimacy on the world platform?

BK: Oh yes. Because what we could do, we did very well, which was to jam the Vietnamese at every turn when they were trying to break out of diplomatic isolation.

Ong Keng Yong (OKY): We even posted a diplomat at toilet doors you know.

BK: To make sure that even if delegates had to go to the toilet, they would come out in time to vote the right way, which meant against Vietnam.

OKY: One of my jobs was to be at one of the toilets at the UN.

BK: Please don't write it in your exam because you will fail. Your teacher may not understand.

Question: You talked about difficulties in integration in ASEAN right? But considering how far we've gone in terms of being able to churn out FTAs, do you think that we could or should aspire towards the ideals that the EU-centric economic model aspires to?

BK: The essential difference between ASEAN and the EU is this: ASEAN is an inter-state organisation. The EU deludes itself that it can overcome nationalism and is a post-nationalist construct, a supra-national organisation. Now, it doesn't work. Or it works only up to an extent. You look at what is happening in the EU now. That is all the *denouement* of the internal contradictions of the EU idea. So we are not going to go down that way. We talk about "community". This is a rather deceptive term. Because community implies supra-nationality. But we don't mean it. It's not on the agenda. The only bit of any ASEAN community that can be called supra-national is the dispute settlement mechanism in the AEC. But that has never been tested and I can bet you that it will never be tested. We prefer to go to the World Trade Organization because then we don't have to quarrel directly with each other; it is better for some third party to tell us what to do. If we start quarrelling directly with each other, God knows where it will end up. So I categorically reject — and I am glad to say that no matter what they may say in public, I don't think it has never seriously been in the minds of any ASEAN member — to be like the EU. And what's happening with the EU at present convinces me of our great wisdom.

Question: From an economic standpoint, how far can the countries of ASEAN go? On trade barriers, we made progress. But services, capital, I don't see labour mobility happening in my lifetime. How far do you think we could actually get, and what is realistic?

BK: The short answer to your very good question is nobody knows until you try. The goals are set out. I'm sure you've read ASEAN 2025. Essentially, for the economic community, to have a common market and a common production platform, we have to deal with non-tariff barriers and services and to some degree, labour. Labour is going to be very difficult because if there is totally free labour mobility, everybody will move to Singapore and then where do we stay? So it's going to be very difficult. And as I mentioned, the key success or failure factor is going to be domestic politics of member states. Right now, it doesn't look good. But while I have never been accused of being overly optimistic, it is true that throughout the 49 years of ASEAN, we have surprised ourselves and our critics from time to time. So what we can do — and this is how ASEAN works — is to set a goal. Then after all members have agreed on the goal, you try to keep it in sight even though sometimes you can't move, sometimes you only move sideways, and sometimes you may even move backwards a bit. But you always keep the goal in sight and you don't give up and then things eventually change and you move.

ASEAN in its original conception was a Cold War organisation. Five non-communist countries deciding that we'd better hang together no matter how much we hate each other because if not, we would hang separately. As a Cold War organisation, we had a small problem when the Cold War ended. What should we now do? Of course, what we did was what we always said we would do but didn't really for a long time: economic integration. There were a lot of agreements signed during the 1990s. Very few of them were implemented. There were some ASEAN secretariat studies done that showed something like 30% or less were implemented. We nearly fell apart when the Asian economic crisis hit in 1997. But a near death experience focuses the mind. After that, and because of the rise of China and India, we realised we'd better get our act together and do what we always said we were doing because we are fated to live in between these two giants and if we don't integrate we are finished. That remains the strategic impetus for economic integration. It doesn't look good at present, but we shouldn't give up because something may happen, things will change.

Question: What do you see as the role of Australia on ASEAN policies and economics, and particularly in the context of US-China relations?

BK: In the broad context of US-China relations, Australia is an adjunct to the US — an Australian Prime Minister once said it is the "Deputy Sheriff". So it does not really have much of an independent role in that context. But in other areas Australia has a major role to play and *is* playing a major role in ASEAN. In economics, in capacity-building in the less developed ASEAN countries, in a whole host of things. Australia is one of ASEAN's most important partners in this region. There are some dialogue relationships that seemed a good idea 20 years ago. We now wonder why we established those relationships but are stuck with them. To be polite we call

all dialogue partners important. But Australia is permanently part of the region, will get closer to the region, and it is *really* one of ASEAN's most important dialogue partners. Some of our ASEAN colleagues like to multiply dialogue partners in the name of "centrality". But what we should be trying to do is think how we can deepen relationships with countries like Australia that are substantive dialogue partners.

Question: In your talk today, you spoke of China's influence *vis-à-vis* ASEAN. Singapore, among ASEAN countries, stands out in its racial composition as a majority Chinese country. Do you see this as an advantage or disadvantage for Singapore in this context of dealing with China? For instance, could we be China's portal for dealing with ASEAN?

BK: It has both advantages and disadvantages. The advantage is obvious. Many Singaporeans speak some version of Chinese. And I guess it helps. It doesn't hurt, particularly in economic relations, for business. The disadvantage is that China keeps referring to us as a "Chinese country". We keep telling them that we are *not* a Chinese country. Yes, the majority of the population may be of Chinese origin but this is not a Chinese country. They don't understand, or don't want to understand. And that is a liability because when they say you are a Chinese country, they don't mean it as flattery. They mean that because you are Chinese, you should know your position in life better than the others and help us explain to the ASEAN countries where their position is. Of course we cannot do that.

OKY: And just to remind ourselves. When the late Lee Kuan Yew conducted his relationship with Chinese leaders, he never used the Chinese language although he perfectly understood it.

BK: It's been the same for subsequent Prime Ministers.

OKY: Ladies and Gentlemen, thank you all for being such a good audience, and I hope you have taken away some of the important messages that Bilahari has delivered in this lecture.

Lecture IV

THE MYTH OF UNIVERSALITY: THE GEOPOLITICS OF HUMAN RIGHTS

As I stand here before you, at least three different things are happening simultaneously: what I think; what I say to convey what I think which, because of the limitations of language or by design, will not always be the same as what I think; and what you hear and understand of what I had intended to convey, which is again not necessarily the same thing. Misunderstanding of some degree is inherent in all human communication; indeed in all human perception. One might call this the "Rashomon phenomenon" after the title of the short story by the Japanese author Ryunosuke Akutagawa. Human rights and democracy more than other subjects are particularly susceptible to this phenomenon. Anything really "universal" ought to be less prone to misunderstanding. In fact the evidence of our senses tells us that the most salient characteristic of the world we live in is diversity, not universality.

To explain why universality is a myth, I must beg your indulgence to recount how some of my personal experiences intersected in a minor and tangential way with international developments. Had the Institute of Policy Studies and the Lee Kuan Yew School of Public Policy not been so foolishly reckless as to invite me to deliver this series of lectures, I would not inflict my stories on anyone. They are of little inherent interest except, I think, to explain why I came to this conclusion and in the process draw some of the threads of my previous lectures together. My focus is on human rights and democracy promotion as an element of statecraft; in relations between states.

I served as a junior diplomat at our Embassy in Washington DC from 1984 to 1987. Mikhail Gorbachev had been appointed General-Secretary of the Communist Party of the Soviet Union in 1985 but the Cold War was still quite warm and the Soviet bloc seemed on the rise. The Soviet Union had invaded and occupied Afghanistan. With Moscow's support, Vietnam had invaded and occupied Cambodia. The revolutionary Sandinistas had come to power in Nicaragua. Cuban troops were fighting in Africa. That the Cold War was in fact nearing its end and that the Soviet Union would collapse only six years later was not evident at that time, at least it was not evident to me. I had never paid much attention to human rights and democracy as factors in international relations and I do not think they played any significant role in US diplomacy during the Cold War except perhaps as a tactic. The US has of course always seen itself as the Exemplar of Rights and Democracy to the World. But during the Cold War this was more propaganda than policy. The key American foreign policy considerations were strategic. If the US had any qualms about pursuing policies that did not meet its own notions of human rights and democracy, it hid them well.

These subjects certainly did not occupy much of my time in Washington. Our major preoccupation at the Embassy was the Vietnamese occupation of Cambodia. There was an element of our work that obliquely touched upon human rights when we had to explain why ASEAN supported a resistance coalition that included the murderous Khmer Rouge. We did not deny that they had committed genocide. We pointed out that the Chinese-backed Khmer Rouge was the most effective fighting force in the resistance and words alone would not get the Soviet-supported Vietnamese out of Cambodia and give the Cambodia people an opportunity to determine their own future under UN-supervised elections.

It was an argument that I now admit was a little disingenuous. But in the context of the Cold War, I do not recall that we had much difficulty in getting officials of the Reagan administration to accept it. As I recounted in my last lecture, at one point the US had even sided with China and the Khmer Rouge against ASEAN. Insofar as American officials were uneasy, it was about supplying non-lethal assistance to the non-communist components of the resistance. Some American officials were then still so traumatised by the Vietnam War that they imagined that supplying a few pairs of boots, some ponchos and radio-sets would again lead them down a slippery slope into another quagmire.

There was a little more difficulty with Congress which tends to be purist about human rights and democracy. But there we had the staunch support of a key member of the House of Representatives, the late Stephen Solarz, the Chairman of the House Asia-Pacific Sub-Committee. Mr Solarz was generally very liberal and I wondered why he supported us until one of his staff explained that his district had many former refugees from the Soviet bloc. They hated the Soviet Union. Since the Soviet Union was supporting Vietnam, they were for anything that was against Vietnam. As the votes went, the Congressman followed. Mr Solarz was not atypical.

In the Philippines, the Marcos regime was under pressure after the assassination of Benigno Aquino — the current Philippine President's father — in 1983. "People's Power" eventually forced Marcos to flee the Philippines in 1986. Still, our main concern, and the main concern of the Reagan administration, was what Marcos' fall after 20 years in power would mean for the stability of the Philippines and Southeast Asia and not primarily as an opportunity for the promotion of democracy. In 1987, human rights was briefly forced upon my attention by the necessity of dealing with the fall-out when a group of lay Catholic social workers, returned overseas graduates and radical theatre enthusiasts were arrested under the Internal Security Act. But this was mainly to help the administration cope with pressures from NGOs and their supporters in Congress. To our friends in the administration, this was a distraction from the strategic issues of the day. We had to do our bit by running interference — to use an American football term — to help keep the administration focused.

By the end of my term in the US, events were moving more quickly and with greater significance than anyone could have foreseen. Gorbachev had introduced *glasnost*, was attempting *perestroika* and, overcoming initial scepticism, was taking important steps to improve relations with the West. In 1986, the US and the Soviet Union had reached a major understanding on nuclear arms control at the Reykjavik Summit. The same year, the Geneva Accords set a timetable for Soviet withdrawal from Afghanistan. As the Cold War wound down, events began to break in East Asia as well. In 1987, martial law was lifted in Taiwan; that same year, mirroring events the previous year in the Philippines, student demonstrations pushed President Chun Doo-hwan from power in South Korea. I began to sense that something was shifting in US attitudes towards human rights and democracy, but only very dimly and inchoately.

It was not until 1988, after I returned to Singapore and found myself peripherally involved in the expulsion of a US diplomat stationed in Singapore, one Hank Hendrickson, that it clearly dawned on me what had changed. Singapore had been consistent in supporting the US presence in Southeast Asia, at least as consistent if not more so than formal US allies, Thailand and the Philippines. We had done so even when it was unfashionable during the Vietnam War when the US was in dire need of Asian political support. We had volunteered support because it was in our interest. But it was a calculation of interest that we need not have made — notwithstanding the "Special Relationship", even the British were half-hearted in their support for the Vietnam War — and a calculation that was not without domestic risk for the government. After the Hendrickson affair broke, I recall Mr Lee Kuan Yew saying that the US should not assume that our ground was naturally in support of America. It was a choice the Singapore government made and, having made, had to politically sustain. It was not unreasonable to expect the US government would help and not hinder us.

Yet here was an accredited diplomat from a friendly country, with the support and encouragement of his immediate State Department superiors, and in defiance of all diplomatic practice enshrined as international law in the Vienna Convention on Diplomatic Relations, enthusiastically promoting opposition to the People's Action Party (PAP) government, promising shelter and succour to the chosen ones if they ran into trouble. Clearly, advancing human rights and democracy was now American policy and not just propaganda, an interest that the US considered central enough to risk a long nurtured and mutually beneficial relationship. Why? It was not as if they wished us ill. I was acquainted with Mr Hendrickson and his State Department superiors. I was sure they were not enemies. They did what they did simply because we did not fit neatly into their theories of political development. Now that the Cold War was ending, they saw an opportunity to nudge us in the direction that the Philippines, South Korea and Taiwan had taken. In their minds, they were doing us a favour.

I do not think it was a mistake to have supported the US then and to continue to support the US now. But there was a lesson to be drawn from this episode. The lesson is not that the US was ungrateful. Gratitude is not a concept that is greatly relevant to the understanding of international affairs. If you expect gratitude in international relations, adopt a dog and name it "Foreign Policy". The relevant concept is interest; interests change and they do not change to suit our conveniences. It is therefore vital to try, the best we can, to look over the horizon to see what may be coming our way. I decided to study human rights and democracy more closely than I had hitherto done to try to better understand their evolving role in post-Cold War geopolitics.

In 1992, I wangled a three-month sabbatical at one of the older British universities. The first, most valuable and enduring lesson I learnt was from the don assigned to guide my studies, although it was perhaps not the lesson he would have chosen or intended to impart. He was a very distinguished historian of Southeast Asia, with a contemporary interest in human rights in what was then known as Burma and East Timor; so immensely learned that he had probably forgotten more about the region than I could ever hope to learn. But the Southeast Asia he talked to me about — and he spoke very eruditely and with great passion about human rights and democracy in our region — seemed to me to bear little relationship to the place I actually lived in and had dealt with in my previous work as Director for Southeast Asia in the Ministry of Foreign Affairs. We met only once. I never went back to see him again and he never asked to see me again. It was probably for the best.

The lesson I took away from this encounter was simple: when thinking about human rights and democracy, Conviction, however fervent, and Authority, however majestic, are not the same things as practicality or even reality. Common sense, you may think, but this is an idea that is akin to heresy in the human rights community which too often confuses feeling Good with doing good.

I began this lecture by pointing out that the shade of Rashomon constantly lurks around talk about human rights and democracy, making it particularly susceptible to misunderstanding. So please do not misunderstand me. Let me state my position plainly and unequivocally: I am not against human rights; I think human rights are one of the most important ideas that the human species has ever invented. What I am sceptical about — deeply sceptical — is what I have termed the Myth of Universality: the assumption that when we speak about rights or democracy we will all always mean the same thing just because we use the same words, and that the same words will always be applicable in the same way everywhere.

The Myth of Universality is what I called in the first of these lectures, a "false framework": an ontological device into which we try to force a stubbornly elusive and ever shifting reality in order to comfort ourselves with the illusion of comprehension. I argued that resorting to false frameworks in the more than usually ambiguous and uncertain post-Cold War times that we are experiencing is dangerous. This particular false framework is perhaps more dangerous than others because human rights and democracy seem to be the one reliable fixed point of reference in an age without definition.

No country has rejected The Universal Declaration of Human Rights. Since the Universal Declaration was adopted in 1948, an elaborate apparatus of international and regional human rights treaties, declarations and institutions have enmeshed relations between states and, whatever their actual practice, states can no longer credibly argue that their internal affairs are in principle entirely only their own business. During the Cold War, the US and the Soviet Union validated their policies by opposing ideas of universal norms. After the collapse of the Soviet Union, only one definition of the Universal seemed to be left standing.

Only the exceptionally obtuse would cling to a false framework that is demonstrably false. But all I have just described is *not* demonstrably false, only partially and contingently true. This is a more subtle concept and therefore more difficult to grasp. Any idea that is only partially and contingently true is an intellectual shape-shifter. What is true and what is not true is in flux and thus elusive, particularly when there are no clear or attractive alternatives.

The brief post-Cold War American unipolar moment has passed. Europe lacks the power to force acceptance of its ideas which in Europe's present predicaments are in any case not particularly appealing, even to many Europeans. Post-Soviet Russia seems to have reverted to an older idea: that of the great 19th century Russian philosopher, Pyotr Chaadaev, who said of his country "We never went with other peoples". China is not interested in promoting any idea of the Universal except its own intrinsic superiority as a normative value, and that primarily in East Asia where it is contested. India may accept western universal values, but I think only with regard to some of its internal arrangements and not as an over-riding international authority.

There are also more fundamental conceptual problems with the notion of universality. The idea that runs through the work of Isaiah Berlin — a liberal British political philosopher who deserves to be more widely read and understood than he is today — is that there is not one Good but many conceptions of the Good, each of which may have its own validity but which are not necessarily reconcilable or capable of simultaneous realisation. This is an idea that many liberals seem to find hard to accept: there is nothing more intolerant than a liberal in full bray in defence of liberalism asserted, somewhat self-contradictorily, as an absolute value. This often leads liberals into thickets of paradox, confusion and contradiction. Examples are not hard to find. Earlier this year, some students at Yale-NUS called for Ambassador Chan Heng Chee to be sacked from the school's Board because they took offence at her defence of Singapore's position on Lesbian, Gay, Bisexual and Transgender (LGBT) rights at Singapore's Second Universal Periodic Review at the United Nations Human Rights Council in Geneva. Curiously, it did not seem to occur to the students that the value of a liberal education is precisely to instil openness to other views even if you do not agree with them.

After the terrorist attack on *Charlie Hebdo* in Paris, it struck me that there was a similarity in the modes of thought of the terrorists and the cartoonists, not moral equivalence in their actions because there is clearly none, but a similarity of thought processes: both held their values so absolutely that they thought it justified anything. Murder is wrong, but is lampooning a religion right? The fact that the terrorists held a completely mistaken view of Islam is beside the point. The point is that they believed in it; believed in it as fervently as the cartoonists believed in freedom of expression.

I wrote an article for *The Straits Times* along these lines. The French ambassador took umbrage, at what exactly I am still not quite sure. He wrote a letter to *The Straits Times* to refute me. That was his right. I did not find his arguments convincing and explained why in a response to his letter. But he went further and complained to my bosses about me and got his own boss to do so as well, clearly to try to shut me up. In other words, he attempted to mobilise superior force to deprive me of my freedom of expression; the very freedom the French state, indeed all Europe, defended in the case of the cartoonists. My bosses quite properly told the Ambassador that my views are my own and if he did not agree with them to talk to me to convince me of the error of my ways. He has not done so. I do not in any way blame the Ambassador for trying coercion rather than persuasion. In his position I would have done the same. But then I have never been accused of being a liberal. Perhaps he secretly isn't a liberal too.

These are trivial anecdotes. But there is a serious point to them. If there is not only one Good but many Goods which are irreconcilable, then we must either impose our concept of the Good by force, which in history has occurred all too often with very bloody consequences — or moderate our own ideas to minimise friction and seek some *modus vivendi* between different conceptions of the Good in order to lessen the probability of conflict. As Isaiah Berlin said in his famous lecture "Two Concepts of Liberty": "Freedom for the pike is death to the minnows: the liberty of some must depend on the restraint of others."

The idea of human rights is qualitatively different from the idea of a rock or a stone or a tree or the idea that the earth is round. A rock is a rock irrespective of whether or not we believe in it and the earth remains round even if we think it is flat. The idea that human rights have an autonomous reality or are somehow "natural rights" is, as the 19th century English philosopher Jeremy Bentham famously said, "rhetorical nonsense — nonsense on stilts". Some legal scholars have argued that human rights are now *jus cogens.* Louis Henkin has, for example, argued that human rights reflect a "new law of fundamental values adopted by the international system". But I don't see how Bentham's basic point can be avoided by dressing up "nonsense on stilts" in lawyer's Latin. This does not mean that human rights and international law can be dismissed as unimportant. What it means is that international law and human rights are, as I alluded to earlier, human inventions: civilising myths that we have chosen to believe in so that we may at least occasionally live in a civilised manner; faith, not objective reality. The apple will always fall even if I stubbornly choose not to believe in gravity. Faith is subjective. There is no reason to assume that we will all always believe in the same thing in the same way even when we appear to do so. Violent quarrels have erupted even in monotheistic religions.

Although the idea that humans have rights of some sort has won general acceptance, most specific rights are still essentially contested concepts where superficial agreement, sometimes no more than agreement over vocabulary, masks deep conflicts over interpretation and implementation. This is true even with something as basic as the right to life where there is fundamental and visceral disagreement over capital punishment, mandated by Sharia law, and abortion, which some Christians equate with murder. If Life itself can be disputed, how much real agreement over the ever expanding range of other ideas claimed as rights can we realistically expect? Advocates argue that human rights are aspirational global norms. I do not disagree. But that does not get around Isaiah Berlin's insight into the plurality of values and the essentially contested nature of many rights held up as aspirations.

Failure to recognise these realities leads either to a mindless formalism — a numbers game of encouraging states to sign human rights instruments that they do not have the capacity or even the intention to implement — or leads back to coercion. Anyone familiar with the United Nations has witnessed the less than edifying spectacle of western diplomats threatening, sometimes subtly, sometimes otherwise, but always apparently oblivious to the irony of their actions, to withhold desperately needed aid from less developed countries unless they supported some human rights resolution or another. I am not shocked by such behaviour. It is entirely understandable. Many a career in multilateral diplomacy has hung on a comma or a word in some obscure resolution and some countries need to find grounds for believing that they are still world powers. These are perfectly logical and justifiable reasons for what they do. But we should not call it promoting human rights. We should not forget that the promotion of human rights and democracy is not just a high moral calling but also an industry.

When I returned from my sabbatical at the beginning of 1993, I became involved in preparations for the United Nations Conference on Human Rights that was to be held in Vienna later that year. It was intended to be a festival celebrating western victory in the Cold War. The beginning of the 1990s was, however, a period of great potential geopolitical complication. After the Cold War the West was drunk with hubris; China was beginning to take off and, freed of the imperatives and constraints of their *de facto* anti-Soviet alliance, the US and China were beginning to eye each other warily, particularly after the Tiananmen incident. President Bill Clinton had been elected in 1993. The Democrats had been out of power for two decades, except for the atypical four years of the Carter administration that even Democrats seemed eager to forget. Clinton had accused his predecessor of "coddling dictators" and an inexperienced administration seemed somewhat more than merely inclined to take a harder line with China and give human rights and democracy promotion a more prominent role in US-China relations. But these were issues on which the Chinese Communist Party would never compromise. The potential for trouble in US-China relations seemed great and if trouble broke out it would have rocked our entire region. Our memories of the Hendrickson affair were also still fresh — I hope my younger colleagues have not entirely forgotten it — and the new Democrat administration did not know Singapore or the region as well as the Republicans. The Asia specialists in the new administration, who did know us very well, did not appear to be the most influential voices in its inner counsels.

This was the context of what came to be known as the "Asian values" debate which was more about geopolitics than values of any description. The goals of the debate were modest: to encourage a more complex and realistic view of political development in East Asia and buy some time for the passions of a new administration to cool and common sense and the imperatives of *realpolitik* to prevail. But it made for a fraught run-up to the Vienna Conference. More fraught than I thought at that time.

An Asian Group preparatory meeting for the Vienna Conference was held in Bangkok in April 1993. Prior to the meeting a friend in the US Embassy in Singapore had taken me aside and rather cryptically sounded a cautionary note about the American diplomat who had been assigned by the State Department in Washington to observe the meeting. She was, he vaguely intimated, inclined to ingratiate herself with the new administration and so I should make a special effort to keep her thoroughly briefed. It is one of the minor regrets of my career that I did not take his advice seriously enough. But it would have in any case been difficult to take his advice because I never set eyes on the lady. God only knows where she was, how she got her information and what she reported. My regret is minor because

I doubt it would have made much difference if I had made more of an effort to track her down. I later heard she had been given a junior ambassadorial appointment sometime after she returned from Bangkok.

The Bangkok meeting was split on the core issue of the universality or otherwise of human rights and democracy. The basic division was between the more western oriented members of the group such as Japan and South Korea who were clearly and reluctantly under instructions to act as American proxies and countries like Iran and China on the other end of the spectrum of opinion. The majority, including Singapore, were somewhere in between. The final compromise was contained in Article 8 of the Bangkok Declaration that reads as follows: "[Ministers and representatives of Asian governments] recognise that while human rights are universal in nature, they must be considered in the context of a dynamic and evolving process of international norm-setting, bearing in mind the significance of national and regional particularities and various historical, cultural and religious backgrounds."

This was taken as a challenge to the western idea of universality and provoked a storm of controversy after Bangkok and at Vienna. I confess to having played a role in suggesting the idea and drafting the language of Article 8. The controversy bewildered me then and baffles me still. My approach was historical and the text was intended to be, and I still think is, no more than a straightforward statement of fact. All norms evolve. How we conceived of, say, women's rights or LGBT rights 50 or 20 or just 10 years ago is not how we conceive of them now and we will not conceive of them in the same way a hundred years hence. The evolution of rights and political systems must necessarily be conditioned by responses to specific events and issues including, among other things, history, culture and religion, and our understanding of all these and many other factors also evolves over time. There is no reason to expect that evolution of rights must necessarily be teleological or a Whiggish story of ever advancing progress up and up and on and on.

It is with a tad of *schadenfreude* that I watch the EU and Australia struggle with refugees. Singapore was once roundly criticised by these countries for defying what they maintained was established international law on the rights of refugees by not recognising an automatic right to asylum and taking a tough stand to deter Vietnamese boat people from seeking shelter here. I do not think that the problems Europe and Australia today face can be managed within the existing framework of international law on refugee rights which was established in 1951 essentially to deal with displaced persons, mainly of European origin, after the Second World War. The magnitude, causes and quality of refugee flows are today entirely different. The 1951 UN Convention on Refugees and its 1967 Protocol are obsolete. But it is extremely unlikely that the domestic politics of key countries will allow these instruments to be updated in any way that will allow them to provide an adequate international legal framework for managing contemporary refugee flows. Consequently, countries will do what they must.

Australia has already changed tack and adopted refugee policies harsher than we ever did. Last year the Human Rights Council criticised Australia for breaking international law. I think Europe will eventually have to do so too. It will be far more difficult for the EU and its member states to make adjustments because the refugee crisis confronts Europe with existential questions about itself and member states are divided on what adjustments to make. The EU is now desperately trying every other expedient to avoid having to face the issue squarely. But reality cannot be evaded forever. As Mr Lee Kuan Yew once said apropos the Vietnamese boat-people, "you have to grow calluses on your heart or bleed to death".

The refugee crisis in Europe is a vivid example of value pluralism and how different conceptions of the good are not necessarily always reconcilable. It is good to abide by international law. It is good to take care of refugees. It is good to ensure that one's own citizens feel secure and comfortable in their own country. Can all three goods be simultaneously realised? I doubt it.

I must stress however that value pluralism is not the same thing as value relativity. Although these concepts are sometimes confused, they are in fact diametrically opposed because value pluralism implies no hierarchy of values whereas some notion of hierarchy is implicit in the idea of relativity. It is precisely because value pluralism assumes no hierarchy that conflicts of values arise. And when such conflicts arise, the process by which states try to reconcile them or at least reach a *modus vivendi* between differing conceptions of the Good is a political process.

Last year at a conference in Switzerland, I listened to Mario Monti, the former Prime Minister of Italy and former EU Commissioner admit that the root cause of the refugee crisis in Europe was failure in the domestic politics of EU member states. He argued that while EU institutions worked reasonably well, the idea of "Europe" was too abstract for the peoples of member states to understand and consequently their politics were driven by short-term considerations. Mr Monti's analysis was correct but did not go far enough.

The EU's idea of "Europe" is utopian and unsustainable — one is tempted to call it the Soviet Union with human rights — and the divergence between the ideals of the EU elite and their peoples has led to the rise of anti-EU, anti-migrant and in some cases, anti-Semitic, right-wing movements. Much of the same phenomenon is present in the US. The outrageous comments Donald Trump has made on women and minorities taps into the anger of his white working class base who feel culturally as well economically insecure because a once familiar America — perhaps imagined but nevertheless real in their minds — had been "stolen" from them by liberal elites and mainstream political leaders who have promoted women's rights, gay rights and the rights of minorities and migrant workers. That the President is African-American does not help either. When the gap between what elites consider desirable and the general public considers comfortable grows too wide, democratic politics becomes dysfunctional.[1] It is a lesson we should think about in Singapore too.

In the 21st century, a fundamental *structural* contradiction may be developing between the ideas of "democracy" and "human rights". Democracy is a protean term. Western liberal democracy is one historical variant and even that variant has changed over time and will continue to change. But what all variants of democracy have in common is the idea that first emerged in Europe at the end of the 17th century and gathered force during the 18th century: that sovereignty resides in and derives from the Will of the People rather than from Divine Right, the Mandate of Heaven or Bloodline or some other principle. It established itself as the dominant legitimating idea during the 19th century. Today all political systems, except for a handful mainly in the Middle East, legitimate themselves by this general principle. During the 20th century, three models of mass politics based on this idea emerged: western liberal democracy, fascism and communist "people's democracy". All three still exist, even fascism in the thankfully

---

[1] As "Brexit" has dramatically demonstrated.

much attenuated form of extreme right-wing movements. One may have a preference for one model or another, but all share the same intellectual roots and it is ahistorical and pretentious to claim an unquestionable superiority or universality for your preference.

Sovereignty resides in the will of the people, but who are "The People"? The meaning of the phrase is not stable. It steadily expanded in the course of the 20th century to include women and minorities. But the idea of "The People" is now being deconstructed by the centrifugal forces unleashed by the collision of 18th century political philosophy with 21st century communications technology in the form of the Internet and social media. Moreover "The People" today claim — or have claims made on their behalf by self-appointed activists whose visions and concerns are generally narrow — an ever-expanding slew of rights, some of which are contradictory, and claim them in an ever more absolutist manner, a process again accentuated by the Internet which has also enabled the idea of "The People" to escape the boundaries of the nation-state. All these forces are loosening, perhaps irrevocably, the sense of national community and national solidarity that I think is essential to democracy. Politics is fragmenting, making government and the pursuit of coherent public policies more difficult everywhere.[2] In my darker moments, I wonder whether the rigidities of ideological faith have caused the technologies that were the fruits of human ingenuity to far outpace the capacity of human ingenuity to adapt our political and social institutions to deal with them. We cannot abandon the technologies. The answer cannot be just more faith in human ingenuity. Faith is nothing but hope which might well prove forlorn.

Western confidence in the superiority of its model was based on the link between Western political forms and processes and the superior outcomes those forms and processes produced, particularly economic outcomes.

---

[2] The theory is that from political debate and the clash and clamour of ideas, the "Truth", or at least something approximating it, will emerge. Social media has undermined this always unwarranted assumption: "facts" are what you happen to believe or can be made by whatever means to believe; or opinion is conflated with information and both with entertainment, and expertise devalued. During the "Brexit" debate, Michael Gove dismissed all the economic arguments for staying in the EU by saying "the people are tired of experts", unfortunately with great effect. Furthermore, social media creates echo chambers: you listen to only what you already believe. This accentuates polarisation and undermines national cohesion.

China's growth challenges confidence in that link at a time when the link is already looking shaky in the West. But China is no real alternative. In Europe and the US, political dysfunctionalities are far more advanced. Nevertheless, as I argued in my second lecture, we are all "western" now and no country in any region is entirely spared. Since the communist system developed from the same 18th century political philosophy and China cannot insulate itself from 21st century communications technologies, China too suffers from its own strain of this global disease — insecurity is one of the causes of its overly assertive nationalism — which may prove equally resistant to treatment.

Political dysfunctionalities are not going to be resolved by trying to delink the political process from outcomes through the now-fashionable but bloodless concept of "governance", as if valid universal principles of public policy can be somehow neatly abstracted from an increasingly messy and diverse political reality. Public policy is not some Platonic Ideal stored up in heaven waiting to be discovered by the contemplation of superior minds serenely detached from the hurly-burly of events. A policy that cannot be sold politically is not a policy. If some principles are truly universal, the commonalities exist only at such a high level of generality that they have little practical relevance as guides to how different societies and cultures should actually govern or organise themselves. Charles S. Maier, a distinguished historian of the modern state, called governance "the utopia of the Masters of Public Policy", a thought that the school under whose auspices these lectures are being held and the prissier sort of civil servant would do well to always bear in mind.

While writing this lecture, I came across a commentary in the *Financial Times* of 20th April which described Europe and North America as suffering from what the author termed "sophisticated state failure". This, he argued, "fuels the Donald Trump and Marine Le Pen insurgencies and endangers the ability of advanced societies to secure a bright future for their citizens". Sophisticated state failure occurs when "by and large everything works as it should in mature democracies", yet little actually gets done, including economic reforms that everyone acknowledges are necessary, because governing is very difficult, voters are fickle, majorities are unstable and hence politicians unwilling to take risks. This sets up — and this is my paraphrase of the author's argument — a vicious cycle of increasingly frustrated voters disillusioned with the political process. He called it "a cancer eating away at societies in the west and undermining the liberal world order". The author, the Director of Carnegie Europe, had observed much the same dysfunctionalities as I did. His solution? "The only lasting way out of sophisticated state failure is for responsible politicians to worry less about getting re-elected and to start risking their political careers for things that need to be done." This is advice that only a desperate intellectual would give, and only angels in heaven would take.

Failure to free oneself of the shackles of the false framework of Universality leads to such tautological "solutions". A better if partial answer is to take a practical and not ideological approach to human rights and democracy: to hold our beliefs in these values loosely, contingently and transactionally. Human rights and democracy are not just desirable ends in themselves, but also means that should be evaluated and implemented on the basis of their utility. Any good idea taken to extremes becomes absurd or self-defeating or both. In December last year the *New York Times* reported that one of those responsible for the terrorist attacks in Paris earlier that month may have escaped arrest in Brussels because of a law banning police raids on private homes from 9pm to 5am. Human rights have historically been rights held by the individual against an overly powerful state; democracy a means of taming Leviathan. But what if Leviathan is now metamorphosing into Gulliver held down by myriad silken threads of Rights?

Men of goodwill believe that education and dialogue will enable us to arrive at consensus between different conceptions of the Good, or if not consensus at least peaceful coexistence or common space. But those inclined to participate in such dialogues and respond to education are usually those who are already inclined to seek common ground or coexistence and hence are least in need of education or dialogue. Consensus and common space are in any case always tentative and in constant renegotiation. It is the fundamental purpose of politics and government to hold the ring as neutral arbiter and to maintain whatever consensus or common space may pertain at any point of time, if necessary by the exercise of the coercive powers that are the legitimate monopoly of the state, including the pre-emptive or prophylactic exercise of such powers. This is a particularly urgent function of the state at a time when few countries are homogenous, when multiculturalism frowns upon attempts to homogenise a country and identity politics is spreading.

When conflicts of values lead to violence, as they did during the attack on *Charlie Hebdo*, it is because of state failure: because the state was lulled into complacency or hamstrung by its own ideology; because the state was too weak or too timid to take decisive action; or because the state was unable to resist the temptation to seek political advantage by privileging one group or system of values over another. And lest you think I am unduly smug about the situation in the West, let me remind you that we need not look very far from our own borders to find examples of such situations existing or developing. We can find examples of groups seeking special privilege for their values — thankfully as yet without success — even within our own borders.

I am not arguing that the traditional concept of rights held by the individual against the state has become unimportant. But that concept of rights is at best only a partial answer to the perennial problem of balancing justice with order. Order requires justice, but there can be no justice without order which must include a minimal societal consensus and a functioning political process. Justice is itself a contested concept and, since what one group sees as "Just" another group may regard as an intolerable tyranny, there must be some means of adjudicating between different conceptions of the "Just". Every country must find its own balance in the context of its particular circumstances. Democracy is a self-indigenising concept, greatly influenced by the *terroir* in which it is planted. This also makes it extremely difficult to impose any particular variant of democracy from the outside. Once any balance is disrupted by internal or external forces pushing too far or too quickly in one direction or another, it can be extremely difficult to restore a sensible equilibrium. President Obama's election can be seen as an attempt to restore balance to the American system after the post-9/11 excesses of the Neoconservatives. I am not confident that he has yet succeeded.

Some of you may consider that I have strayed too far into the abstract. But I thought it important to expose some of the conceptual complexities of the ideas of human rights and democracy that do not often enough see daylight. "Democracy" and "human rights" are not magical incantations that when uttered make all problems vanish. They are important but contested and sometimes internally contradictory concepts that may create new problems even if they solve others. Understanding the concepts better makes it more likely we can assess them clinically, implement them practically, and not unthinkingly fall under their thrall.

Ideological blinkers and political dysfunctionality have led to deficits of political leadership in major countries that exacerbate the uncertainties of post-Cold War international relations. Since leadership failures are not just the results of the deficiencies of individuals but have structural and conceptual causes, we will have to suffer them for a long time to come. In my previous lectures I briefly sketched some examples of how false frameworks have led to geopolitical complication: the knots that Europe has tied itself into; failure to anticipate Moscow's response to the feckless attempt to draw Ukraine away from Russia; the disastrous interventions in the Middle East and North Africa; and the idea that economic reform must lead to political reform that is the root of the strategic mistrust that complicates US-China relations. What all these examples have in common is the cardinal sin of foreign policy: wishful thinking, mistaking hopes for reality.

The effects of wishful thinking are not confined to the immediate regions where the error occurs, are unpredictable and can linger long after the error was committed. The descent of Iraq and later Libya and Syria into chaos after western interventions — these countries cannot be put together again and exist only as names and flags — did not initiate, but almost certainly accelerated and accentuated, the influence of Middle Eastern varieties of Islam, sectarian tensions and terrorist ideologies on Southeast Asian Muslims. This has changed the texture of Muslim communities in Southeast Asia and hence the relationship between Muslims and non-Muslims in the plural societies of Southeast Asia. The consequences will be difficult to manage and will unfold for many years, perhaps decades, to come.

The ill-considered American intervention in Iraq elevated Iran's regional position, shook Saudi Arabia's confidence in the US, promoted an apocalyptically existential view of Sunni-Shia competition — a proxy for geopolitical fears of Iran – which has led Riyadh into policies in Yemen and elsewhere that may well undermine what stability, including its own, that remains in the Middle East. If this occurs, it will certainly have further consequences for our own region.

The Middle East distracted the US from responding effectively for a critical decade when China was consolidating its position in Southeast Asia and trying to shape the regional architecture to its advantage. It was only at the very end of the George W. Bush administration that the US began to be persuaded that the game was worth the candle and the US has been playing catch-up ever since. The western response to the so-called "Arab Spring" — the very choice of metaphor illustrates the depth of wishful thinking: summer inevitably follows spring and Arab summers are notoriously hot — compounded the effects of American distraction. Within the space of a mere week, the US went from standing by Mubarak as a staunch 30-year ally, to refusing him a dignified exit from power and unceremoniously dumping him. By comparison, the Hendrickson affair was very small beer. Mubarak's treatment recalled the US treatment of Suharto, another 30-year friend, in 1998. And both the treatment of Mubarak and Suharto were starkly different from how the US had arranged safe passage to Hawaii when Marcos fell. Even the dregs of Cold War imperatives had a moderating influence on the US response at that time. But how the US treated Mubarak and the echoes it sounded with Suharto's treatment raised doubts about the reliability of US commitments at a time when China was emphasising its inescapable geographic reality to ASEAN. And despite President Obama's attempts to "rebalance" US attention, the now more than usually turbulent Middle East will be a continuing distraction for his successors.

I could go on multiplying examples, but there is no need to belabour the point. It is not my argument that the Myth of Universality was the only cause of these and other blunders. No country ever looks at the world only through a single lens. No country can pursue policies that are perfectly consistent with any principle. But the distortions of the Myth of Universality have in my view had a particularly deleterious effect on post-Cold War international relations. We should not underestimate the enduring power of its attraction. It is a mode of thought that I think originates in the monotheistic Christian traditions that are the foundations of even the most secular of western societies and so deeply a part of the western worldview and sense of self that nothing as mundane as empirical evidence of error can loosen its hold on the western imagination. If today the US again focuses less on what it considers the inadequacies of political systems in Southeast

Asia, this is perhaps due more to the imperative of dealing with US-China competition and terror than any genuine change of mind. As it did during the Cold War, I think the US has only decided to bide its time.

Nor are American dogmas the only ones to reckon with. American ideology may be disciplined by strategic realities, but Europe plays no significant strategic role in our region and therefore can afford the luxury of assuming moralistic postures. Not long before I retired it was my not entirely uncongenial duty to take to task a European diplomat who had crossed the boundary of acceptable diplomatic practice in his dealings with our opposition. This was an experienced diplomat who knew full well that there is a difference between *cultivating* the opposition to gather information — this is acceptable diplomatic practice and our diplomats do so too — and interfering in our domestic politics by *encouraging* the opposition. He did so entirely conscious that he was crossing a boundary. He chanced his hand, hoping we would not notice. After our last general election it was reported to me that some other European diplomats were grumbling because the natives — that's us by the way — were not wise enough to vote in accordance with *their* preferences. Why should we? But as I said in an earlier lecture, it seems very difficult for the white man to lay down his burden. We have to understand the Myth of Universality because it is one of the many uncertainties — domestic and international — that we will have to manage for the foreseeable future.

Questions and Answers

Gopinath Pillai: Ladies and Gentlemen, I feel privileged to have been asked to moderate this session. I do not agree with everything that Bilahari says. But I'm not here to debate with him but I'm here as a traffic policeman to regulate the traffic. I could carry on, for as you know, it's very difficult to detach an Indian from a microphone, but I will resist that temptation and I will open it to the house.

Question: If a country which is not a signatory of a particular convention acts in a fashion that is diametrically opposed to the convention, does that mean it is in breach of international law? What exactly is international law? Can a country be in breach of it when its conduct goes against a code that it never signed up to in the first place?

Bilahari Kausikan (BK): International law, as I said in passing, is not an autonomous reality. It's not a rock, a stone, or a tree. It is something we choose to believe in because it is in our interest to believe in it. In other words, it is one of a range of instruments available to a state to advance its national interests. I think you were alluding to the Refugee Convention. The fact that we were not a signatory was irrelevant to those who criticised us. They mobilised international law because they believed it was in their interest to get us and other countries of Southeast Asia to take in as many of these refugee boat people as possible so that they would not reach their own shores. So it was an instrumental use of international law. And that is precisely why now, kind as I may be in my heart, when I look at what's happening in Europe, I feel a little bit of *schadenfreude*. Just a little bit.

Question: What do you think about ends and means in human rights? For example, the US ignored international law in a case of gross travesty in Kosovo in 1999, and perhaps also in defence of their own interests, they went and conducted some bombing to help the Muslims there. Another question is that for a small state like us, what do you think our stand should be, like in the case of the Romanian diplomat?[3] How do you think we should act? Should we be more forceful if a more serious case happens in the future?

BK: As I said earlier, International law is an instrument — states use it when it suits them, they don't use it when it doesn't suit them. As a small state, we say that generally, a world governed by international law and international rules is in our interest. And that's of course true. But is this really such a world? At best, only occasionally.

As for the Romanian diplomat, we were not going to invade Romania and declare war against Romania because of this guy, as unsavoury a character as he may have been. But we did quite a lot. We put a lot of pressure on Romania and other EU states to ensure this guy was hounded and harried, and he could not find any safe refuge. And so he was put on trial in Romania. The trial was reasonably fair. He was bankrupted in the course of the trial so I was made to understand. He died in jail which is not something I lose any sleep over. So in this case, some form, if not of justice, of revenge was extracted. How? By holding the EU to the ideals it said it adhered to. Romania is a member of EU so we told Romania and the other EU countries, "You believe in the rule of law and you go around the world lecturing on it. Please apply it in this case and we are watching you." We sent people from our Attorney-General's Chambers and our Ambassador in Brussels to every

---

[3] Former Romanian diplomat Silviu Ionescu fled Singapore after a deadly hit-and-run accident in Singapore in 2009. He was later convicted and sentenced to jail by an appeals court in Bucharest, Romania.

stage of the trial to keep watch and report. We made sure our newspapers were kept informed so if there was any deviation we would make sure that there was going to be a lot of egg on the collective face of the EU. And I think the EU ambassadors here knew us well enough to know that we would have done it and they put some pressure on Romania.

Question: This is about the people of the Rakhine State, the Muslims there or Rohingya as they are also known. When the sailing season comes, they will leave Myanmar again. Your earlier response makes it clear that we're not bound to accept them. But how should ASEAN deal with this issue and how should human rights factor into their decision? And of course, not just within ASEAN but perhaps the inflated expectations of others.

BK: Very good question. But before I try to answer it, I must remind you that I'm a pensioner and this is only a pensioner's answer. I don't know what ASEAN is going to do when the next sailing season comes, but I can tell you what ASEAN did in previous seasons because I then witnessed it firsthand.

First of all, there was no ASEAN country that really wanted to take any of them, for the same reasons that we refused to take Vietnamese boat people. Some ASEAN members said it was raised in ASEAN circles. It is true that the word "Rohingya" was uttered a few times when ASEAN met and therefore we were not entirely unjustified putting it into statements. And it is true that some ASEAN Foreign Ministers made well publicised trips to Rakhine state. But that's as far as it went. I think Indonesia and Malaysia were ultimately compelled by their domestic politics to take some Rohingyas. And they took them on the basis of guarantees by the United Nations High Commissioner for Refugees (UNHCR) that resettlement will be found for them. This is purely domestic politics because they well knew that those guarantees by the UNHCR are worth nothing. The UNHCR cannot guarantee resettlement. Only sovereign states can guarantee resettlement. And sovereign states who are very loud in proclaiming their sympathy for these poor people — not one of them volunteered to take substantial numbers of them. Not Europe — maybe that's understandable, they have their hands full — but none of the Arab states and these are fellow Muslims. So why should the Southeast Asian states be different? Based on this experience, I do not expect anything different to happen the next season

Question: I would like to raise a question on migrant labour in the ASEAN context. There are certain human rights issues involved in migrant labour, because all ASEAN countries tend to be involved in it, either as receiving or sending countries. ASEAN has got a human rights convention which it just adopted. But recruitment agencies have hefty charges called placement fees which are illegal under various laws in different countries. Labourers may work for six months to a year without getting paid. Why can't ASEAN come up with a labour migration treaty under the human rights convention of ASEAN?

BK: I doubt you can get such a treaty because there are fundamental differences between the interests of sending countries and the interests of receiving countries and that is not going to change. That is a circle that is not going to be squared in any satisfactory way. All you can do is to ensure that if you are a receiving country as we are, the people you receive are treated in a decent way. And I think we do, not perfectly, as we can certainly do better, but we do treat them on the whole decently. If you are waiting for an ASEAN-wide instrument or an agreement, you're not going to get it. So all you can do is to hope that both the sending countries and the receiving countries, within their own national frameworks, treat these people in a decent manner.

Question: Singapore is subject to a relationship with larger global structures and those are what we navigate, so that is why we reject this universality you talk about. But within a country, the government is the one that enforces universality. Within state borders, universality is legitimised by state force and I think the voter's mandate. So, what do you think about the perhaps risky use of voter pressure to perhaps modify the state's attitudes or methods?

BK: You are absolutely correct. The idea of universality can only be imposed by a predominant power. And in the international system, there is no longer any predominant power. If there was, it was only for a very short period after the Cold War. Within state boundaries, ideas of what is right, what is good, are ideas of the government of the day. In democratic systems, they have to validate themselves by periodic elections. I think this is the best we can do in this imperfect vale of tears we call the world. Is it risky? Yes, of course it's risky. Democracy is full of risk. It doesn't mean that just because you have elections, a person with ideas that are useful will be elected. What's "useful" anyway? Someone may think certain ideas silly, others might think otherwise. There is that inherent risk. But is there a better way? There isn't. This is an imperfect world. I don't see that there is a better way than these periodic risks that we call elections. And no better way than the government of the day defining the good. If you have a government that is wise, it would not try to define everything because that is impossible. Even in the most totalitarian of systems, it is not possible. If a government is wise, it will try to define the main parameters, it will try to create some common space and defend that common space knowing full well that a different government may have a different notion of common space based on different assumptions.

It is a serious problem for a young country like Singapore. What are our common assumptions in Singapore? There are some, I think. But I also think that if we start debating the matter, we will find that we each have our own ideas about what our common assumptions are. Whereas if we have a history of 500 years, a thousand years, there are certain common things embedded in the collective subconscious. In Southeast Asia, I think there is in almost every Vietnamese a subconscious assumption that they have to live with China but also resist China to maintain their identity. And they don't even have to think about it; it's just there. We don't have that because we're only 50 years old, which is nothing in history.

Question: How will our new geopolitical environment with a more multipolar world affect the development of human rights? For example, President Xi Jinping came out and said that his view of Asia is an Asia that is run by Asians and for Asians, and with a predominantly Chinese perspective in terms of how they see human rights.

BK: Insofar as a multipolar world develops, there will be less international consensus on what constitutes, let's say, the interpretation of the Universal Declaration. Nobody is going to dismantle the apparatus of human rights treaties, of institutions and so on that exist. But the fact is that these concepts, the interpretations, the implementation, are going to be more and more contested. Do the BRICS — Brazil, India, Russia, China, and South Africa — have a consensus on what constitutes human rights? If they have one, is it the same as what the US and Europe would think of human rights? Or Japan? I don't think so. I'm not saying that human rights are not important. You have to have an ideal. But the interpretation of the ideal is always going to be different, it will not be agreed, except in very general terms, and the interpretations are going to change over time.

Question: Do you think the EU will still be around in a decade, especially in light of the migration crisis? And if it is around, or not around anymore, how do you think this will impact human rights and this universality issue in future?

BK: Well, first of all I don't think there is any issue about universality because I think it is a myth and irrespective of what happens in Europe it will not cease to be a myth. The EU's definition of Europe was an overly ambitious one. The idea that nationalism could be overcome was a utopian one. I wasn't entirely facetious when I compared the EU to the Soviet Union. This idea that you can create a Pan-European man reminded me very much of the Soviet idea that you could create a new Socialist man. It didn't work. The Soviet Union was around for 70 odd years. When it collapsed suddenly everybody again became Kazakhs, Uzbeks, Belarusians, Ukrainians and so on.

I think the EU will survive but it will be a different concept of Europe. A humbler concept of Europe; one more in line with human nature. But I also think it's going to be a huge struggle for Europe because they will have to confront very basic questions about themselves and that internal European conversation has only just begun and only begun in a very tentative way. Right now with reference to the refugee issue, they are trying almost every other expedient to avoid having to confront it. I hope they succeed.

I used Europe a lot in this lecture because it is the most fertile source of examples, because they have taken things furthest. As to what a shrunken concept of Europe is going to mean for human rights, refer to my answer to the previous question: a multipolar world will still have an ideal of human rights but it will be a far more contested ideal of human rights because different countries are going to have different conceptions of what it means and Europe will be only one voice. Maybe I should explain one thing before I stop talking and we can wrap this up.

When I say international law and human rights are not autonomous realities, I mean these are human ideas. They are good ideas; they are ideas that should be pursued. But because they are human ideas, they do not exist independent of our apprehensions of them. And our apprehensions will always vary. The earth is round even if I sincerely believe it is flat. But human rights and other political concepts are not like that. They are fundamentally different in nature from concepts like the earth being round. And that is a hard fact that people who are fervent supporters of human rights have difficulty accepting because they generally think *their* definition of a concept must be the only possible one. And that is what I don't agree with and call the Myth of Universality.

Lecture V
CAN SINGAPORE COPE?

Singapore is in much better shape than in 1965. Our economy is more robust and diversified, linked by a network of Free Trade Agreements (FTA) to the major economies. The Singapore Armed Forces (SAF) is strong and deterrence keeps our neighbourhood honest. We enjoy good relations with all the major powers. We have a wide and respected diplomatic network. Our city is safe with public services provided at a level of efficiency that is the envy of other cities. Of course, we are not perfect and as Mr Lee Kuan Yew has observed, Singaporeans are also champion grumblers.

That we have this dubious distinction is perhaps a measure of success. Some years ago, we had flash floods in Orchard Road. A Vietnamese friend happened to be in Singapore for an ASEAN meeting. He had read in *The Straits Times* about floods in Singapore. Where? He asked. Outside your hotel, I replied. He laughed. In Hanoi we only call it floods when the water reaches our waist, he said.

I am old enough to remember when we regularly had floods in my friend's definition. I can remember a poor, disorderly, dirty Singapore without a proper sewage system and clean water for every household. I can remember riots and curfew. But I belong to probably the last generation that has personal experience of such a Singapore.

Fifty years is only the blink of an eye in the history of a country. Our survival, let alone success and prosperity, was not preordained. It was in fact most improbable: the result of the government and people pulling together to defy the odds, much sweat and sacrifice, and a little luck. Can we cope with the many international and regional complexities of the post-Cold War world that previous lectures have outlined? Before I answer the question, let us remind ourselves of some of the enduring realities that confront a small city-state in Southeast Asia.

The US shrugs off political dysfunctionalities to remain the preeminent global power. China and Russia have endured traumas that would have caused small countries to vanish without a trace. Japan, Germany and South Korea have recovered from self-inflicted wounds that would have killed smaller countries. In Berlusconi's Italy, politics was theatre, but Italy remains a member of the G-7. Cocooned by the EU, between 2010 and 2011, Belgium went without a government for almost 20 months. Indonesia absorbs governmental incoherence, inefficiency and corruption but remains relevant despite everything because it is rich in resources and, more importantly, big.

Small states are vulnerable. The margin for error is narrow. The government's role is essential. Thanks to what was achieved over the last 50 years, the threat is no longer that we will disappear as a sovereign and independent country, although that can never be entirely discounted. The threat is now more insidious. The danger is that our autonomy could be compromised even though we remain formally independent and sovereign. We will still have a flag and a seat in the United Nations (UN). No one will stop us from singing "*Majulah Singapura*". But if we are clumsy in our external relationships or mishandle our domestic politics, the freedom to decide our own destiny could be severely circumscribed. That is in fact the condition of many small states who are members in the UN.

Small city-states have no intrinsic relevance to the workings of the international system. Relevance is an artefact, created by human endeavour and, having been created, must be maintained by human endeavour. The world will probably get along fine without a fully sovereign and independent Singapore. We perform no function that we did not in some way serve as a British colony and as part of Malaysia. Autonomy has enabled us to raise the level at which we perform such functions and prosper. But there is little reason to assume that we cannot in some way serve these functions even if we were under someone's thumb. It need not be only the panda's paw or eagle's claw to which we may succumb.

We are an anomaly in Southeast Asia. Singapore is a Chinese-majority state in a region where, typically, the Chinese are a less than entirely welcome minority. We organise ourselves on the basis of multiracial meritocracy in a region where other countries, explicitly or implicitly, typically organise themselves on the basis on the dominance of one ethnic group or another.

This confronts us with a paradox: an anomaly can only remain relevant, survive and prosper by continuing to be an outlier. We cannot be just like our neighbours. We cannot be only just as successful as our neighbours. If we were only just like them, why deal with us rather than bigger and more richly endowed countries? To be relevant, we have to be extraordinarily successful. But this does not endear us to our neighbours.

The basic issue in our relations with our immediate neighbours, and in varying degrees with other countries in Southeast Asia, is not what we *do* but what we *are*: the implicit challenge that, by its very existence, a Chinese-majority Singapore organised on the basis of multiracial meritocracy poses to systems organised on the basis of different and ultimately irreconcilable principles. That we have the temerity to be more successful adds to the offence. But we have no other choice.

No one who is even minimally familiar with our neighbours should have any illusions that they mean to surpass us and put us in what they consider to be our proper place, which is not, believe me, where the sun shines on first. This attitude was virulently explicit when Dr Mahathir was Prime Minister of Malaysia but muted under Prime Minister Najib. Indonesia makes no secret of it, even though President Joko Widodo is not hostile to us. It is never absent even when relations are at their friendliest, not because they necessarily hate us, but to validate their own systems.

This does not mean we cannot cooperate with our neighbours. We must, we can and we do. But we must do so from a position of strength. Strength is not to be defined in purely military terms. The SAF is of course vitally important. But strength, success and relevance must first of all be defined in economic terms. To put it crassly, small countries will always have fewer options and operate on narrower margins than big countries, but rich small countries will have more options than poor small countries. The management of the paradox I set out a moment ago — to survive and prosper we must be extraordinary but being extraordinary does not make us loved — lies at the heart of our foreign policy. It prescribes our most fundamental approaches: maintaining an omnidirectional balance in Southeast Asia by facilitating the engagement of all major powers in our region, while fostering regional cooperation through ASEAN; maintaining our economic edge and keeping our powder dry. It is a delicate balancing act.

What could make us trip and fall? To adapt a phrase from the great American folk philosopher, Pogo: "I have met the enemy and he is us".

I am quoting from a comic strip by the late Walt Kelly. But my point is a serious one. We can cope with the more complicated post-Cold War external environment provided we get our internal environment right. A successful foreign policy must always and everywhere rest on a sound domestic foundation. There are three aspects: politics, policy and social cohesion.

Ideally, politics should stop at water's edge. This is an ideal realised nowhere on earth. It is therefore not surprising that in Singapore, partisan politics has begun to creep into foreign policy. Political debate over foreign policy is not necessarily a bad thing if it is conducted within and leads to a domestic consensus on the parameters of what is possible and not possible for a small city-state in Southeast Asia.

In countries with long histories, partisan debates over foreign policy are generally conducted within such a framework of shared assumptions, often unconscious, on what ought to be in the fundamental interests of the country irrespective of which party holds power. With only 50 years of history, I am not sure we have a framework of shared assumptions about the national interest in Singapore. Perhaps we will develop one in time. But so far the manner in which the opposition has approached foreign policy does not inspire confidence that they have any concept of the fundamental national interest — that should hold irrespective of partisan ambition — or that they really understand Singapore's place in our region and the world.

In 2013, Mr Pritam Singh of the Workers' Party (WP), who should have known better, asked a question in Parliament about our Middle East policies that could have stirred up the feelings of our Malay-Muslim ground against the government. He did not do his homework. It is not difficult to demonstrate that Singapore has been consistently even-handed in our relations with Israel and Palestine.

The Arab countries understand our position and have no issue with our relations with Israel. Some years before I retired, I was in an Arab country for talks with my counterpart. It happened to be during Operation Cast Lead, the Gaza War of 2008–2009. The Israel Defense Forces had moved into Gaza to stop rocket attacks against civilian targets in Israel. Horrific pictures of death and destruction were splashed across the front page of that country's English language newspaper. I went to the talks expecting an earful about the inequities of Israel. And I indeed got an earful — for about five minutes. My counterpart spent most of the rest of our hour-long meeting talking about the threat that Iran's nuclear programme and the Shia posed in the Middle East. And as he walked me out after the meeting, my counterpart whispered to me, tell *your* friend not to wait too long. I don't think he was referring to the US because America is his country's friend too.

If the Arab countries do not think that our relations with Israel and our position on Palestine are problems, why was the WP asking questions about our Middle East policy? Was it to try and stir our Malay-Muslim ground against the government? Will Singapore benefit if Singaporean Muslims become alienated from the government or non-Muslim Singaporeans? The answers ought to be obvious. But the following year Mr Singh again asked another question in Parliament about our Middle East policy that could have inflamed our Malay-Muslim ground.

Nor is the Workers' Party the only opposition party to play fast and loose with foreign policy for partisan purposes.

On 29th January this year, coincidently the day I delivered my first lecture in this series, *The Straits Times* published a letter from Dr Paul Tambyah in his capacity as a member of the Central Executive Committee of the Singapore Democratic Party (SDP). The SDP has advocated a reduction in our defence budget in favour of health spending and Dr Tambyah was responding to a People's Action Party's (PAP) MP's parliamentary speech about this policy. One of the arguments that he advanced in support of the SDP's position was so breathtakingly naïve or so breathtakingly irresponsible that it is worth quoting.

"Singapore has a long history of being non-aligned in our foreign policy", Dr Tambyah wrote. "Such an approach has served us well. Getting overly entangled in regional conflicts, especially through military means, may not be in the interests of the people of Singapore".

I agree that Singapore should not get entangled in military conflicts if at all possible. But the purpose of a strong SAF is to *deter*; that is to say, to prevent military conflicts from breaking out in the first place, and if deterrence should fail, to prevail. If the good doctor really thinks that being non-aligned is an adequate substitute for deterrence through a strong SAF, he ought to consult a doctor of another sort without delay: a psychiatrist.

You cannot remain safe by shutting your eyes to unpleasant realities, lying low and hoping for the best. Being non-aligned did not save Sihanouk's Cambodia or Souvanna Phouma's Laos from getting entangled in military conflicts with very tragic consequences for their peoples. Contrary to what Dr Tambyah seems to think, Singapore is a member of the Non-Aligned Movement (NAM) not because it makes us feel safe, but because we are vulnerable.

It is precisely because a small city-state gives itself hostage to fortune if it ignores the possibility of military conflict, that we cannot concede any forum to any possible adversary. If deterrence fails and conflict breaks out, we must mobilise the diplomatic support of the 120 members of the NAM to try and shape a political context in the UN which will enable the SAF to do its job as expeditiously as possible. Every war must eventually end. The political context within which a war was fought will be a significant influence on whether the conflict will end on the best possible terms. Many wars have been won on the battlefield only to be lost at the negotiating table. War and diplomacy are not alternatives; they are different sides of the same coin that complement each other.

We live in a region that, for all the reasons I advanced in my previous lectures, is going to become more uncertain. One of my previous lectures analysed the strengths and limitations of ASEAN. Regional cooperation is not a substitute for a strong defence; it is the stability in relationships created by a credible deterrent force that makes regional cooperation possible.

As our population ages, we will certainly need to devote more of our budget to healthcare and other social spending. The government has predicted that by FY2020, healthcare spending alone will outstrip defence spending.

How is this to be financed? Obviously we will need to continue to grow to afford more social spending. We cannot live on our reserves indefinitely. But how are we going to grow in order to afford more social spending?

The SDP and other opposition parties have never given any answer to this question that I have found convincing. The results of the last general election and the recently concluded by-election suggest that my scepticism is shared by many. Dr Tambyah's boss in the SDP, Mr Chee Soon Juan, has written articles attacking our FTAs, as if the people of a small city-state could make a living only by taking in one another's laundry.

A city-state with a small domestic market has no other economic choice but to be open to the world. Openness could well accentuate our vulnerabilities. All the more reason why the insurance policy of a strong deterrent is vital. If a strong deterrent can be maintained at lower cost, well and good. But would we be a desirable economic partner or an attractive investment destination if we could not defend ourselves?

This brings me to policy and the role of the civil service. The traditional role of the Ministry of Foreign Affairs (MFA) of every country is to be the principal interlocutor of the country with the world. This concept of diplomacy is obsolete.

No MFA anywhere can now be the sole or even the main interlocutor of a country with the world. Of course, there are some things that only MFAs can do. But after the Cold War the distinction that used to be made in international relations between "high politics" and "low politics" is blurring. Any MFA that tries to be a country's main interlocutor with the world is bound to fail its country: it can only pursue defensive interests — essentially just say "no" — because it will lack the domain knowledge to advance positive interests across the broad range of often highly technical issues that are now prominent on the international agenda, many of which span traditional bureaucratic boundaries.

This is confronting civil services across the world with unfamiliar challenges. All domestic agencies now have to engage internationally. There is no important policy domain that is now entirely "domestic". The only question is the degree to which an issue is "international". Within a country's civil service, agencies are being compelled to work with each other in new ways. This requires not just new structures and processes; that is the easy part. More crucially, it requires them to learn new ways of thinking and acting. This is difficult. Inertia is not a force to be underestimated in all bureaucracies. Any experienced civil servant anywhere can readily find reasons why something new should not be done, and as effortlessly find ways of presenting existing practice as new.

How does Singapore do? I can say accurately and without false modesty that the civil service of which I was proud to be a part, does not do badly. We do better than other civil services in East Asia and generally better than many civil services across the world, including those of larger and more developed countries. But is this good enough for a small city-state in the more complicated external environment that we will face? There is room for improvement.

A more uncertain external environment and the strategic imperative of avoiding being forced to make invidious choices or foreclose options in the midst of heightened US-China competition, places a premium on what have always been imperatives for the foreign policy of a small city-state: alertness, agility and an appreciation of nuance. But there are certain features of the way in which our civil service is currently organised that may have begun to degrade these qualities at a time when they are becoming even more important.

I am not referring to big decisions taken deliberately by our political leadership as foreign policy decisions or to decisions taken with conscious-ness of their external implications. Here I think our current structures and processes do quite well.

The challenge is more subtle. In a previous lecture I argued that a new US-China *modus vivendi* will not be determined by a deliberate process of negotiation but will be the consequence of many ad hoc responses to situations taken at various levels and in different domains. Similarly, I am concerned about the accumulation of many small decisions, perhaps with no obvious foreign policy implications, taken by different parts of the civil service for sound institutional reasons, but the cumulative effect of which may one day place us in an external position we do not want or intend to be.

Although the civil service now stresses a "Whole of Government" approach, it is my impression that — left to their own devices — agencies tend to take a more narrowly transactional approach to their institutional interests and hence in some ways operate more in institutional silos today than when I joined the civil service. This degrades nimbleness, narrows vision and is making us risk averse. It is always safer to remain within institutional boundaries.

It took me about a year or so to get an inter-agency consensus for Singapore to join the Kyoto Protocol on climate change and this was an international agreement that imposed absolutely *no* obligations on Singapore. We subsequently did very well in arriving at national positions for the complex negotiations in the Conference of Parties (COPS) to the UN Framework Convention on Climate Change, which could serve as a model for inter-agency discussions on national positions. But this was after a Deputy Prime Minister was placed in charge of the process.

The issues in COPS certainly warranted that level of political attention. Most bureaucracies operate better top down and we are no exception. But as our domestic politics place ever increasing demands on our elected leaders, they will have less time to devote to lower order decisions. Yet it is the accumulation of such lower order decisions that could lead us to places we do not want to go. Slowly, but I fear, steadily the central organising concept of our civil service is eroding the alertness, agility and appreciation of nuance that we will need to cope with a more complex external environment.

Let me give you two examples:

- In 2011, MFA concluded that Singapore should try to become an Observer in the Arctic Council. Global warming could eventually change sea routes with potentially profound implications for us. It was only prudent to have early warning of what could become possible in the Arctic. The criteria for Observership spanned several agencies. Their responses were luke-warm. It was the long odds against a small tropical island succeeding and the lack of any immediate institutional advantage that put them off. MFA decided to go ahead alone and placed one of our most wily and experienced Ambassadors in charge. Only when his efforts began to gain traction did other agencies come on board. Singapore was elected as an Observer in 2013.
- In 2014, the SAF conducted a military exercise with the People's Liberation Army (PLA) in the Nanjing Military Region in China.

We must build a relationship with the PLA as part of our overall engagement with a rising China. The Nanjing Military Region is responsible for Taiwan, with which we have long-standing unofficial ties. The headquarters of the PLA Navy's East Sea Fleet which covers the Senkaku/Diaoyu islands, whose sovereignty is disputed by China and Japan, is located at Ningbo within the region. The PLA then had six other military regions. Nothing was said, but eyebrows must have been raised in Tokyo and Taipei, and perhaps Washington too, at the choice of Nanjing.

None of these episodes resulted in irreversible damage to Singapore's interests. But they are symptoms, the ultimate cause of which is, I think, the concept around which our civil service is organised.

At the apex of our civil service is the Administrative Service. This is based on the idea that senior public service leaders should be generalists, capable of taking on a range of appointments in different domains. Most senior appointments in the Ministries and Statutory Boards are filled by Administrative Service Officers rather than officers from specialist services. But in my view, very few people can be equally good at everything. I for example, would have been utterly useless in any other Ministry than MFA.

The idea that generalists make the best senior public service leaders is based on a prior, perhaps largely unconscious, assumption: that there is only one type of logic that is valid across all domains. This is an assumption that has led to mistakes in domestic policy[1] and is particularly antithetical to the requirements of a successful foreign policy.

A world of sovereign states is a world of different and competing logics because, in principle, a sovereign recognises no authority except its own. I do not want to push the point too far. In practice, states hold many basic assumptions in common. Otherwise international relations as we know it would not be possible. But this still leaves a lot of space for what I termed in the previous lecture the "Rashomon phenomenon" to operate within the

[1] An example is "A Sustainable Population for a Dynamic Singapore: Population White Paper" published in January 2013. Its economic logic was impeccable but it failed to take into account political logic. We are still trying to recover.

ever shifting kaleidoscope of possibilities that is the world of foreign policy. This is not a world that the Administrative Service generally finds congenial because control of events is not in its hands. But every Ministry must now, at least to some degree, be responsible for conducting diplomacy.

In a world of competing logics, it is the function of diplomacy to reconcile logics or at least minimise friction between different logics, or when logics are irreconcilable, to ensure that your logic prevails. This requires first to recognise and accept that there are other valid logics than one's own. Every successful diplomat from any country I have met has one quality in common: empathy. By empathy I do not mean warm and fuzzy feelings but the ability to see the world through another's eyes and think as he does, the better to persuade him or out-manoeuvre him. This is not something that comes naturally to many senior Singapore civil servants.

I do not want to leave you with the impression that all is lost. All is *not* lost. Our elected leaders understand that policies that are not or cannot be communicated in political logic — that is to say a logic that will appeal to and can be understood by the intended audience — are policies that will fail. Political communication is improving. I am less confident however that this has yet been adequately hoisted in by all senior civil servants.

Still, where politicians go, the civil service must eventually follow. The idea that the civil service is or ought to be politically neutral or independent is a myth. A "politically neutral" or independent civil service is to be found nowhere on earth. This is for the simple reason that the civil service is always and everywhere the instrument of the government in power. The civil service has a responsibility to give its political masters objective advice. But that is not the same thing as being "politically neutral" or independent. The civil service is obliged to carry out the instructions of the government irrespective of whether those instructions are in accordance with its advice.

I find it remarkable that so many people, even some very senior civil servants, do not seem to understand the relationship of the civil service to the government. Perhaps they do not want to understand.

But ours is a pragmatic system that changes when it must. In 2013, a new programme was introduced that enabled members of specialist services to be appointed to senior positions hitherto reserved for members of the Administrative Service. This was in effect an implicit admission that the assumption that there is only one sort of logic valid across all domains is wrong. It was a good first step. What is not clear to me is whether individuals chosen to take up senior positions under the new programme must leave their own services and join the Administrative Service in order to do so, or if allowed to remain in their own services, be remunerated on par with Administrative Service Officers holding similar appointments. Unless this is so, a caste may be perpetuated.

The mindset of a caste is dangerous for a city-state. C.P. Snow attributed the decline of another city-state to its prior success: "They were fond of the pattern", he said of Venice. "They never found the will to break it."

None of this is a criticism of any individual. My criticism is of a *system* that incentivises certain modes of thought and certain patterns of behaviour. There is no doubt that the system is changing. Whether it will change fast enough and far enough is another question. But even within the existing system there are always exceptions: my two immediate predecessors and my successor in MFA are examples.

In case any of you are wondering, I have held these views throughout my career and never made any secret of them. The Public Service Division (PSD) was probably relieved when I retired. I found the PSD's announcement of my retirement in 2013 tellingly amusing. It said I had 31 years of service. But I joined the Foreign Service in 1981 and was shanghaied into the Administrative Service only in 1983. Do the math. It was as if the PSD by some Kafkaesque conjuration had caused the time I spent as a Foreign Service Officer to vanish because a specialist service did not matter. In fact nobody seemed to be able to make up their minds about how long I served: the customary letters and certificates of appreciation I received all credited me with different lengths of service. Changing mindsets is always difficult.

Now, social cohesion. The US and China will take many years to reach a new *modus vivendi*. I doubt either will eschew any instrument as they compete for influence in our region. Our politics is becoming more complicated; the political space is more crowded with civil-society organisations and advocacy groups as well as opposition parties, all vying to shape policies. This is a favourable environment for external parties to try to cultivate agents of influence which need not always be witting. As the only country in Southeast

Asia with an ethnic Chinese-majority population and arguably the most cosmopolitan and Westernised elite, Singapore faces unique vulnerabilities.

My last lecture recounted how we once had to expel an American diplomat for trying to interfere in our domestic politics and alluded to the attitudes and activities of some European diplomats as well. Were these exceptional incidents never to be repeated since they had been caught with their hands in the cookie jar? I doubt it. The attitudes that gave rise to these episodes are so fundamentally a part of the Western sense of self that they will never go away. But now that the fierce glow of post-Cold War hubris has been dampened by its Middle Eastern misadventures in nation-building, and with China a growing preoccupation, I doubt too that the US has much appetite for trying to effect political change in Singapore in the same way as they tried in the late 1980s. At least for now, the Americans, and the Europeans, will indulge their missionary instincts with occasional meddling in second or third order issues.

They will have opportunities to do so. The culture wars are upon us. Some part of our population is clearly attracted to western attitudes towards such issues as the death penalty and Lesbian, Gay, Bisexual and Transgender (LGBT) rights. Are these Singaporeans typical? I share some of their attitudes but I don't think so. Most Singaporeans are much more conservative. In any case, fundamentalist versions of both Islam and Christianity are not absent in Singapore too and have very different attitudes which cannot be ignored whatever we may think of them. These issues are not going to be resolved anytime soon. Sooner or later, some Western diplomat blinded by ideology to our social and cultural fault lines will again breach acceptable diplomatic conduct by trying to tip the balance in favour of some group he thinks shares values he believes to be universal. We'll just have to paddle their bottoms when we catch them.

China poses a more delicate and fundamental challenge. A previous lecture had drawn attention to the manner in which growing economic ties with China were changing calculations of interests in Southeast Asia and even in US allies such as Australia. China's relationship with the overseas Chinese communities of Southeast Asia is a closely related issue.

Two years ago, the Seventh Conference of Friendship of Overseas Chinese Associations was held in Beijing. President Xi Jinping's speech at that conference was entitled "The Rejuvenation of the Chinese *Nation* is a Dream Shared by All Chinese" [emphasis added]. The specifics of the relationship of overseas Chinese communities to the Chinese Communist Party's (CCP) narrative of the "Great Rejuvenation" beyond the obvious contributions to China's growth were not, undoubtedly deliberately, defined in detail. But the boundaries of the concept of "nation" are wide enough and vague enough to leave a lot of room for what was left unsaid. At the end of his speech, President Xi called upon the overseas Chinese to "better integrate themselves into their local communities". But the emotionally charged language of the speech made clear enough that the CCP also has other expectations. President Xi described overseas Chinese as "members of the Chinese family", rejuvenation as a "shared dream", enjoined them to "never forget…the blood of the Chinese nation flowing in their veins" and called upon them to promote "understanding" to "create a better environment for achieving the Chinese dream".

Historically, China's approach towards the overseas Chinese of Southeast Asia has waxed and waned according to China's shifting objectives. Southeast Asia was once an area of intense competition between the CCP and Kuomintang (KMT) for the allegiance of overseas Chinese. By the mid-1950s, with the KMT penned in on Taiwan and wanting to cultivate friends at the Afro-Asian Bandung Conference,[2] China disavowed responsibility for overseas Chinese communities in Southeast Asia, telling them to be good citizens of the countries in which they resided. That did not stop the CCP from using "United Front" tactics during the 1950s and 1960s to advance the interests of the Southeast Asian communist parties it supported, notably the Malayan Communist Party which consisted mainly of ethnic Chinese.

When Vietnam with the support of the Soviet Union invaded and occupied Cambodia in 1979, the imperatives of Sino-Soviet competition and rallying ASEAN against Vietnam took priority. China ceased all support for Southeast Asian communist parties. The Cambodian issue preoccupied China in Southeast Asia throughout the 1980s. The priority

---

[2] The Asian-African Conference was held in Bandung, Indonesia from 18–24 April 1955, with representatives from 29 African and Asian nations.

was consolidating official relations with the ASEAN governments. From the 1990s, with Cambodia out of the way, China turned its attention to deepening and consolidating economic and diplomatic ties with Southeast Asia. The overseas Chinese communities were then largely regarded as a source of investment and economic expertise.

In 1998, vicious anti-Chinese riots broke out in Jakarta during the run-up to Suharto's fall. China issued a mild admonition to Jakarta to treat Indonesian Chinese better and punish those responsible. Mild as it was, this broke with the practice of 40 years. Last year, shortly after racially fraught demonstrations in Kuala Lumpur, the Chinese Ambassador to Malaysia made his way to Chinatown and close to where police had to use water-cannons to break up a potentially violent anti-Chinese demonstration, pronounced the Chinese government's opposition to, among other things, any form of racial discrimination, adding for good measure that Beijing would not stand idly by if anything threatened China's relations with Malaysia.

What was the Ambassador trying to do? Was he really trying to help the Malaysian Chinese? If he was, I don't think he did them any favours. Or was he trying to highlight China's clout in the context of rising competition with the US? The Chinese Foreign Ministry spokesperson defended his actions as "normal".

This apparent shift towards positioning China as the protector of Southeast Asian Chinese has created many uncertainties with direct implications for Singapore. If anti-Chinese violence should again break out in Indonesia or Malaysia — a possibility that unfortunately cannot be ruled out — how would Beijing respond? Since China has associated the overseas Chinese with the CCP's narrative of the "Great Rejuvenation", can Beijing still respond in as carefully calibrated a manner as it did in 1998? Will its own people let it do so? In 1998, the Internet was in its infancy in China. There are now some 700 million netizens in China, easily aroused through social media. How will China's response affect our neighbours' attitudes towards us? How would non-Chinese Singaporeans react? After 50 years, does our collective Singapore identity now override ethnic identities?

Chinese leaders and officials refer to Singapore as a "Chinese country" who should therefore "understand" China better and hint at their generosity if we should "explain" China to other ASEAN countries. We politely but clearly and firmly point out that Singapore is not a "Chinese country". We know all too well what they really mean by "understand" and "explain". But they persist. The idea of a multiracial meritocracy is alien to China which seems incapable of conceiving of a Chinese-majority country in any other way than as a "Chinese country" and a potential instrument of its policy.

This mode of thought is deeply embedded in Chinese culture and political practice and will not change. As China becomes more confident and assertive, it will probably become more insistent. It would be prudent not to underestimate the resonance that the idea of Singapore as a "Chinese country" linked to a rising China could have with some sections of our population. We are not immune to these visceral seductions or to the economic inducements that some other ASEAN countries have eagerly embraced. There are many potential avenues through which China could bypass the government to try and directly exercise influence on our people.[3] China still has a United Front Work Department under the CCP's Central Committee.

If we were ever foolish enough to accept — or are compelled to concede to — the characterisation of Singapore as a "Chinese country", this would not only provoke a counter-reaction from other major powers; more critically, the multiracial compact of social cohesion which is the foundation of independent Singapore's success would be at least severely strained if not entirely broken. Once lost, this foundation will be extremely difficult, perhaps impossible, to rebuild. But it would also be foolish to alienate China which must be a significant factor in our economic future. Maintaining a good relationship with China, while preserving the autonomy to pursue our interests as we define them is the fine line we must walk.

We have so far managed this delicate balancing act. But Singapore is only 50 years old. I doubt all our compatriots fully understand the complexity of the contradictory forces at play upon us. Many younger Singaporeans who

---

[3] The Global Times, published by the CCP's mouthpiece People's Daily, ran an article on 21 September 2016 accusing Singapore of raising the South China Sea dispute at the Non-Aligned Movement (NAM) Summit held in Venezuela on 18 September 2016. Singapore's Ambassador to Beijing Stanley Loh refuted this, prompting Global Times editors and Chinese officials to weigh in. This is an example of an attempt to influence Singaporeans through coercion and united front tactics referred to in this lecture. Such coercive tactics began to be deployed in 2004 when then-Deputy Prime Minister Lee Hsien Loong visited Taiwan. They are reminiscent of Communist United Front tactics of the 1950s and 1960s.

take the only Singapore they have known for granted are sceptical about our inherent vulnerability, an attitude encouraged by some attention seeking academics. Some dismiss vulnerability as a scare tactic designed to keep the PAP in power.

Since we do not yet have a self-correcting internal equilibrium, sooner or later equilibrium may have to be enforced by the coercive powers that are the legitimate monopoly of the state, including the powers of the Internal Security Act (ISA). It would at least be prudent to keep such instruments in reserve and not discard them as some opposition parties would naïvely have us do. The use of the ISA for this purpose will almost certainly be depicted as "political" by those who seek its abolition and cause problems for us with the US and Europe. But that would be the lesser cost.

We need to do a much better job of national education and are paying a price for deemphasising history in our national curriculum. What now passes as national education is ritualised, arousing as much cynicism as understanding. Knowledge of our own history should not be only a matter for specialists. The controversy over the 1963 Operation Coldstore and whether those detained were part of the Communist United Front exposed the extent to which the public lacuna of understanding may allow puerile and pernicious views to gain currency. Our understanding of history must of course be constantly revised. But critical historical thinking is not just a matter of braying black when the established view is white. This was not just an academic exercise. For some, it was a politically motivated attempt to cast doubt on the government's overall credibility by undermining the government's narrative on one particular historical event. I understand that steps are being taken to revise our history curriculum. It will take time for this to have an effect but the problem is at least recognised.

Mine is a counsel of realism, not despair. I am not pessimistic about Singapore's ability to cope with the complexities ahead of us. We have coped with far worse with far less on our side. We will cope if we continue to be clinical in our understanding of our own situation and hard-headed about what may need to be done. We will fail only if we lose our sense of vulnerability because that is what keeps us united, agile and alert.

Questions and Answers
Moderator: Janadas Devan

Janadas Devan (JD): Thank you, we've come to the end of this lecture series. I'd hoped to get through all five without causing undue controversy. The wish was granted for the first four lectures. I don't think this lecture would pass similarly unnoticed. You've taken to task the Workers' Party, Singapore Democratic Party, the admin service, the Singapore civil service and China. I'm sure there are lots of questions and hopefully lots of demanding questions.

Question: You've focused on states, Asian states, and their actions but what about non-nation state actions, like for example climate change and also a post-antibiotic environment and their respective impacts on Singapore?

Bilahari Kausikan (BK): The issues you mentioned were the consequences of human action although not always state action. But you need state action to deal with the issues. We can do what we can do, but these are international issues. Effective international action needs leadership. The US is the only remaining global power. But after the Cold War, there was no strategic imperative for any country to follow US leadership except on an ad hoc and sporadic basis. One of the consequences is that international action on issues such as those you mentioned is going to be suboptimal. The climate change conference came to some sort of conclusion in Paris but it was widely recognised that while this was the best there could be, it was not good enough. Even if everybody does everything they said they would do, it would only slightly slow global warming and not really deal with the core of the issue. I would guess the same would be true of antibiotics and nuclear proliferation and all kinds of other transnational global issues.

Question: I was rather startled by Indonesia's reaction to us when under the Transboundary Haze Pollution Act, we moved to go after companies linked to fires in Indonesia that resulted in last year's haze. The reactions seemed disproportionate — they raised questions about whether we were undermining their sovereignty, and said that there would be a review of all kinds of partnerships and collaborations. Could you help explain what's going on and whether Singaporeans should be alarmed?

Second, you said there might be ways in which we can discuss foreign policy more calmly, more clinically and more broadly so that not just politicians but citizens would have a way to share our views. How do you envision this happening?

BK: I'm surprised that you were surprised at the Indonesian reaction. I was not at all surprised. When you have the Vice-President of a country telling you to be grateful for the oxygen his country supplies and to forget about the haze, why should you be surprised? It's quite typical. If you recall, the Minister of the Environment and Forestry Siti Nurbaya Bakar said Singapore should do its part [to combat transboundary haze]. But when we did our part, she got upset.

Indonesia has not yet reached a stable post-Suharto equilibrium. It is still struggling to impose coherence on a fairly incoherent polity. That was perhaps understandable in the immediate aftermath of Suharto's fall, but that was in 1998, how many years has it been since? President Susilo Bambang Yudhoyono did manage to restore some coherence, but what he did seems to be slowly unravelling with different ministers saying different things and the same minister, as I just pointed out, saying different things on the same issue at different times.

What underlies it all is a huge sense of nationalistic entitlement. There is a very strong belief in Indonesia that we are a Chinese country and they project upon us all their anxiety and angst of their attitudes towards their own Chinese population. In a sense, the Indonesians see us as a *cukong*[4] writ large; they believe that our prosperity is by their favour and gift, because of their kindness and generosity, and therefore we owe them. So when they burn down forests and pollute the atmosphere, we should just shut up. But of course we can't because we are a sovereign state. We have to do what we must. As you pointed out, this guy defied our laws and we have to take some action. I don't see how it's a derogation of their sovereignty because he broke *our* law; he obviously broke their law too, but that's for them to take action against him. But the law he broke was the law for not turning up when he was told to turn up, legally required to turn up, and that's a Singapore law.

But there is also another aspect of Indonesian nationalism that is not merely loud and assertive but in which the loudness and assertiveness actually masks an inner insecurity. The question is always asked, somewhere in the sub-consciousness of Indonesia: how is it that we, a huge country with very talented people and vast natural resources, do not do as well as we think we ought to do, as befits a country with long historical tradition with all the advantages we have. The answer is always that it must be somebody else's fault. Because otherwise it requires them to confront their own shortcomings and nationalism prevents them from doing that. This gives a sharper edge to some of their dealings with us.

We live next to Indonesia, so we had better understand Indonesia because they're not going to change. And we are not going to change, we are not going to accept the position they want. As I've said in my lecture, the position they would like us to be in is a subordinate one. Can we as a sovereign state accept that? Can we breathe haze happily because of the oxygen that Indonesia provides in other months of the year? What will our own people think of our government if we do so?

Now your second question, I think it really boils down to national education; as I mentioned briefly at the end of the lecture, we don't do a good enough job. I don't think our universities, at least in the political science departments, do a good job of teaching international relations in a way that is relevant to us. It's not really the university's fault because the

---

[4] *Cukong* is an Indonesian word referring to Chinese-Indonesian businessmen who control many business assets.

entire field of international relations as well as many other social sciences, has turned inwards on itself and scholars are just speaking to each other rather than to a wider audience. You don't get any points for speaking to a wider audience, you don't get tenure, and you don't get any credit if anybody actually understands what you say, your university's rankings don't go up. We can't do anything about the general trends in academia but we can do something about our schools. If you recall, I think it was during my third lecture, a Junior College student asked a question which she said was based on something her teachers had told her. I found this so shocking that I went to the Ministry of Education and said let me look at your history curriculum. And they told me it was in the process of being revised, which is a good thing. I think they are going in the right direction. But it will take time. In the meantime, we can have more discussions like this. One of my purposes in these lectures was to expose some of these things which are quite obvious to people in the Foreign Ministry and maybe in the Ministry of Defence and some other ministries, but not very obvious to the population as a whole. It's a start. I don't know what ultimately will become of it but that's all you can do.

Question: You cautioned us about the risks of parts of the civil service working in institutional silos but on the other hand you seem critical of the administrative service and its approach to training generalists that are exposed to the challenges of different portfolios. So it seems to me that there is a bit of tension here.

BK: There is indeed a tension. I'm not advocating getting rid of all generalists. My quarrel with the Administrative Service is what I tried to explain about it; that the way it is positioned in the civil service creates certain less than ideal behaviours. You need some generalists, there is no doubt about that. But the assumption until relatively recently when they tweaked the policy a little bit, was that only generalists should serve in all the senior positions. Now I think this is contrary to human nature. People cannot be equally good, no matter how smart you are, at everything. The underlying assumption that there is only one kind of logic that is valid across any domain is simply not true; it is certainly not true in the foreign affairs field.

This idea has not entirely gone away but is changing. Is it changing fast enough? Is the acknowledgement that there is not only one kind of logic internalised enough? I'm not so sure. I'm very sure our political leadership has internalised it far more than our civil service because if they don't, they will lose their jobs. If politicians cannot explain things to the people in terms of political logic, they will lose elections. Political logic is required to explain complex things in a way that can be understood by everybody. It is not the same as, say, economic logic or other kinds of logic.

I am not too pessimistic because if the political leadership changes, the civil service must follow because every civil service is the instrument of whatever government may be in power. And if you don't know that as a civil servant, you aren't going to be a civil servant very long or you aren't going to be progressing in your civil service career.

You need generalists and you need specialists. The mixture you need of generalists and specialists is a constantly shifting target and that kind of tension, the tension to determine a shifting balance, can be creative. What is not creative is if you insist there is only one logic and so only generalists should take all the top positions, which was the attitude and I suspect deep down is still the lingering attitude of some senior civil servants.

Question: I think that the lack of National Education has gone on for so long that the prevailing sentiment that I see among my younger teaching colleagues, especially those in their 20s, seems to be that they think that anyone who tells them about Singapore's vulnerabilities is spewing propaganda. With that kind of a backdrop, no matter how much National Education changes, I worry that the message will not get across to the students because the teachers themselves don't buy it. How might we be able to reverse this especially when we are talking about adults and not just at the student level?

BK: You are absolutely correct. I had exactly the same discussion with the people in the Ministry of Education who are trying to revise the history curriculum. I asked them who is going to teach this. The people revising the history curriculum are historians, or at least they have access to historians, but the problem is really with the teachers. Not that the teachers are bad; but for the reasons you said, the teachers don't know enough except what they read in the curriculum which they may not believe or understand. It is a serious problem. There used to be a programme, I don't know if it's still going on, where Permanent Secretaries and Deputy Secretaries were asked to go and talk to groups of teachers about various aspects of national policy, not necessarily only foreign policy, and answer questions and try to help in whatever small way, to give them a better understanding so that they know something of the considerations that went into certain policy decisions, so that they can explain things better. I think you have to do that. We've got enough people, you can get ex-civil servants, you can get ex-military officers, you can get ex-politicians too to talk to teachers, to open themselves to be questioned by teachers because you're absolutely right, you have to educate the educators first.

JD: So speaking about Singapore's vulnerabilities — water, our small size, our regional relations — very few Singaporeans are aware of our vulnerabilities, very few people remember the historical reason for our vulnerability. Just across the Causeway, any number of Malaysians are still aware of those things. Why? Because those vulnerabilities have still not been resolved for them. It means issues of race, language and religion are still very much present over there. In some ways, we are paying the price for being successful.

BK: Well, the best National Education actually comes from events. When something happens, you take advantage of it. When, for example, Indonesia makes contradictory statements, you should try to take advantage, use a real event to explain. That's better than an abstract explanation. For example, I always credit Dr Mahathir with NEWater,[5] or helping us gain public acceptance of NEWater. He just made everybody so fed up that our people thought, okay, we will do it, we will drink our own urine. So one thing the government can do is when some event happens, use it, take advantage of it, try to explain what it means for us.

---

[5] NEWater is the brand of reclaimed water by Singapore's Public Utilities Board. It is produced from treated and highly-purified waste water.

Question: You said a small city state should be open for trade and free goods for economic viability. Would you say the same for labour mobility?

BK: If you have perfect labour mobility in ASEAN, everybody will come here and what will happen to us? Consistency is an overrated virtue. It was a great American who said a foolish consistency is the hobgoblin of inferior minds. You have to pick and choose. We already have a lot of political controversy in Singapore over foreign labour which we do need and there is a very controlled sort of entry on foreign labour, but still it causes controversy. So we'll have to find some sort of balance. Other ASEAN members have their own concerns. You cannot have perfect labour mobility within ASEAN. There is an ongoing discussion in ASEAN to determine how far we can go on this issue.

Question: You mentioned that we don't understand our history and that National Education has become ritualised. And yet you seem to be disdainful of the notion of competing historical narratives when it comes to, for example, Operation Coldstore. Putting aside the validity of those alternative narratives, don't you think that in order to revive National Education and build interest in it, we would need to have that kind of open discussion and debate?

BK: You are right that there needs to be open discussion and debate. My quarrel is with the puerile way in which the alternative narrative of our political history has been formulated. They denied that there was ever any such thing as a Communist United Front because the people involved were not all communists. Of course, not everybody in the Communist United Front were communists and they wouldn't know who the communists were because that's the essence of what is a United Front and how it operates. It is this kind of silly debate that I object to, where if the establishment's view is black, say white. That is not to my mind, a critical debate. That is just being contrarian or attention seeking. There is room for critical debate over our history and, as I said, our understanding of history is constantly being revised. But there must be some connection with reality in the revisions. You can't just say I think this is not so because the government said so, which is what debate on the Internet and social media usually amounts to.

I used Operation Coldstore as an example of a stupid debate that happens because there isn't a wide enough understanding of some basic facts. If there was a broad enough understanding of basic facts, I don't think the people that started the debate could have got away with the silly arguments they made. They got away with it only because most people didn't know facts because they don't know enough about our history.

Question: Singapore is in between Malaysia and Indonesia and with the rise of Islamic fundamentalist values, what's in store for Singapore?

BK: Well, it is a matter of concern. Malaysia has changed, it is unrecognisable compared to Malaysia 30 or 40 years ago and I don't think it can go back to that. Indonesia is a bigger country, changes are diffused. There is obviously a debate or a struggle going on in the Muslim world. Not every Muslim in Malaysia is equally happy with the direction in which Islam in Malaysia has drifted; ditto for Indonesia. That is something for the Muslim community to settle. No outsider can really play a role in this debate. What can we do? We can watch it, we can try to understand it and we can prepare ourselves for all eventualities. That is one of the reasons why we have to be strong and we need a strong deterrent so that no matter the eventuality, we at least keep our neighbours reasonably honest in their dealings with us. We also need strong social cohesion. A lot of things for a small country are like the weather. The American election is a weather factor. Our neighbours are weather factors. You can't change it so you have to adapt yourself to it, prepare yourself for it. If you think it is going to rain, for heaven's sake buy an umbrella and keep it handy.

Question: We've succeeded, done so much and are really acknowledged very widely. In view of this changing technological era that we are now in, is our top leadership, our civil service, capable of the new forms of thinking and acting which you spoke about earlier?

BK: I think we are capable of what is necessary, but I also think the civil service needs to do a few things which I spoke about that will make them even more capable. What you are talking about are big technological disruptions to the established way of doing things. Some changes we can anticipate, I mentioned the Arctic Council because the ice is sooner or later going to melt. That's not really a technological disruption but we are looking forward. We probably do more looking forward than other people in this region, but whether that is enough or not I don't know. That is the burden of what I was trying to say. In fact, you have recast my essential point in another way. Are we aware of the new kinds of vulnerabilities that may be emerging? Is awareness enough? I quoted what C.P. Snow said of Venice: "They were fond of the pattern; they never found the will to break it." The quote actually goes on to show that Venice actually did recognise things were changing but still did not have the will to break it. If you go to Japan, they obviously need a new labour policy, a new immigration policy, they need a new foreign labour policy. The Japanese know this but they don't yet have the will to do it. We are not so bad, we are much better, but you have put your finger on the nub of the challenge. I think we do anticipate change, not perfectly and we certainly can do better; there is room for improvement. But we will not really know if we have done enough until the challenge is upon us.

APPENDICES

1

Lee Kuan Yew's Cast of Mind and its Lasting Influence

By Bilahari Kausikan

Lee Kuan Yew, Singapore's first Prime Minister, passed away on 23 March 2015. This speech was delivered at "The Legacy of Lee Kuan Yew and the Future of Singapore", a conference organised by Fitzwilliam College, University of Cambridge, on 31 October 2015. Mr Lee was an alumnus of Fitzwilliam College.

My generation of Singapore Foreign Service officers were privileged to have had the opportunity to work with Mr Lee and his comrades: Dr Goh Keng Swee and Mr S. Rajaratnam.

These three men defined the essentials of our foreign policy. Their ideas were formed by the imperatives of survival in the less than benign environment in which Singapore found itself on 10 August 1965, the morning after what was politely termed "Separation".

My colleagues and I learnt our trade from them. We did so in very humble capacities: taking notes at their meetings or seeing to the necessities of their travels, but still privileged to observe them at close quarters and absorb something of their modes of thought and operating style.

It was a unique apprenticeship. Then as we assumed more senior positions, we came to understand a little more of their considerations by sitting-in on their policy discussions and even occasionally contributed our mite to their decisions.

Some of us had studied international relations as an academic subject before joining the Foreign Service. But after 35 years, I have concluded that any resemblance between what I had studied and what I eventually did for a living was purely coincidental. Our real education in the realities of the diplomacy of a small country only started when our professional lives were touched, however tangentially, by Mr Lee and his comrades.

The most valuable thing they imparted to us was a cast of mind.

Mr Rajaratnam, our first Foreign Minister, has described his first meeting with the international press as Foreign Minister. It was only a few days after we had independence thrust upon us. Relations with Malaysia were fraught with racial tension; Sukarno's Indonesia was still fighting an undeclared war against us and to our north in Indochina, the Cold War had turned hot. The newsmen were braying for information on how newly independent Singapore would conduct itself.

What, Mr Rajaratnam told us he asked Mr Lee, shall I tell them? "Just wear a tie, Raja", was the answer, "you'll think of something".

Big countries may delude themselves about being always in control of events. Small countries cannot afford such illusions. For small countries, foreign policy is usually a series of not always neat or consistent improvisations to a messy and unpredictable reality. The future can at best be only dimly glimpsed and in any case cares not a whit for your concerns. So you must pragmatically adapt yourself to it.

One must of course set goals. But having done so, more often than not the most one can do is keep a distant star in sight as one tacks hither and tither to avoid treacherous reefs or to scoop up opportunities that may drift within reach.

Successful navigation requires a clinical — indeed cold-blooded — appreciation of the world as it is and not as you may wish it to be. This is harder than you may think. Diplomacy is an area of human endeavour that is more than usually susceptible to self-deception and wishful thinking.

Mr Lee and his comrades were not devoid of idealism. Singapore as it is today would not otherwise exist. They risked their lives to make it so.

But idealism must be rooted in a hard-headed understanding of the realities of human nature and power. Without power nothing can be achieved. And even with power not everything desirable will always be feasible. No matter how fervently one may wish that they may be liberated from the surly bonds of earth, pigs are never going to sprout wings and fly.

Understanding requires information. Mr Lee had intense intellectual curiosity. He sought information without regard for hierarchy. He was tolerant of alternate views or at any rate, he was tolerant of the young and brash desk officer as I then was who, too green to know that the tiger is dangerous, ventured on occasion to argue with him.

The tiger's roar is fearsome and its fangs are sharp. Mr Lee sometimes tried to intimidate you into agreement. But if you stood your ground with reasoned arguments, he listened even if he did not agree. And I am here to tell the tale.

Mr Lee and his comrades were impatient of complexity for complexity's sake; for the sake of showing off how clever one was. He did not suffer fools. If he sought a view, it was to be taken for granted you had something useful to say and would say it in the fewest possible words. And if you didn't know, say so.

What Mr Lee and his comrades possessed to a greater degree than anyone else I have ever met, was an uncanny ability to zero into the core of even the most complicated problem or situation. They wielded Occam's razor with great intellectual ruthlessness, slashing through the pious obfuscations which too often shroud international issues.

Margaret Thatcher once said of Mr Lee: "He was never wrong". That is of course, not true. Nobody can be always right, particularly in international affairs where most of the time most of the factors are going to be unknown or only partially known and where even the effort to know may change what you are trying to know.

But Mr Lee and his comrades were never shy about changing their minds. Again, this is harder than you may think.

Too often, vested interests, stubbornness or just plain pride stands in the way. Too many people believe their own propaganda. Mr Lee and his comrades avoided this most common of pitfalls because their laser-like focus was always on the national interest of Singapore. And they never confused ideology with interest.

Diplomacy is not all about being pleasant or making oneself agreeable. It is about defending and advancing the national interest, preferably by being pleasant and agreeable, but if necessary by any appropriate means. In this respect, having to stand your ground in the face of the tiger's roar — and in the shadows of diplomatic politesse lurk many wild beasts — was another valuable lesson.

This is particularly so in Southeast Asia, where a Chinese-majority Singapore which organises itself on the basis of multiracial meritocracy, is something of an anomaly. We live in a region where the Chinese are typically a minority and not a particularly welcome one, and where our neighbours organise themselves on the basis of very different principles.

Perhaps Mr Lee's greatest mistake was, during the period when we were part of Malaysia, to underestimate the lengths to which the Malay leadership in Malaysia would go to defend "*Ketuanan Melayu*" — Malay dominance. It was not a mistake that he or any of our leaders ever made again.

The basic issue in Singapore's relations with our neighbours is existential: the implicit challenge that by its very existence a Chinese majority Singapore organised on the basis of multiracial meritocracy poses to systems organised on the basis of different and ultimately irreconcilable principles. That we have the temerity to be successful adds to the offence.

None of this means we cannot cooperate with our neighbours: we must, we can and we do. But we must do so from a position of strength. Mr Lee was a lawyer and had a deep belief in the rule of law. Yet as a former Chief of the Malaysian Armed Forces has recounted, Mr Lee told him: "If PAS[1] comes into power ... and tries to meddle with the water in Johor Bahru, I'll move my troops in. I will not wait for the Security Council to solve this little problem."

But Mr Lee also once told an Israeli General, who had helped start our armed forces, that Singapore had learnt two things from Israel: how to be strong, and how not to use our strength; meaning that it is necessary to get along with neighbours and no country can live in perpetual conflict with its neighbours.

But we are different and we must remain different to survive. Small countries have no intrinsic relevance. To small countries, relevance is an artefact created by human endeavour and having been created, must be

---

[1] Parti Islam Se-Malaysia (Islamic Party of Malaysia).

maintained by human endeavour. To remain relevant we cannot be ordinary. We cannot be just like our neighbours. We have to be extraordinary. Yet being extraordinary does not always endear us to our neighbours.

The management of this paradox lies at the heart of our foreign policy and prescribes our most fundamental approaches: maintaining balance in Southeast Asia by facilitating the engagement of all major powers in our region, while fostering regional cooperation through ASEAN and maintaining our edge and keeping our powder dry.

Singapore and Southeast Asia in 2015 is obviously not the same as Singapore and Southeast Asia in 1965. But some things do not change: our geopolitical situation and how our neighbours choose to organise themselves.

The parameters of choice for small countries are never overly broad. The approach that Mr Lee and his comrades bequeathed to my generation of Foreign Service Officers and which we have tried to impart to our successors still serves us well.

Our environment is still complicated and perilous. The US and China are competing for influence with a greater than usual intensity as they grope towards a new accommodation with each other and the region. Malaysia is on a political trajectory that has heightened racial and religious tensions and may well lead to violence. The haze that regularly envelopes Southeast Asia is a reminder that post-Suharto Indonesia is still an incoherent and rent-seeking polity which has yet to reach a stable political equilibrium.

The key challenge is internal: that a new generation of Singaporeans will take the achievements of Mr Lee and his comrades for granted as the natural order of things and be persuaded that we are no longer vulnerable.

Some opposition politicians and their fellow travellers among the intelligentsia have tried to do just that. They either do not understand their own country and region or place their ambitions above the national interest. Fortunately, as the results of our recent General Election have demonstrated, the majority of my compatriots do not believe them.

2

A Tribute to S R Nathan (1924–2016)

By Bilahari Kausikan

S R Nathan, Singapore's sixth President, passed away on 22 August 2016. *This eulogy was delivered at "Reflections", a private rememberance ceremony for Mr Nathan at Singapore's Ministry of Foreign Affairs (MFA) on 24 August 2016.*

Mr Nathan influenced me even before I joined the MFA. One of Mr Nathan's best friends was the late Chia Cheong Fook who was also once Permanent Secretary of MFA. Mr Chia was my father's best friend. I grew up vaguely conscious of Mr Nathan as a background presence — obviously a personality to be reckoned with, but without clear resolution.

It was only in the earlier part of the 1970s that Mr Nathan acquired sharp focus in my consciousness. I was then pretending to study in the University of Singapore. I did something that could potentially have had serious ramifications — what it is I am never going to say, so don't bother to ask. Nobody knew what I did except my fellow conspirators — or so I fondly believed — but things began to go pear-shaped and I thought I'd better come clean before everything crashed.

I telephoned my father, who was then Singapore's Ambassador in Moscow. Before I could say anything, on a line that like all Embassy lines was obviously tapped, my father said he knew about it and told me to tell Mr Chia.

I dutifully called Mr Chia. Again before I could say anything, he said he knew about it, and told me to go and meet Mr Nathan at MFA which was then in City Hall, now the National Gallery Singapore.

With more than a little trepidation, I made my way to City Hall and was tremblingly admitted into Mr Nathan's presence. He wasn't then working in MFA. He must have just borrowed an office in MFA to meet me as he was then in a department whose very existence a callow youth should not know about let alone visit.

Again he already knew all about what in the innocence of youth I had thought was secret. Why did you do it, he demanded. I answered the best I could. Mr Nathan sat in grim faced silence, apparently pondering what I said.

"Who else was involved?", he suddenly barked at me. "No one", I said. "Don't lie", he said. "No one", I insisted. Again he pondered in silence. I sat before him nervously for what seemed an eternity.

"Will you take responsibility?", he finally asked. Exasperation momentarily overcame fear. "That's what I've been trying to do", I snapped.

"What's the worst that can happen to you?", Mr Nathan snapped back. "I don't know", I replied, puzzled. "Will you be hanged?", he asked.

"I don't think so", I replied, by this time thoroughly discombobulated, which I now realise was his intention.

Mr Nathan broke into a smile — and those of you who know him should know he had a very charming smile. "So what are you worried about?", he asked. "You did what you thought was right, it was stupid, but you won't be hanged. Go", he said.

I got up and made for the door. He called me back. "Good that you are willing to take responsibility for what you thought was right", he said. "Never evade responsibility, but if you want to play such games again, ask someone who knows how", he said.

I fled.

I then had no idea that I would one day join MFA. But I tell this story in his memory because it eventually dawned on me that the lessons he intended to impart were of great and continuing relevance to foreign service officers.

I lived my career in MFA by those lessons and today, in Mr Nathan's memory, I pass them on to you, my younger colleagues.

First, clever as you may be, you are not as clever as you may think. You need others. Work as a team.

Second, take responsibility for what you do; do your duty without fear. Be loyal to your team.

That was not to be the last time I made my way to Mr Nathan's office with trepidation. Subsequent occasions were as a foreign service officer.

Mr Nathan was tough on us. He had to be to whip us into shape. He had high standards that he would not compromise. He treated service to the country with high seriousness and taught us to take service seriously too. He was our mentor — a lifelong mentor.

Mr Nathan left an indelible mark on MFA and all who worked for him. All subsequent Permanent Secretaries only built on the foundations Mr Nathan laid.

Today MFA is an organisation that is respected worldwide. You can be proud of being part of an organisation Mr Nathan shaped. MFA is his monument. Do not let him down.

In March this year, Mr Nathan hosted lunch for a group of the survivors of MFA's City Hall days; as many of the aged but alive, ambulant and in country, of the old guard that could be rounded up, as well as (former senior civil servant) Benny Lim for whom Mr Nathan had great respect and affection.

I was hard on you, he told us, but you all always served me faithfully and I may not have told you before, but I want all of you to know that I appreciate it as this may be the last time we can meet together.

These were not his exact words — I was too moved to remember exactly; in the old days if he had known I didn't take precise notes, I would have been in for a scolding — but that was the gist.

As hard-bitten a crew as those at that lunch all were, I'd bet that the others were as moved as I was.

When Mr Nathan was taken ill, I went to see him in hospital. His daughter told me that of all the many and varied appointments in which Mr Nathan served, he told his family that MFA was special to him, the others were duty.

We may have on occasion grumbled about him being a hard task-master, but I think all those who served him knew that MFA was special to him.

Mr Nathan demanded loyalty: Loyalty to colleagues, loyalty to the organisation and above all, loyalty to Singapore. But he more than amply repaid loyalty with loyalty; he took responsibility for us and never denied responsibility for us even when we were the brunt of well-deserved criticism. He scolded us when he had to; he never let us down. Work done, he treated us as family. Long after he left MFA, he kept a paternal eye on us. I suspect he's doing so still.

And thus Mr Nathan in turn inspired loyalty, respect and affection. That is why to those of us who were privileged to serve him, Mr Nathan will forever be The Boss. I can now almost hear Mr Nathan's shade growling in my ear: Stop the long palaver and get back to work!

Rest easy Boss, we will not let you down.

About the Cover Illustrator:

Caleb Tan is an illustrator from Singapore. He graduated from the School of Technology for the Arts, Republic Polytechnic, in 2009 and has been under the tutelage of experienced illustrators. He has also completed a Singaporean children's book together with Direct Life Foundation and AF Storytellers, which was launched in May 2016.

LACAN'S CLINICAL TECHNIQUE

LACAN'S CLINICAL TECHNIQUE
Lack(a)nian Analysis

Antonio Quinet

R Routledge
Taylor & Francis Group

LONDON AND NEW YORK

First published 2018 by
Karnac Books Ltd.

Published 2018 by Routledge
2 Park Square, Milton Park, Abingdon, Oxon OX14 4RN
711 Third Avenue, New York, NY 10017, USA

Routledge is an imprint of the Taylor & Francis Group, an informa business

British Library Cataloguing in Publication Data

A C.I.P. for this book is available from the British Library

ISBN-13: 9781782205500 (pbk)

Typeset by Medlar Publishing Solutions Pvt Ltd, India

CONTENTS

II. CONDITIONS FOR ANALYSIS

III. THE ART OF THE ANALYST

ACKNOWLEDGMENTS

I wish to express my deepest gratitude to my team here in Rio, who helped me prepare the manuscript. Without them, this book would never have been ready for publication. To Roberto Previdi, my editor, revisor, and this book's first critical reader, and to Bruno Luz, my research assistant, who helped me to find all the references, designed the graphic elements and mathemes, formatted the final draft, and prepared the bibliography.

Spanning a career of nearly thirty years as a writer and a practising psychoanalyst, **Antonio Quinet** from Rio de Janeiro (Brazil) is one of the founders and member analysts of the EPFCL-Brazil (Psychoanalysis School of the Lacanian Field Forums).

As an international lecturer and four-language polyglot *par excellence*, he has been a guest speaker all around Latin America as well as in Australia, England, the United States, Spain, and France. His busy teaching, clinical, and lecturing schedule has also taken him all over Brazil, where he is currently one of the country's most outstanding scholars and thinkers in psychoanalysis. As one of the first translators of Lacan into Portuguese, he collaborated on *Seminars* 2 (1985), 7 (1988) and *Television* (1993) and many other miscellaneous texts published in Brazil.

A graduate in medicine from the Universidade Federal do Rio de Janeiro (UERJ) where he majored in psychiatry, he later moved to France and obtained the Certificat d'Études Spéciales de Psychiatrie at the Université Paris-Sud and the degree of Ancient Interne des Hôpitaux Psychiatriques de la Région Parisienne (A.I.H.P.R.P). Dr Quinet is guest professor at the Psychiatric Institute of the Universidade Federal of Rio

de Janeiro (UFRJ), where one of his ongoing projects has been interviews with ward interns.

From 1979 to 1989, Dr Quinet lived in Paris, continuing his studies
with Lacan's students at the École de la Cause Freudienne and receiving
the Diplome d'Études Approfondies du Champ Freudien (University
of Paris VIII—Vincennes) with a Master's Thesis on Psychosis in Freud
and Lacan and went on to become Assistant Professor at the Pyschoanalysis Department at the same university. And under Alan Badiou,
Dr Quinet also defended his PhD in Philosophy at the University of
Paris and published his thesis (*Un plus-de-regard*, 2003) in France and
Brasil. Dr Quinet is currently co-editor of the French-language psy-
choanalystical journal *L'en je-Lacanien*. The French edition of his book
Pyschosis and Social Bonds is forthcoming in 2017.

Currently adjunct professor of the graduate-level Programs in
Psychoanalysis, Health, and Society at the Universidade Veiga de
Almeida (UVA) in Rio de Janeiro, where he teaches and coordinates
graduate-student research projects on Subjectivity in Health Science
Practices as well as Psychoanalysis and Theatre. Dr Quinet founded the
Unconscious On Stage Theatre Company, to stage his own plays and
provide opportunities for professional actors interest and theatre and
psychoanalysis.

A life-long lover of the arts, literature and theatre, Dr Quinet made
his debut as a playwright and director with the staging of *Charcot's
Lesson* (2004), followed by *X, Y e S—Strindberg's Intimate Theatre* (2005),
and *Artorquato* (2006)—based on the life and work of Torquato Neto
(2006) in Rio de Janeiro and major Brazilian capitals. From 2007 to 2009,
the Unconscious On Stage also put on *Óidipous, Son of Laius* (2007–2009)
in Rio de Janeiro, São Paulo, Belo Horizonte, and other Brazilian cities.
Freudian Variations 1: The Symptom (2010–2011) received its international
debut in Rome, Italy, and then in Brazil's major capitals. Other plays
include *Open up, Hysterics!* (2012), first staged in Brazil and then as *La
leçon de Charcot—théatre hystérique* in Paris (2013). *The Act—Freudian
Variations 2* had a successful season in Brazil (2013–2014). All of his
plays have been published in Portuguese in Brazil.

In 2007, he appeared acting in the role of Dr Freud in his own play
Hilda and Freud: Collected Words at the Freud Museum in London and
in many major cities in Brazil and Latin America (translated in Spanish
as *Hilda y Freud—La laguna creativa* and performed in Argentina and
Colombia). The play, published by Karnac (2015), has been performed

to critical acclaim throughout Brazil and mostly recently, Dr Quinet was invited to stage it with his company in Melbourne, Australia (2017) during an international seminar where he was the keynote speaker.

The author of eleven books (several translated into Spanish and French) published in Brazil on psychoanalysis including *Theory and Pyschosis Clinic* (5th ed., 2011), *The Discovery of the Unconscious* (5th ed., 2016), *A Further Look: Seeing and Being Seen in Pyschoanalysis* (2nd ed. 2004), *Charcot's Lesson* (2005), *Psychosis and Social Bonds* (2nd ed. 2006), *The Strangeness of Psychoanalysis—Lacan's School and its Analysts* (2009), *The Others in Lacan* (2012), etc. His latest *Oedipus to the Letter* (2015): an in-depth examination of Greek tragedy in Lacan and Freud, shortlisted for Brazil's most prestigious literary award—the Prêmio Jabuti—in the category of psychology in 2016. His prolific output also includes numerous articles, reviews, and essays both in Brazilian and international specialised journals and media as well as many book chapters.

As co-author, editor, and organiser, Dr Quinet has also published: *Jacques Lacan: Psychoanalysis and its Connections* (1993), *Psychoanalysis—Convergences and Controversies* (2001), *Detours of Desire—Depression and Melancholy* (1999), *In Desire's Aim* (2002), *Love and the Couch* (2013), and also *Homosexuality and Psychoanalysis* (2013), shortlisted for the Prêmio Jubuti in 2015.

Dr Quinet's Lacanian clinical technique book *As 4+1 condições da análise* (1991) is now in its fifteenth edition and has been a best-seller in Brazil and Latin American (translated into Spanish as *Las cuatro condiciones del análisis*, 1996) pyschoanalytical circles. *Lacan's Clinical Technique—Lack(a)anian Practice* (Karnac, 2017) is a greatly updated and expanded sequel of the book's core ideas on clinical technique.

Further information at: https://www.antonioquinet.com/

PREFACE

Darian Leader

What do psychoanalysis and theatre have in common? According to most of the histories of Freudian practice, analysis begins where theatre ends. After his initial awe at the theatre of the Salpetriere, where patients acted out to the suggestion of their doctors, Freud moved from a clinic of the eye and the visible to a clinic of the ear and the invisible. The rule of free association and the use of the couch, we are told, signalled this decisive break from the space of the spectacle.

It's a nice story, but as Antonio Quinet shows, theatre has never been lost in psychoanalytic practice. The error here is to equate theatre with the visible effects of suggestion, rather than with the more fundamental question of drama and its function in human life. Quinet has a unique perspective here: a psychoanalyst trained in the Lacanian orientation, he also writes, produces and directs plays, working closely not only with his patients but also with actors and all those involved in the *mise en scène* of drama.

In this book he introduces the essentials of Lacnian clincial technique effortlessly and with great humour. Conceptual issues are linked directly to the clinic, and the rationale of the Lacanian approach is explained with clarity and ease. Transference, the use of the couch, the modulation of time, the place of money and the form and aim of interpretation are all explored carefully and succinctly. But running through these discussions is the overarching question of analysis as a kind of theatre, with the analyst as actor.

If Lacan's early advice to the young analyst was to do crossword puzzles, his later work implies, as Quinet shows, both a textual practice and a dramatic one. Lacan may have begun by elaborating a theory of interpretation, but he would later nuance this with his concept of the analytic act. And indeed, when we survey the numerous examples of Lacan's clinical style, we find plenty of word plays, yes, but the interventions that have the most powerful effects are those which involve a theatre, as Lacan uses his body and his voice to touch, to mimic, to reach and to impact his analysands.

To the analysand's talking cure, Quinet opposes the analyst's acting cure. But this is a special kind of acting. Focusing first on the desire of the analyst, Quinet shows the centrality of the utterance, the conveying of the interpretation rather than its content as such. The analyst performs, acting out the *semblant* of the object, in a strange kind of role-play. This isn't exactly show-business, as he reminds us, but practices constitutive of theatre are equally formative of the analytic encounter. Theatre, after all, has always been about how to convey those things which cannot be said directly.

In a sense, this is the logical consequence of Lacan's position from the late 1950s that desire is incompatible with speech. If desire cannot be given any ready propositional form, it will articulate itself in different ways, in the cracks and furrows of discourse, and in the relations—or sets of relations—between terms. To put it as the Russian Formalists did, what cannot be inscribed as a meaningful proposition will take the form of a relation.

When Theseus set sail for Crete, he tells his father he would hoist a white sail if he was successful in his mission of killing the minotaur. After he slays it, he forgets his promise, and his father throws himself off a cliff. In the first part of this story, a son deliberately kills a non-human adversary. In the second part, a son accidentally kills a human non-adversary. The Oedipal proposition is not directly sayable, and is inscribed not in the first or the second part of the story but in the relation between the two parts. This is the structure of Lacanian desire, which eschews any propositional representation.

If you take this seriously, as Lacan did, analytic practice has to change. New ways have to be found to access what is unsayable, to touch the points of real in each person's life. Analysis here is not simply a subversion of everyday forms of dialogue, but involves a more radical engagement with the real, an engagement which, as Quinet shows, means that the body and the voice have to be put into play. This is the kind of theatre that Quinet has in mind, and we will be both instructed and delighted at how he introduces it to us in this book.

PRELUDE TO THE AFTERNOON
OF AN ANALYST

> But where and how is the poor wretch to acquire the ideal qualifications which he will need in his profession? The answer is, in an analysis of himself, with which his preparation for his future activity begins.
>
> —"Analysis Terminable and Interminable", Sigmund Freud

This is not a do-it-yourself book or a step-by-step manual for psychoanalysts. You will not find any easy recipes or a tidy formulaic and prescriptivist approach to Lacanian praxis. Each of the chapters herein is an autonomous essay that can be read independently or studied as a separate unit from the others.

Psychoanalytical technique is grounded in and subordinated to the structure of subjectivity and psychoanalytical ethics. The main treatment guideline is getting the analysand to speak and plunge into free association. This golden rule of psychoanalysis stands above all others. Nevertheless, Freud highlighted some key "initial conditions" such as tentative treatment (preliminary interviews), use of the couch, and the handling of time and money. Accordingly, Lacan lays down a transference strategy as *semblant* and interpretation tactics as poetical. Nonetheless, hovering far above these initial considerations is the analyst's own analysis—the key prerequisite for effective psychoanalysis. This book is an overview of the Lacanian concepts related to analytic practice and a summation of my own thoughts as a clinical practitioner.

Analysts need not be dogmatic sticklers to Freud's framework. But they must know the "whys and wherefores" of their technical approach and also surrender themselves to the same structure of analytical procedures.

As all speaking beings, analysts too are subject to castration and must be aware that the Other is also castrated and branded by a *lack*: this is what makes the Other so slippery and vacuous. Hence, analysts cannot place themselves in the place of the Other, because, according to Lacan, the Other is lacking.

They may, however, guide treatment to unravel the threads of alienation signifiers and help patients recognise the lack behind desire that no signifiers can cover or disguise. This process allows patients to unhinge themselves from alienating signifiers. It is here that both analysts and analysands come to the place where all utterances have finally been exhausted: this moment represents the potential end of analysis. Analysts can "promise" to lead the analysand to unveil the object of his or her fantasy in the *locus* of the lack—that thing which exists as an answer to the enigma of the Other's desire. Throughout this process, therapeutic effects can be remarkable.

During treatment, analysts do not act as ego-endowed persons with their own agendas and a personal vision of reality, or as desire-driven subjects plagued by symptoms. Rather, they play the role of the *semblant* of analysand's *object a* and will only be successful if they themselves too have undergone analysis and reached their own lack point. It is at the end of analysis that they will discover the "analyst's desire". This "desire" is the Lacanian ethical operator that guides all the analyst's acts and steers the treatment.

The analyst's desire and act

The analyst's desire is not a formation of the unconscious. It is not to be found in the subject's chain of signifiers, life story, or entangled with the Other's desire. Hence, the analyst's desire is not decipherable and cannot be located among desires and in the aspirations of any pantheon of familial longings. It is not the *prêt-a-porter* desire of the Other analysands can decipher through their parents. We can only know this desire through our own analysis. The analyst's desire is one brought on by analysis.

The unconscious desire as the Other's desire– that desire belonging to something else which precedes and moulds our own—is handed down from parents to son, from generation to generation. Psychoanalysis has invented no wheel or gunpowder here. The Greeks knew as much before us. After all, says Lacan, the subject's very desire belongs to the Other, since it is "dated", "received", and interwoven with the desires of those occupying the Other's throne in the subject's mind. The very signifiers the infant is bombarded with since or even before birth are the ballast and meanings of the Other's desire: they are baggage the child will haul along throughout life.

The analyst's desire is not bound to the desire of being or having a phallus: it is not desire connected to the demand for love or sex, and much less a clear-cut answer to the Other's burning desire. It is neither desire as passed down from father to son, from analyst to analysand or any other kind of bequeathal. The analyst's desire is not found in Freud's *Traumdeutung—The Interpretation of Dreams*. That seminal text is a precious record of Freud's desire to analyse himself: a stunning portrait of self-discovery and self-knowledge in which the young analyst learns that the true interpreter of dreams is himself.

The desire Freud discovered in the formations of the unconscious (i.e., dreams), is one linked to something lacking and is therefore always an unfulfillable want. It is a desire knotted in sexuality and signified in the child's earliest representations. It is desire running wildly after signifiers and images to represent, construct, depict, and stage itself. Desire is obsessed with its linguistic signifier "selfies", yet these only reveal it incompletely, because it is always slipping away along the signifier chain; you cannot catch it by the tail.

The analysand's desire for knowledge differs from that of the analyst's. In pursuit of knowledge, analysands, as subjects of their desire, hike along the pathways of sex in the great psychic hinterlands of love—that undiscovered country where their frustrations are reborn and re-enacted in relationships. But the analyst's desire is the cause that empowers analysands to decipher their own selves.

The analysand's "desire for knowledge" is like a "desire for gold" and it is embedded in the formations of the unconscious. Analysands chase after answers like diggers after gold: they think this knowledge is supposedly part of the Other's treasure. Analysands, like Alcibiades who lusted after Socrates's "golden knowledge", want to be moonstruck by some new insight or knowledge about themselves. The analyst's desire has an entirely different meaning. If gold can be a signifier of desire, like a "golden desire" (in honour of the golden number that Lacan uses to refer to *object a*), the analyst's 24-carat desire is the result of his or her personal encounter with the *not-all*: it is a *"not-all"* knowledge. It is a desire that glitters with epistemic colours, that is to say, it is caused by the surplus jouissance which extracts its truth from knowledge about the non-existence of the sexual relationship, which Freud called castration. This knowledge is the very hollowness of human desire.

Analysts do not convey their desire like other types of knowledge, "like a wire transfer" (Lacan, 1969–1970, p. 23), an email or WhatsApp message. It is not, therefore, a neat and orderly Power-Point presentation of statements of knowledge. It is a *sui generis* conveyance, inasmuch as "the analyst's desire is its own enunciation" as Lacan says, in "The Proposition" and thus equates it with the analysand's *x*. (Lacan, 2001, p. 251).

The analyst's desire is not sexual, nor marked by childhood wish fulfilments. It is not representable, stageable, interpretable and, as such, it is unattached to any lack.

Foremost, the analyst's desire is an "answer"—the very answer they have found for themselves as analysands. Thus, analysts use this "answer" as an enigma for analysands to figure out. This is the radical element that upholds the ethics of analysis. All rules and principles governing our practice stem from it and orbit around it like gravity-bound satellites. But, alas, it is unutterable even though its presence is expressed in ways that transcend the verbal and the rational. Whereas this ineffable enigma is not a pure Real and does not have, nor can have, signifiers to label it, but it can indeed get the analysand's symbolic juices flowing.

The analyst's desire prevents him or her from acting on patients out of sexual desire or to meet cheap-spirited demands for love from them. The analyst's desire is devoid of that subjectivity which comes in the form of wanting to cure, care, nurse, protect, love and be loved. Decipherable desire, whose Symbolic, Real, and Imaginary coordinates can be located through analysis, is unconscious desire ciphered in signifiers. This is not the case of the analyst's desire, which is the logical operator of analysis.

The analyst's desire is not desire grounded in lack-of-something as an unconscious desire which is a negative and translated into unfulfilled, impossible or forewarned desire, which characterise hysteria, obsession, and phobias respectively. The analyst's desire is signposted by assertiveness, open acceptance of the overflowing and plentiful void rather than negativity, denial or need for fulfilment: it is the desire, says Lacan, to obtain the pure difference. It is desire of having other individuals engender an absolutely unique and personal difference that sets them apart from the hypnotised crowd "all marching in step". Therefore, the analyst's desire, at the end of treatment, is linked to that individual uniqueness which goes against the grain of thinking of analysts (or anyone, for that matter) as a cohesive, classifiable, and definable group. At best, collective categorisations are as meaningful as, say, an expression such as "a ship of fools". The analyst's does not engage in Orwell's "group-think", and rejects all simplistic social labelling that pigeonholes human beings. Once again, this is only possible when analysts undergo analysis themselves to the end. Hence, the analyst will shy away from any little club or group representing the vested interests of some S_1 agents playing the Master or their peers and friendly competitors.

Deciphering unconscious desire—that psychic stuff whose structure reveals the blatant lack in the human condition—is fundamental for subjects to review repeatedly through roll-calling signifiers or symbolic coordinates until they hit upon that affirmative and causal dimension of desire—*object a*, which fires up and fuels the "warp drive" of desire and jouissance. Only after stripping away layer after layer of signifiers, metonyms or metaphors, do we hit upon the core essence of desire divested of its wardrobe and make-up. Desire's Real is found in its cause, which springs forth contingently as surplus or left-over jouissance. Thus, the final (if we can even think in those terms) frontier is not a set of laws governing the unconscious, but rather that very unshiftable thing that lies beyond desire's tricky, multi-masked signifiers and always remains outside the Symbolic. The analyst's desire is related to the leftover *object a*—desire's real fountainhead.

The analyst's act

The analytical act and the analyst's desire are strictly enmeshed with each other. They are the final aim and the highest aspiration of analysis. The act also starts analysis.

In the beginning was the Freudian act. This Freudian parody of *Genesis* is the psychoanalysis creation story through the act of making the unconscious known through its myriad of perplexing formations. Underlying all signifiers, there still remains a formless void that is beyond the realm of words, concepts and signifiers. The concept of the unconscious is a watershed in human culture, an insight that brought us a little closer to understanding the underpinnings of our psychic life, but it is also a discontinuity. Because it is an open-ended concept with such a cutting edge, it by no means represents a ready-made tool, approach or technique. Freud left us the task of recreating and reinventing his original act in each session with patients: he has left some guidelines, but we must fill in the blanks before commencing any analysis.

An individual sets up an appointment with an analyst to start treatment: the how, when, and why of the session will all depend on the analyst's personal decision. But what is the linchpin of this decision-making? Some probably think that going by the book and using free-association as the basis and benchmark of the "analyst–analysand contract" regarding setting, time, and value will ensure the best results.

Lacan thought otherwise. Instead of rules cooked up by psychoanalytic societies that aim at homing in on the Other's various manifestations or guises, he introduces the concept of the psychoanalytic act, thereby shifting psychoanalysis from the rulebook to the sphere of ethics. The unconscious comes to life through the analyst and the psychoanalytical act, and each individual case recreates psychoanalysis *ex nihilo*. Thus, the start of analysis is a psychoanalytical act—it is the condition of the unconscious whose status is ethical rather than ontic and it relies on the analyst's act. Lacan's concept of analysis act reveals that the "contract"—the start of the analysis—takes the burden of responsibility off the analyst's shoulder for this act.

The psychoanalytic act *par excellence* is the one in which the analysand becomes the analyst. Therefore, analysts will only understand this if they themselves have crossed this threshold. Lacan's calls this *la passe*, which I translate as the crossing-through-and-over (*la passe*) that point in analysis wherein analysands face their own hollowness. The analyst's act has the markings of this crossing. From Freud, we learn that the analyst's own analysis is the groundwork of the psychoanalytical act. And from Lacan, we see that only the analytical process can actually turn the analysand into analyst. This crossing takes place inside and never outside of analysis.

Lacan's seminar on the psychoanalytic act appears simultaneously alongside "The Proposition of October 9 on the Psychoanalyst and the School" (2001) where he infers how a theory of the aims of analysis

would affect institutions and predicates the psychoanalyst's qualifica-
tion on the analysand's end result. The psychoanalytic act takes place
when the subject finally perceives itself as an object (i.e., the object that
the subject thought it, in its fantasy, represented to its mother). It is afterwards, after crossing-through-and-over (*la passe*) and going beyond this
fantasy, that the analysand then becomes an analyst. In this condition,
the analyst is now able to deal with the *semblant* of the object causing
desire for the analysand. The psychoanalytic act in one's own analysis
provides the framework for Lacan's aphoristic and oracular statement
in the pre-Socratic style: "the analyst is only authorized by himself"
(Lacan, 2001, p. 243).

The analytic act is incompatible with the paralysing hesitation of the
split subject. For neurotics, parodying Hamlet's soliloquy, "to do or not
to do" is the big question. Like those suffering from obsession, neurotics
put off doing something or are so plagued by doubts that even simple
tasks blow up to Herculean proportions. And similar to hysterics, neurotics prefer complaining to acting or striking while the iron is is hot.

The analytic act is in double time: first during the analyst's own
analysis (the act of becoming an analyst) and second, when the analyst
treats the patient.

The clinical analytic act shows the *not-all* of knowledge and is devoid
of premedition. During the act, the analyst is an object rather than
a subject. By its very nature, the act springs forth uncontrollably and
unpremeditatedly. Analysts do not act as subjects of a voluntary act, but
are rather impelled by the urgency of their analytical act which pulls
their strings, so to speak.

Freud demonstrated with many examples in *The Psychopathology of
Everyday Life* that the subject performs the act without thinking, in a
purely accidental way, in other words unconsciously. But the analytic
act is based on knowledge which includes:

- That analyst's knowledge of how the unconscious works obtained
  during his or her analysis;
- The analyst's newly acquired knowledge of the analysand during
  analysis;
- Awareness of the *lack* which underlies being, knowledge and desires.

The awareness of the lack and incompleteness inherent to jouissance
is particularly important since it is a key factor involved in pinpoint-
ing the impossibility of having all we want, of complete knowledge

or full satisfaction or finding that perfect harmony in a relationship with another person. In Lacanian terms, a sexual "relationship" is non-existent. But each case must be appraised independently. There is no "general panacea" in psychoanalysis.

The first analytic act is performed by analysands—they are not on the receiving end of perennial wisdom and timely insight like a team getting a pep talk from the coach—but rather at a crossroads with the analyst where a demolition is underway. According to Lacan, the psychoanalytical act is usually scandalous for the analysand, since it reveals the failure of the subject-supposed-to-know that foggily appears in a glimpse here and there and shocks the patient undergoing treatment.

So, analysts only find the reason for the analytical act itself at the end of their own analysis. Can individuals who have never worked out their own fantasies even work as psychoanalysts? How will they interact with analysands? As subjects, they would place the patient as the object of their personal fantasy ($\mathcal{S} \lozenge a$)[1] and overplay their burning passion with him or her. Or, analysts would situate analysands as subjects (a $\lozenge \mathcal{S}$), and participate as objects in a perverse fantasy that has all the ingredients of prostitution. Acting as the *semblant* of the object is not the same as acting as the analysand's fantasy object.

The psychoanalytic act traces its origin back to Freud's timely portrait of the analyst as a young analysand in *The Interpretation of Dreams*. The analyst's act, based on the analyst-as-analysand assumption, re-enacts Freud's breakthrough and makes it new again in every encounter with the analysand. This is the *sine qua non* condition for starting analysis. With this in mind, let us now proceed to examine Lacanian clinical techniques.

* * *

This book aims primarily at bringing out the artist in every clinical practitioner of psychoanalysis. I always recommend we read poetry and literature to interpret texts, watch movies and plays and bring out the actor in ourselves.

During his early years, Lacan told analysts to do crossword puzzles. In his later years, Lacan focuses on poetry and states that analytical interpretation must be poetic to be effective. The analyst's know-how or *savoir faire* is poetic and theatrical artistry is living poetry. Analysts must be artists to do their job.

I

THE ANALYST'S DISCOURSE

Freud listed three impossible professions: governing, educating, and analysing. All are limited by a real and unendurable structural resistance that makes the tasks of the professions practically a hopeless case. Those ruled find their governors unbearable whereas students refuse to submit to teachers and analysands resist analysis. It is also impossible to perform these tasks satisfactorily because there is always something lurking in the background that threatens to disrupt these professions. People are unruly, students are unteachable, and analysands are always ungrateful as they refuse to improve from analysis. Lacan formulated the discourses to represent the social bonds inherent in these impossible missions:

- The Master's discourse (MD) corresponds to ruling over people.
- The University discourse (UD) corresponds to educating people.
- The Analyst's discourse (AD) corresponds to analysing people.

Lacan further discovered yet another social bond which stems from clinical practice: the Hysteric's discourse (HD), whose purpose is to provoke desire or that which makes someone desire something (*faire*

3

désirer). Lacan dignified hysterical neurosis by promoting it to the level of a social bond. HD is also the analysand's discourse.

The AD is the flip-side of the MD whereas the HD is the reverse of the UD. The MD and the UD are the discourses of domination; the former through rule over subjects, the latter through knowledge. Lacan's theory of discourses represents power as S_1 (unitary signifier) and knowledge as S_2 (binary signifiers) and these are the agents in these social bonds. The HD agent is the subject of the unconscious ($\mathcal{S}$) and the AD agent is *object a* (object-cause-of-desire and surplus jouissance). The latter two discourses go against the grain of the MD and UD.

The whole of our society is grounded on these particular discourses (capitalism now appears as a deformity of the former MD discourse). All of these discourses are embedded in the field of jouissance which Lacan called the Lacanian Field. In this section, I will provide a brief overview of Lacan's theoretical framework for this field and the discourses as an essential background for the reader to understand the analyst's place and techniques as an agent in the social bond with the analysand.

Civilisation and its jouissance

Just what is this field called jouissance that Lacan introduces in *Seminar XVII* and calls "the Lacanian Field"? Therein, he resorts to Freudian concepts such as Repetition, Death Drive, Beyond the Pleasure Principle, and the superego which he equates with *object a*. This latter is defined as *plus-de-jouir*[1] or surplus jouissance or the waste or trash civilisation rejects. It is in this part of the drive where, according to Freud, civilisation forces subjects to surrender something which they regurgitate as guilt feelings thanks to that psychic cop, watchdog, and lawmaker known as superego.

The field of jouissance is, primarily, a linguistically structured conceptual and operational field. Moreover, jouissance spins its web with the thread of discourses, which are among its many toys and tools. Jouissance redefines whatever falls into its clutches and, even if it itself cannot be caught entirely, there is no universal or generic jouissance since, if the signifier is sex, it cannot be reduced to merely sex or a phallic signifier, because it is all that and much more. In its abundant overflowing, jouissance is a true "signifier-buster": it catches the signifier without being caught by the same. Regarding jouissance, Lacan says that, "[...]

once inside, you do not know where it will end. It begins with a trickle and ends in the blaze of a gasoline fire" (Lacan, 1969–1970, p. 83).

Titanic *or jouissance on a sinking ship*

James Cameron's blockbuster film *Titanic* (1997) illustrates jouissance's tidal overflow and the signifier's inability to completely contain it. The established order and organisation—social/class boundaries—are clearly marked in first class and steerage. The passengers all have their own stories, dreams, and pain. After some mix-ups, mishaps, and plot twists, Jack and Rose meet and fall in love, but, catastrophe strikes, or rather, the Titanic strikes ... an iceberg, and the unsinkable vessel is suddenly going down. Slavoj Zizek points out this departure from the standard Hollywood fare in which great disasters take place so two people can fall in love such as in *Reds* (1981) or *Dances with Wolves* (1990). In the former, the Russian Revolution really only "happens" to bring Warren Beatty and Diane Keaton together for some hot romance; in the latter, "boy meets girl" thanks to ... a tribal massacre. *Titanic* represents a noteworthy shift from this Hollywood tradition. While Jack and Rose are experiencing the equivocations of language, jouissance carries on like a well-behaved youngster. On board, social classes and different aspects of reality are literally compartmentalised: if it is time to rock and roll down in steerage, in first class everyone is *ennui*-stricken or annoyed. Whereas the boiler room is hotter than Hades, the first-class tea room is as cold as the iceberg up ahead. The raucous sensual power of the lower classes is in sharp contrast with the futile snobbishness of the crusty aristocrats. Since a social symbolic order is present, these two kinds of jouissance are like oil and water because their symbolic function screens them from each other like apartheid.

Spruced up as an aristocrat at a swanky tuxedo dinner party, Leonardo di Caprio's character (Jack) illustrates a weird jouissance expressing the mood of the scene: Jack's awareness of something so "thick in the air you could cut it with a knife" makes him wobble uncomfortably. When Jack and Rose finally consummate their frenzied sexual passion in the automobile, she outdoes the young Madame Bovary by getting out of the car and venting her annoying and whining dissatisfaction. This can be seen as that moment when, even if a desire has been indulged, the unfulfillable jouissance of the Other (*object a*) floods the subject's awareness. The former order collapses and the jouissance of dissatisfaction and lack burst forth like water out of a ruptured damn. At the same time, the mighty liner fatally grazes the iceberg and things will soon become quite watery for crew and passengers. In my reading of this film, the ship is to phallic jouissance as water is to the jouissance of the Other.

Social order and class rank go down the drain before the ship does. Grammar gives way to drama, melodrama, and chaos. The water "democracy" (it really is for everyone) washes away the first-class totalitarianism even as it attempts to exclude steerage access to the lifeboats. A new "one-water" order rules everyone. Crew and passengers must all deal with this overflowing and rapidly spreading Other which wreaks havoc of boundaries, barriers and bulkheads and flushes away the new unsinkable technologies and delightful consumer dream called Titanic. The marriage between the signifiers of science and capital is unable to contain the jouissance of the Other signified by the invading water.

Before finding her Romeo, our Juliet (Rose) attempts an interpretation in the name of Freud: the ship materialises as its builder's phallic jouissance. In her passionate ignorance, she asks if Dr Freud might be one of the first class passengers. No, Freud was never booked on this soon-to-be leaking liner, nor, as he incisively states in *Civilization and its Discontents*, did he share the American "put-your-pedal-to-the-metal" dream of economic growth!

Hollywood shows us how catastrophes are proportional to the infatuation with phallic power, just as jouissance's vital flood is commensurate with an unflinching refusal to castrate or be castrated. Moreover, in *Civilization and its Discontents*, Freud stresses how the play of the death drive may be equated with omnipotence and narcissism.

Phallic jouissance's One is represented by the builder-captain pair. The former is accountable for the sinking whereas the latter must go down with his ship. The outcome of the action of opposing—albeit complementary figures of bad master and good master—is the segregation of life (the class apartheid I mentioned) and the lack of lifeboats for all. Nevertheless, some half-filled boats are dropped anyway as if they were choice box seats from which the masters could comfortably watch the reality show of hundreds being flushed down into the sea.

The movie ends with a survivor—a woman—telling the Titanic's tragic tale. She is the character of the timeless (or eternal) woman (she is over a hundred) who kept the diamond—the film's causal object. An object which is lost as soon as it is found in the depths of the ocean.

In throwing the diamond into the sea, our Madeleine-Medea narrator amply demonstrates her awareness that the object's desire-causality only comes into play when the object—the "die-amond" as the object-cause of love—is lost.[3] That consumer dream (or nightmare) called the Titanic sinks, but that which causes desire forever remains. No wonder they say diamonds are forever.

The field of jouissance

Jouissance always spills forth like water over the floodgates, but in Lacan's structured field, we witness its multiple manifestations. First and most obvious is *object a*, an object which condenses jouissance, albeit episodically. Knowledge as S_2 (the slave) is defined by Lacan as "means of jouissance". For S_2, knowledge is the tool of jouissance, which is a different form of jouissance as expressed by the Master signifier. In the field of language, S_1 functions as the Name-of-the-Father which bars the mother's jouissance. However, the field of jouissance as a whole renders S_1 powerless to exclude anything. On the contrary, it celebrates the eruption of jouissance, as in the trauma.

Thus, the field of jouissance instrumentalises S_1, S_2 and *object a* and transforms the subject into the Real's answer. In other words, the subject is the effect of his or her traumatic encounter with the sexual Real and as such retains the representation of that clash as the traumatic S_1 that experiences jouissance.

Although Lacan again returned to Freud (and to the field of jouissance) during the 1970s, he had set out earlier in 1968 as a contingency of the May 1968 Student Movement revolt against authority and established order (or what was once called "The Establishment"). As usual, Lacan delivers something truly innovative by returning to the Freudian source and coming back with an absolutely new reading. We may interpret Seminar XVII *The Reverse of Psychoanalysis* as a Freudian based reading of social bonds and a return to key Freudian texts on culture (particularly, *Civilization and its Discontents*) written after Freud had revamped all his theses in light of the death drive (or what James Strachey terms "the death instinct"). But just what is the flip-side of psychoanalysis? It is the MD and consequently of civilisation itself. If psychoanalysis is the reverse of civilisation, Lacan enters psychoanalysis through the back door of civilisation.

Lacan describes this field of civilised jouissance as something structured in the form of an instrument-equipped operational field and propounds what he calls "the discourses and the field of jouissance". The tools that enable this field are the discourses I will address in the next chapter.

It is noteworthy that had not Lacan attempted conceptualising *object a*, the topic of discourses would never have come up. What are the discourses? He defines them pithily as civilisation's social bond. Hence, Lacan's return to the same place where Freud began examining social bonds.

Lacan's starting point is *Civilization and its Discontents*. What does Freud consider the greatest human suffering therein? Is it the unconscious or something else inside us? Or perhaps symptoms since, besides the anxiety and castration they cause, Freud's text unfolds around them. But according to Freud, the greatest causes of human suffering lie in our relationships with others. Foreshadowing Sartre's "hell is other people", Freud posits that there is nothing worse than the other person. We know this from working in corporations or institutions, in marriages or friendships gone astray. In our entire social network, hell is always a definite possibility that materialises in our fellow beings who ambush us unexpectedly.

This is mankind's greatest pain, and granting this assumption, Lacan returns to psychoanalysis as a social bond among others. He delivers an ambitious proposal: to account for civilisation and its structure and the role of psychoanalysis. Seminar XVII is a "seventies-bell-bottom" Lacan-style version of *Civilization and its Discontents* based on the 1968 Student Revolution. At the time, Lacan tried to interpret the unrest of the 1960s, a time when the Master was coming under heavy fire and being questioned. Lacan offers the following diagnosis, which I will here paraphrase in my own words: "… you, who are overthrowing your professors, you who are rising up against your educators, you know what you want? A new Master." Hardly the best way for Lacan to ingratiate himself with hot-headed young rebels. Consequently, the students almost ran him out of the class room for his pointing out that their beloved movement had all the makings of the HD which swaps the last Master for a new one.

We should never underestimate the HD when hysteria has now become an unflattering word even in our own profession. Drawing a parallel, the HD is, *par excellence*, that of the analysand. Here I invite my reader to pause, re-evaluate and redefine the hysteric's discourse as a social bond, and its function in society: that of questioning the establishment.

Getting back to civilisation, Lacan proposes to examine the social Other's structuring bonds and adds another concept regarding structure. This is a shift from the structure of the Subject (singular) to structures (plural) of the discourses. It is through these structures (which are jouissance's tool box) that individuals form bonds with each other. Lacan defines these structures in *Seminar* XVII: "It is a wordless discourse [...]" (Lacan, 1969–1970, p. 11). It is not only what is said (statements, speech acts, and utterances) in verbal exchanges, but also the enunciation's implicit relationships. Furthermore:

> The fact is that, in all truth, it (wordless discourse) is able to subsist without words. It subsists in certain fundamental relations. The latter literally would not be able to be maintained without language. (Lacan, 1969–1970, p. 11)

Lacan here is speaking of "speech-less" structures that are nevertheless not "language-less". Lacan is bipartitioning the function of speech—something he had already completely unified in his work during the 1950s—in the broader field of language. There is a separation: language no longer just deals with speech but also with silence and acts. According to Lacan: "Through the instrument of language, a number of stable relations are established, wherein something much larger may be wired in, something beyond utterances" (Lacan, 1969–1970, p. 11). Something primordial (a kind of *a priori* silent "statement") thus remains concealed yet somehow conveyed in language; something undefinable that manifests itself beyond words in social relationships and actions. Something "in the air" so to speak, like a screaming silence, which may express itself by a wordless act. But what exactly is this primordial statement? For if we can sense it, is it not evident enough to be perceived and ascertained in speech itself and its delivery?

Lacan shifts from speech to the act separating speech from speechless acts determined by language in the field of jouissance. And it is precisely jouissance that will define the latter's structure: there is no discourse which is not jouissance. Despite this, it is hidden; we must figure out the jouissance involved in each discourse.

Psychoanalysis thus aims at the being implied in the jouissance-and-socially bonded subject. Hence, what matters is the subject's jouissance that permeates social bonds.

Object a

In this same *Seminar* XVII, Lacan says that Freud is worthy of a discourse which sticks as closely as possible to the concept of jouissance. What Lacan attempts to demonstrate in his return to Freud is the drive's location in discursive practices. In *Group Psychology*, Freud demonstrated both the nature of the cement or glue of social bonds, as well as a homosexual Eros—an Eros that excludes the Other's sex. Freud asserts that the sublimation of love through identification (I identify with the one I love) is what bonds groups together. This is the Freudian theory of identifications based on an Eros in which I mirror myself in the other and I am the other. Thus, according to Freud, where sublimated homosexuality is present, homo-generalisation, homogeneity or, to put it plainly, the same old stuff follows. Lacan embraces the erotic cement in social bonds but claims it is the heterogeneous *object a* that envelops the four discourses (MD, UD, HD, and AD) makes up the structure of this field of jouissance. Lacan's reasoning enables him to envision and conceptualise *object a* as the most absolutely heterogeneous and radical object in the field of language, and consequently, in the unconscious. Heterogeneous and manifold insomuch as the unconscious can wrap itself up in a host of different signifiers, but radical in the sense that a representation of the unconscious as a whole is impossible. There is no *Vorstellungsrepräsentant* for the *object a*; no adequate fiction, verbal construct or metaphor that can depict it. It is that out-of-bounds part of the drive of which we can only make abstractions. Concurrently, it was the idea of *object a* that allowed Lacan to establish the social bonds and express them as discourse mathemes in order to formalise the place of the analyst in this new social bond created by Freud.

Object a, according to Lacan, is civilisation's default setting of the social Other. Upon re-examining *Civilization and its Discontents*, Lacan retrieves what is excluded from civilisation and shows that this leftover or surplus jouissance structures all of civilisation as "inside outsider". It spans both the spring of our desire and the winter of our discontent.

There is an important reference of Lacan's in a footnote to "On a Preliminary Question for any Possible Psychosis Treatment" (Lacan, 1966, pp. 553–554) in which he comments on the R Schema which refers to the subject and the fantasy object. The R Schema is the schema of reality, structured by the Symbolic, the Imaginary, and the Real. According to Lacan, the field of reality is buttressed only by jettisoning *object a* and yet the very same object provides reality with a frame. *Object a* is part of the Real but does not belong to reality.

When is *object a* not jettisoned from this field of reality? In psychosis. We see precisely a return into reality of *object a* as gaze and voice. And what are the consequences of this? Reality tends to disappear or lack a frame or delimitation, which it usually has in the case of neurosis and which is sometimes also unsettled in the case of depersonalisation of the subject.

So, this object as a leftover fosters stability in reality for a neurotic just as it tends to disorganise the discourses in psychosis. This extraction of *object a* from the field of language is a prerequisite for the structuring of the four discourses and the circulation of the subject within the four discourses. This is what I understand when Lacan says that *object a* allows these four discourses to be seen as a tetrahedron.

Object a appears as this heterogeneous object, organising the field of jouissance. When *object a* is not extracted, reality disappears, as in psychosis, and all the discourses collapse. This is the "outside" of the discourse of psychosis. So, removing *object a* from the symbolic order is a prerequisite that allows the tools (i.e., the four discourses) of jouissance to organise reality. Thus, we see how discourses structure reality in terms of social bonds by situating the remainder (*object a*) in different places. In psychosis, jouissance invades everything; it invades the body, fragments reality, de-personalises the subject, sonorises language and "scopifies" the subject, which becomes a gaze and appears as the consistent jouissance it actually is. When it is extracted by the paternal metaphor, it becomes separated; an object excluded from language and also from culture.

Discontent and guilt

A rereading of *Civilization and its Discontents* will help us understand the nature and reason of society's malaise. Freud equates discontent with what he calls a sense of guilt (a variation of the subject's anxiety in the presence of superego surveillance). According to Freud, guilt feelings stem from civilisation's demands upon the subject's simultaneous surrender of the drive and the drive's demand for satisfaction. The *Rolling*

Stones knew what they were singing about: "I can't get no satisfaction, but I try …" This is a real paradox since the superego demands surrender and fulfilment at the same time. Thus, the mental watchdog sends out conflicting signals regarding civilisation's pains and pleasure in the subject's mind. Like Al Pacino in the *Devil's Advocate* (1997), the superego is constantly reminding its subject to, "Look, but don't touch. Touch, but don't taste. Taste, but don't swallow."

This represents the worst for the subject in civilisation, namely that desire whose flip-side is discontent. Certainly, it does not refer to culture in the sense of the arts, but human culture opposed to nature (as the latter is synonymous with civilisation) and natural urges. But if the superego acting as agency brings civilisation to life in the subject's mind, how does it (the superego) punch in for work? Through constant round-the-clock surveillance of the subject. Perhaps that lovely old Fats Waller song "Ain't Misbehavin' " was inspired by a muse called superego. But what is good behaviour? Satisfying the drive or living up to society's ideal standards? The superego has its eye on us and compares us to an ideal, as Freud says, we will never attain. But, as Lacan points out in *Seminar* XX, this is an impossible demand since the superego is caught in the throes of the same drive it is so keenly trying to stifle. The superego orders: "*Jouir!*" "have jouissance". It is as if, in pornographic terms, the superego forbids pleasure and says at the same time: "Cum! Cum! Cum!!".[4]

Freud brilliantly describes the surveillance and legislative functions of the superego in "On Narcissism: An Introduction" (Freud, 1914c). Never again would he elaborate on that precise description in the essay where, upon ripping off the mask of this mental lawgiver, he reveals its hideous face in paranoia where the subject is scrutinised by the Other's gaze and tormented by hallucinatory voices. Actually, that is exactly what we find: the two superego functions represented by two drive objects Lacan calls the gaze and the voice—the most powerful implements in *object a*'s tool box which Lacan inserted into the series of Freudian objects which follow after the oral and anal objects.

The superego as an object of jouissance

As civilisation's leftovers, gaze and voice, devoid of any demand signifier representations, are objects that both represent desire. We know *object a* is a polysemic word for Lacan, and we find it here in *Seminar* XVII defined not as a cause of desire—as in Lacan's field of language—but as the superego. We have also seen *object a* defined as surplus or left-over jouissance and the superego as one of its "mental institutions". But here *object a* is the mirror image of the superego. It is the flotsam and jetsam of civilisation because the MD is civilisation's standard default setting. *Object a* returns into our civilised society in its twofold nature, it is the Other's gaze and voice embedded in the subject's psychic life.

I want to wrap this discussion up and leave the reader some food for thought on what is apparently a very current issue. Get on any bus in Brazil and you will see stickers that say "Smile, you're on camera!" The ubiquitous gaze is ever with us (in banks, in convenience stores, elevators, etc.) and the stickers actually work even if there is no camera. There are several noteworthy American movies that fictionalise the gaze and the voice returning to society. The main character of *The Truman Show* (1998) discovers he has been filmed since birth. And throughout most of *American Beauty* (1998) the gaze is quite present. Finally, in *Being John Malkovich* (1999), pure gaze is actually the subject and the film shows just how humans beings can be made to act like puppets through a puppet-master character who pulls John Malkovich's strings. What catches my attention in this movie is that the people who enter the site in the movie—it is a sort of cyber-thing—actually enter the mind of John Malkovich and see the world through his eyes: this is the voyeuristic gaze which is a manifestation of the Other, not the Other of language but rather the manifestation of the Other's jouissance downsized to a virtual, circumstantial object chasing the subject.

This phenomenon is also described in Neal Gabler's book *Life the Movie* (2000). Everyday life has become highly profitable entertainment and people get their kicks watching the Kardashians and other reality shows. All around the world reality shows like *Big Brother* are on television. Furthermore, there are internet sites which shows the entire everyday life of a family—you can watch them twenty-four hours a day. To be sure, the advance of science encroaching on our current civilisation's dominant discourses warrants further research. Lacan offered us a timetable of the mainstream discourses, starting in ancient Greece where the dominant MD gave way to the UD (*Akádēmos* as a sort of modern *Magister Dixit*). In *Television*, Lacan highlighted the dominant capitalist discourse in his day. At any rate, far from alleviating the subject's discontent, the advance of science and the discourse of capitalism increasingly instigate and multiply the gaze-and-voice objects. Personally, both voice (over loudspeakers, iPhones, Skype, etc.)

and gaze (video, cameras, screens, etc.) have become increasingly more prominent as we head into the new millennium's third decade. The film *Denise Calls Up* (1995) shows the autism of our relationships and highlights the voice, both of which reveal how, for some time now, we have been in the Big-Brother era: he was the one with an eye on everyone in Orwell's *1984*. Another variation on this theme is the perpetuation of the panopticon which Foucault had already denounced as structuring our disciplinary society. In our time, "selfies" and "likes" in Facebook dominate our life.

Another example of our scopic society is the virtual prison, a kind of bracelet which contains a chip and this keeps you under surveillance twenty-four hours a day. There appears to be a trend towards "no more prisons". Instead, people are watched constantly by a chip. I have given you these examples to lend currency to our theme and to show how these objects—the gaze and the voice—are being produced by our liquid modern civilisation.

Lacanian discourses

My apologies to the sophisticated Phd and medical readers and analysts, but here I am going back to kindergarten to understand and play with Lacan's mathemes before dealing with the analyst's technique. Here are the corner stones of Lacanian mathemes, namely, the elements:

S_1 (Power), S_2 (Knowledge), $\barS$ (Subject), a (surplus jouissance)

The structure of the places of the agent of discourse, of the underpinning truth of that discourse, the place of the other subjugated therein, and the place of the expected production of this social bond can be expressed as follows:

$$\frac{[\text{agent}]}{[\text{truth}]} \to \frac{[\text{other}]}{[\text{production}]}$$

Master's discourse (MD): $\dfrac{S_1}{\barS} \to \dfrac{S_2}{a}$

Hysteric's discourse (HD): $\dfrac{\barS}{a} \to \dfrac{S_1}{S_2}$

16

$$\text{University discourse (UD): } \frac{S_2}{S_1} \overset{\rightarrow}{} \frac{a}{\cancel{S}}$$

$$\text{Analyst's discourse (AD): } \frac{a}{S_2} \overset{\rightarrow}{} \frac{\cancel{S}}{S_1}$$

I want to address the dynamics of these four discourses—the MD, HD, UD, and the AD—where S_1 and S_2 represent subject 1 and 2 and a, jouissance. As for discourse, let us simply say it is an agent who, incarnating some truth or principle, acts on another to produce something or perform some action.

The barred symbol ($\cancel{S}$) separating two elements do not correspond to the Lacanian bar of repression borrowed from Saussure to show signified/signifier. Rather, it represents that mysterious factor which prevents us from perceiving the deeper truth in the agent's (S) discourse, and at the same time, that truth which underpins each discourse and the social bonds produced in the fraction. Thus, we can sum this all up graphically in the following fractions:

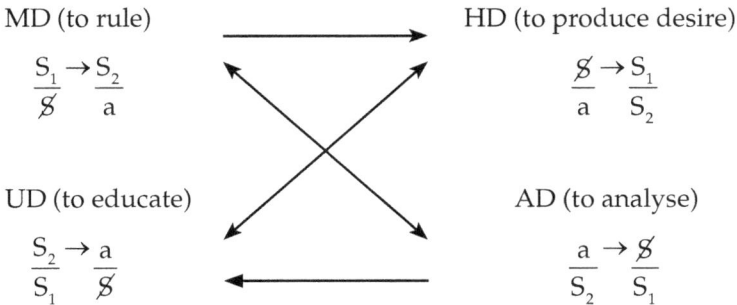

MD (to rule)

$$\frac{S_1 \rightarrow S_2}{\cancel{S} \quad a}$$

HD (to produce desire)

$$\frac{\cancel{S} \rightarrow S_1}{a \quad S_2}$$

UD (to educate)

$$\frac{S_2 \rightarrow a}{S_1 \quad \cancel{S}}$$

AD (to analyse)

$$\frac{a \rightarrow \cancel{S}}{S_2 \quad S_1}$$

Lacan's discourses follow both laws of the unconscious (also represented by S): the metaphor represented by S′ (a signifier replacing another signifier) and metonymy (a signifier to or towards another) represented by → S′:

$$\text{Metaphor } \frac{S}{S'}$$

$$\text{Metonymy } S \rightarrow S'$$

We saw how Lacan conceptualised the fields of language as discourse structure and jouissance as tools of the social bond. The arrow ($\rightarrow$) also deserves another interpretation since, in logic, it is the logical connector of a causality chain: A $\rightarrow$ B (if A, then B). Let us examine how these social bonds work more closely:

- In the MD, the existence of master (S_1) implies that of the slave (S_2) who has knowledge.
- In the HD, where there is a subject ($\cancel{S}$) there is a master (S_1).
- In the UD, knowledge (S_2) presupposes the existence of a student (a) as an object.
- Finally, in the AD, the analyst is represented by a (*object a*) and the analysand as a subject (S).

These are the pairs in different social bonds. This arrow "represents to, towards or for the other". We interpret the bar as that which shows the bond's representation and what is implied therein. But just what is represented? Well, hidden away in that bar ($\cancel{S}$) is the truth of that social bond:

- In the MD, the power (S_1) represents a subject to another S_2 (slave) who must submit to it:

$$\frac{S_1 \rightarrow S_2}{\cancel{S}}$$

- In the HD, the subject ($\cancel{S}$) is what represents jouissance (a) to the master (S_1). Lacan defines the agent in the discourse of hysteria as the symptom—where the symptom is what represents the subject's jouissance, with which the master builds knowledge:

$$\frac{\cancel{S}}{a} \rightarrow \frac{S_1}{S_2} \downarrow$$

- In the UD, knowledge (S_2) is what represents the author (S_1) to the student (a).

$$\frac{S_2 \rightarrow a}{S_1}$$

- Finally, in the AD, it is the analyst (*object a*) which represents knowledge (S_2) to the analysand ($\cancel{S}$):

$$\frac{a}{S_2} \rightarrow \cancel{S}$$

Like a good detective examining the clues, Lacan further interprets the arrow as agency or domination. In such a scenario, the bonds reveal the pecking order:

- In the MD bond the master acts upon the slave to produce the jouissance object.
- In the HD bond, hysterics provoke the master with their symptoms.
- In the UD bond, knowledge has the upper hand over the student.
- In the AD bond, the analyst acts upon the analysand but the agent is exactly what the analysand has exempted from language (*object a*). The analyst decides to act upon the analysand as a split subject to decipher its master signifiers (S_1). *Object a* represents all that is left once discourse has been exhausted. In a word, it is the surplus jouissance or the analyst's desire.

The "dominant"

The agent is the dominant element of the social bond. This was inspired by Roman Jakobson's concept of the "dominant" in his (*la dominante* in his *Questions de poétique*) and this led me to reread the discourses from another angle. According to Lacan, the agent is the place of the dominant ("*la dominante*"), an idea which takes up a theoretical concept from Russian Formalism which Jakobson used to analyse literature and works of art. Jacobson states that:

> […] the dominant may be defined as the focal element of a work of art. It governs, determines and transforms the other elements […] It is a specific linguistic element which dominates the work in its totality. It is imperative, irrecusable, directly influencing the other elements. (Jakobson, 1973, p. 145)

And he illustrates his argument:

> Verse, as such, is not a simple element or an indivisible unit. Verse
> is a system of values in itself; there are many values, but there is one
> dominant value, a value of domination, of mastery, which he calls
> the dominant, without which verse may neither be conceived nor
> judged. For example, in seventeenth century Czech poetry, rhyme
> was an optional procedure, whereas the syllabic scheme was an
> imperative element. A change in the dominant therefore took place,
> for it was no longer the rhyme but instead the way of combining
> syllables and meter. (Jakobson, 1973, p. 145)

Here Jacobson is speaking of a specific linguistic element which dominates the entire work and this is the notion applicable to Lacan's social
bond wherein each discourse supports a kind of act or action. Furthermore, Lacan formalises this with the discourses of the dominant's form
of action—knowledge, S_1, S_2, $\cancel{S}$ or *object a* (as agents)—and then names
the dominant of each discourse:

Social bond	Dominant	Impossible profession
MD	Law	Ruling
HD	Symptoms	Producing desire
UD	Knowledge	Educating
AD	Analyst	Analysing

The dominant characterises the discourse, supports the specific actions
of each social bond and permeates all aspects therein. Law is what characterises governing, though the lawmaker is hidden whereas the main
feature of education is knowledge (always referred to as an author).
There, both the author and the governor occupy the place of the truth.
Regarding hysteria, Lacan states that the hysterics themselves dominate
and are supported by their jouissance. Finally, the AD is dominated by
the analyst not as a subject but as an object: analysts directs treatment
not as subjects but as the *semblant* of *object a* through their theatrical
interpretation acts and role playing I examine in part 3.

The dominated

The place of the other here is occupied by a dominated element. In
Chapter 5 of *Seminar* XVII, Lacan introduces the field of jouissance as
"the Lacanian field" and points out the similarity of all discourse to

MD and states that every discourse is one of domination. Hence, the analyst's dilemma, since his or her discourse ought to be as far removed as possible from any shape or form of domination. Lacan further states that "the reference of a discourse is what it confesses it wants to the master" (Lacan, 1969–1970, p. 79).

Here I shift the perspective from dominant to dominated. Thus, although the arrow still represents the power of domination, the reference now stresses the receiving end:

- Master → slave;
- Knowledge (author) → student—or as Lacan says, the student in the place of the object.
- Hysteric → master dominated, castrated, pushed up against the wall.
- Analyst → analysand.

In both senses, we can assess our place or role in any discourse either through the dominant—sometimes clearer or based on the reference of what the dominator confesses he or she wishes to dominate—or through the dominated individual.

The Lacanian discourses as social bonds mean so much more than their names. When we picture the UD, the image of some college or institution of higher learning pops into our mind. But let us think beyond these obvious and simplistic images and consider the very quintessence that holds the bonds together in the dominant-dominated structure: every relationship which treats the other as object can also be called the UD and, likewise, every discourse which treats the other as a master belongs to the HD. Furthermore, every discourse which treats the other as a slave or employee or can be likened to the MD or the power to exploit. Thus, it treats the other as a source of knowledge that produce objects for one's own jouissance.

Psychoanalysis introduces the concept of psychic causality as its operation base. Let us now examine the causality—represented by the agent—in each Lacanian social bond. Only the agent's acts enable this discourse to exist and function as a social bond. Every cause has a corresponding truth to support a particular social bond. Where we find the agent we will also discover the discourse's cause.

In the MD, power (S_1) is the cause and the truth is the desire subject ($\cancel{S}$) hidden away by the master signifier. What matters is pure power—everything to get, keep, hold and, when necessary, restore power. Power as this social bond's cause is what drives the master/overlord to own and enslave the other and get from the latter a product the former can enjoy. Power's goal here is syphoning out the other's jouissance object for the master's pleasure or benefit. Surplus value is what is at stake in the master–slave/boss–employee, etc. relationship.

In the UD, cause is knowledge (S_2), and truth is the author's power (S_1) Knowledge as cause disguises power which is still at the core of this social bond. We can see this in debates, academic tussles and intellectual rivalries. The university (*universitas*) represents the social engagement on behalf of knowledge but does not take into account the latter's hollowness or the uniqueness of each subject's ($\emptyset$) cause, which bobs up as a symptom of lack—*object a*—regarding the Other's knowledge. The brand of discourse is represented by the intellectually voracious, disgruntled or revolutionary rebel whose emblematic figure is the discontented student.

In the HD, the cause is the subject's split ($\emptyset$) and suffering stemming from civilisation's discontents, and the truth is *object a* which represents the symptom's jouissance. The HD is closest to the AD and its conditions are caused by a subject (S) rather than power (S_1) or knowledge (S_2). For Lacan, that subject is the *manque-à-être* or lack-of-being. Since discourse hysterisation—based on Lacan's four discourses—is a prerequisite for starting analysis, the source of lack-of-being politics in hysteria is the analysand rather than the analyst.

Surplus jouissance

From Lacan's *object a* theory, we may sum up both the analyst's and the analysands politics thus: analysts aim at representing *object a*'s cause through the *semblant* whereas analysands pursue free association to unravel and challenge their desire's signifiers and uncover at least one ideal signifier that has handcuffed them to the Other. What will be missing, therefore, for analysands, is that one signifier that expresses the being of the Other. The analysand's politics are thus found in the patient's hysteria as a split subject.

The lack-of-being politics proper to the HD is the initial condition necessary for the analyst's own politics since it points towards the Other's inconsistency. The HD, is, therefore, a pre-requisite for the analyst's politics. In the crisscross of the discourses as social bonds, the AD is definitely a "step up" over the HD since it aims at toppling those utopic ideals that attempt to envision the Other as that perfect thing which I need and want. Although there are no analytical politics without this prior lack-of-being, the former cannot be reduced to the latter, as we will see in Part III of this book.

The cause of the social bond coincides with the subject's *object a* cause of desire only in the AD and the truth which it underpins is unconscious knowledge (S₂). In all the other discourses, another element appears as causality: power, knowledge, lack, that is, respectively, the totalitarian One in the MD, the *universitas* bureaucracy in the UD and the subject's *pathos* in the HD. We only find the desire object cause in the politics of the AD.

This object, which Lacan called *Mehrlust* (surplus jouissance or *plus-de-jouir*) from *Mehrwert* (Marxist surplus-value) is the product extracted as surplus capitalist discourse, which is our modern updated version of the MD. Surplus value is the cause of desire that is the default setting of the capitalist social bond. It is the product of capitalistic politics which aim at bleeding the other's jouissance through work.

The Marxist cause can be summed up as the end of man exploiting man by getting rid of social classes and then promoting fair income distribution among all and eliminating surplus value. Although Marxist policy in practice has run aground because it was powerless as an alternative to capitalist discourse, Marx's analysis of capital still remains valid even if it did not actually form a new social bond. Would its failure have anything to do with the totalitarian MD and the inefficient and bureaucratic UD?

Despite their affinities, the analytical cause cannot be equated with the Marxist cause: it does not proclaim social distribution justice for jouissance since the latter cannot be split up into shares. And even if it could be, who would distribute it? The fair distribution of jouissance would grant everyone equal rights to enjoy the other as an object just as Sade's republic shows. It would mean the end of each individual's uniqueness and the creation of the empire of the super "I", "Me", and "Mine." But is this not in fact what is at risk in current globalisation politics?

The analytical cause—which Lacan terms *agalma*[2]—desire's essence, is the only one analysts are committed to. "The future psychoanalyst (is) dedicated to the *agalma* essence of desire and willing to pay for it by reducing it and his name to any signifier (Lacan, 2001, p. 254). Here, in a nutshell, is Lacan's ethical and clinical prescription. We will see this in the next chapter.

If the analyst is not dedicated to this clinical cause, no transference can take place, only suggestion. Analysts pay the price by abdicating their being and name as players in the analysand's *object a semblant* and reduce themselves to any signified Sq the subject invests them with during analysis. In a sense, they are "un-being" themselves during analysis.

Agalma is therefore the emergent analytical cause at the end of analysis: the cause of the desire to know, that unprecedented desire which is the "x" of the analyst's desire. If each subject's desire is personal and unique, the analyst's desire that appears at the end of the analysis is an operator without which analysis is impossible.

The analytical cause is not the obsessional's impossible cause or the hysteric's lost one, but the essence of that desire whose truth is unconscious knowledge (a/S_2). The analytical cause does not make the subject subversive—rather, it is what subverts the subject itself because it allows the object to be active. The agalmatic object is the ethical corner stone of psychoanalysis.

The analytical-cause opposes the Other's totalising and unifying utopia and the former is always unwelcome in the Other. The analytical cause may appear and operate anywhere to produce surprise, amazement, disgust, and even horror while always enforcing the unique desire and knowledge of the unconscious where the analyst acts to locate the causality function. The laboratory of the analytical cause is not the psychoanalytic office nor is the classroom its sanctuary. Analysis encompasses the experience of the sexual cause leading to the crossing-through-and-over (*la passe*): the final arrival at the analytical cause where the analysand has become his or her own analyst.

The bond, the analyst, and the object

Among the Lacanian discourses, the AD is the only one—the sole social bond—which treats the other as a subject. Hence the AD goes far beyond the analytic setting.

In the MD, as in that of the unconscious, something pertaining to jouissance bursts out as *object a* comes to light (i.e., hearty laughter as a manifestation of the unconscious). Lacan equates the structure of the MD with that of the unconscious. It may flabbergast us to say that the AD—as the reverse of the MD—actually opposes that of the subject's unconscious. But I want to stress here that AD is most certainly not that of the discourse of the unconscious, but rather the very opposite. If the discourse of the unconscious is the *locus* of the subject's alienation $\left(\dfrac{S_1}{\cancel{S}}\right)$, then the AD aims at freeing subjects from this signifying alienation $\left(\dfrac{\cancel{S}}{S_1}\downarrow\right)$ manifested therein. The master's signifiers are a product of analysis.

Taking the HD as a bridge between the MD and the AD is structural. Hence Lacan's statement that, to reach the AD, we must pass through the "hysterisation" of discourse. This is how subjects plunging into

25

free association are initially able to make a quarter turn regarding their symptoms—as that dominant factor—, and reveal the camouflaged truth of their jouissance to empower and enable the AD.

The capacity of the AD to reveal the master signifier is also another feature of analytic practice. In the MD, S_1 is clearly the law: the master embodies power: commanding a slave, a boss giving orders to his or her employees, a general sending his troops into battle, etc. This dialectic relationship is the "missionary position" of master (on top) slave (on the bottom). In the HD, S_1 is also represented by a master or a doctor who will produce, for example, knowledge, a medical prescription. Finally, in the UD, the master (S_1) is the author. Once again, examining each of these discourses reveals that someone is always lined up as S_1. In the MD, it is the master, the governor, overlord or boss whereas in the UD, it is the author—the referential *magister dixit*—who is also a ruler in the form of an author, an authority, a specialist, a scientist or the "Mr. Know-It-All" of any field of knowledge.

The AD reveals that this S_1 is not a person; it is only a signifier, albeit not always necessarily embodied by a flesh-and-blood creature. It need not be the overlord or the big boss, for here it is merely a signifier: the primordial signifier.

The analyst's discourse (AD)

The AD is the only one that allows us to elucidate the others. Based on it, Lacan formulated the other discourses as social bonds, for the AD reveals *object a* may be found in lieu of any actual human agent, in the role of the dominant. Furthermore, it is the only discourse in which the dominant is that thing excluded from civilisation's discourse.

The MD is civilisation's authoritarian or institutional discourse. It lays down, so to speak, symbolic law and shapes the subject represented in civilisation's symbolic order which demands the surrender of the drive and exclusion of the objects of jouissance such as women in *Totem and Taboo*. The murder of the father and his substitution by a totem set down the law by excluding or forbidding sexual enjoyment with women of the same tribe.

From a Freudian point of view, civilisation's discourse is the outcome of the Oedipus complex which sets up a given institution for the subject. As such, it jettisons (or tries to anyway) jouissance, which returns as discontent, guilt feelings, death instinct and superego examined in

Civilization and its Discontents. Hence, it is precisely what civilisation casts aside which dominates the AD. That's why the MD, as the social bond instituted by civilisation, is precisely "the reverse of psychoanalysis".

All elements in the AD are to be found in exact opposition to those in the MD. The other discourses have never relied on the AD for their existence since they have been in Western society for centuries. But it is Freud's pioneering work that brings the AD into play with the other ones, which, I remind the reader, Lacan later formulated in light of the AD. The discourse of domination belonging to civilisation has existed since the dawn of the human species, and we might say that UD has been around at least since the first European universities were founded in the early middle ages. Lacan shows us that the entire history of Western philosophy is nothing more than the Master usurping the Slave's knowledge in an attempt to appropriate knowledge as the Master's domain.

The HD has always rebelled in various ways against the discourse of domination. In earlier times, necromancers, witches or heretics were once considered hysterics and being burned at the stake since sorcery and witch-craft were a kind of defiant reaction against Western medieval theocratic and church-centred society. Granted that the MD belongs to civilisation, it is also the discourse which institutes the subject and can be represented by the following matheme:

$$\frac{S_1}{\cancel{S}} \rightarrow \frac{S_2}{a}$$

These symbols identify the subject ($S_1/\cancel{S}$) as a representation in the whole set of the signifying chain (S_2). From yet another standpoint, we see that in the MD, the subject is instituted and "owned" by society (like the Master's chattel) and it is diametrically opposite to the AD which aims at stripping the subject of this identity. Adopting the MD, we saw how the primordial identification is what really institutes the subject. Thus, the AD aims at subjective destitution or "de-subjectification"— the subject rids him or herself of an artificial identity through analysis $\left(\frac{\cancel{S}}{S_1}\downarrow\right)$. In a nutshell, analysis aims at stripping away the Other's master signifiers which alienate the subject. Those former rulers in the realm of subjectivity are impeached and banned.

Transference

I would like to examine the analyst's place and role in transference before approaching Lacanian technique.

The analyst cannot be the one who knows and teaches analysands something they do not know about the unconscious because he or she actually does not know. Through free association, using the analysand's utterances and speech, analysts push analysands to become their own analysts. The place and role of the analyst is to represent *object a* as the analysand's cause of desire. That means analysts are not tied in a social bond as an ordinary people with their egos and Imaginary registers (conscious, meaning, imagination, etc.) nor as subjects with their own desires, life stories, and feelings. To do so would risk treating analysands as objects to satisfy their fantasy. The analyst takes on the *semblant* of the analysand's precious object or Plato's golden *agalma*: Lacan's poetic representation of that unrepresentable object, around which the signifiers orbit. The *agalma* is the Symbolic's hollowness permeated by surplus jouissance.

If analysts can make any claim to knowledge on their side as we see in the AD—$\left[\dfrac{a}{S_2} \right]$—it is that they know something about the truth of this bond. But what do they know? Certainly not bookish knowledge that reflects the analyst's culture. Rather, knowledge about the structure of the unconscious, about castration and the lack analysts discover and become aware of during their own analysis and training. It is a unique form of knowledge whose awareness grows with each new discovery: it is the very knowledge about lack and about the impossibility of any absolute knowledge.

To deal with the analyst as *semblant* of *object a*, we must further examine this bond and Lacan's concept of *agalma*.

In the AD, the analyst stands in place of the agent as a *semblant* of *object a* as I am going to further develop in Part 3. This is a role related to transference management that, as Freud pointed out, can be both a motivating factor and a hindrance. Transference love is conveyed in the three registers:

* *Imaginary transference* (a–a') is related to the analyst's personhood through the narcissistic construction of his or her body, manners, dress, appearance, office, personality, etc.

- *Symbolic transference* is related to signifiers the analysand "picks up" in analysts and their environment relocated to the Other's *locus*. The signifiers are related to the ego ideal, or in Lacanian parlance, the Ideal of the Other [IA].
- *Real transference* is represented by *object a*, their analysands chance upon during a fortuitous encounter with someone they choose as their analyst. Lacan discovered this to be the quintessence of transference through the *agalma* or precious object. When real transference takes place, patients feel their analyst is a kind of godsend.

Plato's Symposium

Plato's *Symposium* in which Socrates claims to understand "[…] nothing beyond the subject of Eros" becomes Lacan's central text on transference. It is there that Alcibiades addresses Socrates, because the latter represents the subject who supposedly knows about desire.

The analysand's demand to the analyst instead of to the subject-supposed-to-know (*sujet supposé savoir*) also issues an urgent request for knowledge. This is initially illustrated in the *Symposium*, when Agathon addresses Socrates upon the latter's arrival: "Come and sit here beside me, Socrates, and let me, by contact with you, enjoy the discovery which you made in the porch. You must obviously have found the answer to your problem and pinned it down; you wouldn't have desisted till you had" (Plato, 1951, p. 38). But Socratic irony undoes any claim to knowledge and cleverly underlies the impossibility of such a conveyance:

> It would be very nice, Agathon, if wisdom were like water, and flowed by contact out of a person who has more into one who has less, just as water can be made to pass through a thread of wool out of the fuller of two cups into the emptier. If that applies to wisdom, I value the privilege of sitting beside you very highly, for I have no doubt that you will fill me with an ample draught of the finest wisdom. Such wisdom as I possess is slight and has little more reality than a dream, but yours is brilliant and may shine brighter yet. (Plato, 1951, p. 38)

Agathon is quickly peeved by this Socratic apple-shining which he perceives as sarcasm and he cuts Socrates off. Knowledge transference, like a quick download, is impossible. But knowledge can be conveyed, and so we should ask ourselves how do analysts convey psychoanalytic knowledge?

In "Proposition of October 9 on the Psychoanalyst of the School", Lacan points out that Alcibiades's discourse equates Socrates with both the older mythological satyr Silenus and the precious *agalma*. We assume knowledge can be had by granting the other *agalma*, that is to say, the other has something awesome that I also want. Alcibiades continues:

> I declare that he (Socrates) bears a strong resemblance to the Silenus figures in statuaries' shops, represented holding pipes or flutes; they are hollow inside, and when they are taken apart you see that they contain little figures of gods (*agalmata theon*). (Plato, 1951, p. 100)

Here *agalmata* is the Greek plural of *agalma*. Silenus has two meanings: first, as a mythological figure with a tail and hooves who served at Dionysius's fun fests; second, as a small package, jewel box or gift wrapping for beautiful presents. Further on in his discourse, Alcibiades insists on this comparison and emphasises that there was more to be found in Socrates than just an ugly face:

> I doubt whether anyone has ever seen the treasures (*agalmata*) which are revealed when he grows serious and exposes what he keeps inside. However, I once saw them, and found them so divine and precious and beautiful and marvellous that, to put the matter briefly, I had no choice but to do whatever Socrates bade me. (Plato, 1951, p. 103)

These are the *agalmata*—disguised as knowledge—Alcibiades wants from Socrates, and when the former finds himself alone with the latter, he says: "I should now be able [...] to find out all that Socrates knew." This expectation is based on an equation between what Socrates supposedly knows and on his desire for Alcibiades: "[...] believing that he (Socrates) was serious in his admiration of my charms" (ibid, p. 103). Alcibiades naively supposes he can sleep his way to the top of the philosophical ladder with Socrates.

Eros, and particularly erotic knowledge is what Plato's *Symposium* is about. For the Greeks, *erastes* (the lover) was portrayed as desire's subject or the lacking subject, while *eromenos* (the beloved) had something which "got under the lover's skin", like in the famous Cole Porter song. This two-fold discrepancy for the couple illustrates love's problematical essence: there is no overlapping between what one lacks and what the other has. In the *erastes-eromenos* pair, the perspective of desire reveals desire itself as the concept of lack. When we are in love, what we love is the *agalma* object. It is time to examine a much more appropriate meaning of *agalma* for our psychoanalytical purposes.

What we talk about when we talk about agalma

According to anthropologist Louis Gernet, *agalma*:

> [...] refers to various types of objects, including human beings, as "precious". In most cases, it expresses an idea of wealth, and especially of noble wealth (horses are *agalmata*), and is insepara- ble from another idea, suggested by an etymology which remains perceptible: the verb *agallein* from which it is derived means simultaneously to ornament and to honor [...] It is important to add that, during the classical era, the meaning of offering to the gods became fixed, above all in the form of offerings represented by a statue of the god. (Gernet, 1968, p. 127)

Alcibiades likens *agalma* to the godlike figure he sees and is attracted to in Socrates. As property of the gods, *agalma* are "thought to be 'sacred goods' like tripods, vases, jewelry, and so forth, whose theft is consid- ered sacrilegious" (Gernet, 1968, pp. 128–129).

The term *agalma* thus shows us a concept of value in a pre-currency culture and represents an object invested with magical powers that is transferred to its owner. Gernet further states that "[...] the inherent virtue of *agalma* is, first of all, that of a 'social' power" (Gernet, 1968, p. 176). *Agalma* marks *object a*'s first conceptual appearance as an object of value in Lacan's work. Later, Lacan revamps this idea to include Marx's concept of surplus value in *object a* as surplus jouissance.

For the Greek mindset, *agalma* was endowed with magical powers, whose use—like those idols or icons representing other-world enti- ties—would also bring an added value to those who bond themselves with it like a fetish object. When encountering agalmatic power, Alcibi- ades can only give in and obey out of an overwhelming desire for the *agalma*—that very object which elicits desire and makes him a desiring subject. Subjects are enraptured by this object because they are anchored to it through their jouissance. Furthermore, the gaze and the voice are varieties of *agalma* which bind subjects to their jouissance.

Agalma's root stems from *alamai*, which means "desire" and also "envy" or "jealous". *Aga* is found in Agathon's name and its etymology—*agaston*—means "admirable", whereas *gal* is the same as *galenen* ("shining sea"), and *glene* ("pupil"), hence the association between "eye" and *agalma*. *Gal* also means "splendour" or *éclat* in old French, and is the origin of "gallant" in English. As a magical or gallant object, *agalma* is a charm to entrap enemies, like the huge Trojan Horse or, in Greek, *mega agalma*. According to Lacan, above all else and as an offering "[...] *agalma* arises as a sort of ambush of the gods. There are tricks which catch the eye of the gods, these real beings" (Lacan, 1960–1961, p. 171).

The subject of desire, which is the subject of transference, is moved and affected by this object, which it situates in the analyst's body precisely as Alcibiades does with Socrates. Alcibiades verbalises this process of transference. He transfers and projects this precious and beautiful object—the cause of his stirrings and longings—onto the not-so-handsome Socrates—as analysands do. It is what flies the analysand to the moon or at least to the couch. Hence, the beauty here for Alcibiades is conflated with Socrates's shining and enlightening knowledge. Socrates's knowledge is thus agalmatic, for *agalma* lures with its many-splendored charms.

This is the power of transference whose secret is *agalma*. The nature of adornment and agalmatic object is offered to the gods as a *trompe-l'oeil*, or a kind of optical illusion or ruse which bewitches the beholder's gaze. This is the real trick of agalmatic transference. Certainly, it is a trap, but it is all too real in social bonds. That is why in the AD matheme we find [*a*] representing the analyst as an agalmatic object eliciting the subject's desire to dive into free association and drag up those "remembrances of things past". The goal here is to free the subject from alienating signifiers (S_1). The analyst as *semblant* of *object a* acts using the charming power of *agalma*.

In comparing Socrates's speech to that of Marsyas, Alcibiades stresses the power of its mesmerising charm: "I declare also that he is like Marsyas, the satyr [...]". In this passage, we may interpret this other sort of *agalma*, Socrates's voice as *object a*. As a flutist, Marsyas not only charms men but also puts them into a trance-like state. Alcibiades says that Socrates performs likewise with words rather than an instrument. "What you have said stirs us to the depths and casts a spell over us" (Plato, 1951, pp. 100–101). Such is the mesmerising power of this agalmatic transference. Alcibiades further declares that Socrates is a modern Marsyas and in describing the effect of the Socratic words, he says he is enslaved by Socrates's voice and profound utterances.

In the AD, Alcibiades stands, like the analysand, in the place of the (other) in this social bond. The same position occupied by the slave in relation to the master, as we have seen in the MD. The analyst represents an object that overwhelms the analysand.

In the *Symposium*, an encounter with *agalma* always implies something good—*eutuchia*—that positive *tyché* which denotes the presence of *object a*, the desire's cause. This correlation between *tyché* and *agalma* may be found in Alcibiades's discourse, soon after the passage in which he professes to have found *agalmata* in the personhood of Socrates, the Silenus: "I thought he'd genuinely fallen for my charms and that this was a godsend, an amazing piece of good luck (*eutuchia*)" (ibid, p. 103).

People say, "I'm looking for an analyst. I've seen several but I've finally found *my* analyst." When you find your analyst, you can be certain that your *agalma* in that person is at stake. If the encounter is a flop, it will be very difficult to begin analysis with this analyst. The *eutuchia* is a prerequisite for starting analysis. Let us now further examine the aforementioned associations between *agalma* and knowledge.

A godsend is only possible when *agalma* is at stake. Again, the subject's encounter with *agalma*, which sets off the transference, is concomitant with the subject subject-supposed-to-know, a necessary condition to begin analysis. Once more, I return to Alcibiades's confidence in his sex appeal: "I should now be able, in return for my favours, to find out all that Socrates knew; for you must know that there was no limit to the pride that I felt in my good looks" (ibid, p. 103). Knowledge can, therefore, have agalmatic value for a subject, as does Socrates's knowledge for Alcibiades, demonstrating that *object a* may be found in knowledge. Alcibiades's expectation to swap Socratic knowledge for his good looks appears worthy of consideration, for both are situated at desire's scopic level, a concept developed at length in my book *Le plus de regard* (2003).

In the Greek legend of the *Tripod of the Seven Sages*, the tripod, qualified as *agalma*, is a reward given to whoever is considered the wisest. Thales was the first to win it for his knowledge, yet he relinquishes it to another he considers even wiser, and this sage to a third, and so forth until it is returned to Thales who then bequeaths it to Apollo.

Thus, the agalmatic tripod or assumption of knowledge is transferred from one sage to another and the *agalma* circulates back and forth but it is never for keeps. The precious object handed down like a ring represents *object a*'s slippery quality which none can claim to own for it is ever on the run and is as fleeting as water between one's fingers: indeed, it becomes the perfect metonym of desire's cause. This legend shows how knowledge and that precious object *agalma* always go hand in hand.

In analytical terms, the analyst's agalmatic presence elicits the analysand's desire for knowledge. The analyst does not give this knowledge to anyone, but rather uses it as the basis of his analytical act. This knowledge (S_2) occupies the place of the truth on the bottom half of the AD matheme underpinning *object a*.

How does Socrates react to Alcibiades's discourse which identifies the former as the owner of a precious object, namely, knowledge and the latter as a desiring subject? Socrates eschews the role of *eromenos* and points to Agathon as the object of Alcibiades's discourse. Socrates knows he is not the owner of this precious thing, but only its meaning (signification) and therefore refuses to be identified with it by declaring himself unworthy of Alcibiades's love. The analyst's attitude differs from that of Socrates, because he "dedicates himself to the *agalma* of the essence of desire, ready to pay for this by reducing himself and his name to any signifier" (Lacan, 2001, p. 254). Just like the singer who says the song "is dedicated to the one I love", the analyst is dedicated to *agalma*—not to loving it, but to making believe he has it in order to underpin the transference, or, as Lacan's tersely puts it, to play the role of the *semblant* of the analysand's *object a* as we shall see in Part 3. This is why and how the analyst is an agent in this social bond.

The *agalma* is present throughout the entire analytical treatment. At the end the analysand no longer assumes the analyst owns it. The analysand comes' to realise that this Other owner of the *agalma* is an artificial but necessary mirage. It is a hollow and unsubstantial Other. Finally, the analysand remains with a desire for knowledge no longer connected with wanting the Other. It is this Other-less which will turn the analysand into an analyst. Henceforward, the analysand says goodbye to the analyst who no longer supposedly knows, nor is the owner of any precious object. Now the subject is finally ready to board his or her own streetcar. A streetcar named desire.

II

CONDITIONS FOR ANALYSIS

M y aim now is to "call up to the witness stand" that set of "psy-choanalytical rules" conventionally known as "the setting" starting from Freud's "On Beginning the Treatment" (1913c), where we find them under the heading *conditions*. Freud describes the necessary conditions or prerequisites for treatment that analysts must deal with: the experimental or trial period before signing the patient on, length of sessions/treatment, fees and use of the couch, which are all integral parts of the analytical technique. Thereafter, Freud writes: "The conditions of treatment having been regulated in this manner, the question arises at what point and with what material is the treatment to begin?" (Freud, 1913c, p. 134). These are Freud's default settings or basic preconditions (*Bedingungen*).

It goes without saying that prerequisites are necessary starting conditions rather than rules or norms imposed by Freud, since he holds that the only rule for analysis is free association, which represents the answer to the question regarding the beginning of treatment.

On May 12th, 1889, the "main" or "golden rule" of psychoanalysis was uttered (or dictated) from the mouth of Emmy Von N. to Freud.

At one point treating this patient under hypnosis, Freud interrupts his report to ask her the reason for certain symptoms:

> I took an opportunity of asking her, too, why she had gastric pains and what they came from. Her answer, which she gave rather grudgingly, was that she did not know. I requested her to remember by tomorrow. She then said in a definitely grumbling tone that I was not to keep on asking her where this and that came from, but to let her tell me what she had to say. (Freud, 1893–1895, pp. 62–63)

Freud humbly accepted the Frau's complaint. Meanwhile, as he generalised about it, Freud realised that the analysand's utterances encompass an unconscious knowledge necessary for establishing analysis as a talking cure; a kind of treatment through speech acts and a special focus on words. Freud writes about the analysand at the end of the cited work:

> He is to tell us not only what he can say intentionally and willingly, what will give him relief like a confession, but everything else as well that his self-observation yields him, everything that comes into his head, even if it is *disagreeable* for him to say it, even if it seems to him *unimportant* or actually *nonsensical*. If he can succeed after thins injunction in putting his self-criticism out of action, he will present us with a mass of material—thoughts, ideas, recollections—which are already subject to the influence of the unconscious. (Freud, 1940a [1938], p. 174)

Here then is the sole rule of psychoanalysis, a necessary guideline by which the unconscious may be elicited. It is noteworthy that this rule applies to the analysand rather than to the analyst. Indeed, we are dealing with a rule correlated to the very structure of the psychoanalytical doors opened by Freud. It is free association that signals the dawn of psychoanalysis and also the start of all analysis: it is only there that analysis must necessarily begin. Freud's single rule of thumb deals with free free-floating attention on the part of analysts, namely, that they focus not so much on the sense of the words being uttered from the patients but on the equivocal linguistic twists or unconscious wordplay that spontaneously arise. Free-floating attention is to the analyst what free association is to the analysand; that is why analyst–analysand is not a dialogic social bond in the ordinary sense. From its very inception, the psychoanalytical setting was never strictly defined but allowed leeway provided it was guided by the ethical principle of the analyst's desire. The Lacanian matheme that describes this ethical principal corresponds to the one for the AD seen previously.

A case in point. A document drafted by an IPA member society dogmatically set down Freud's conditions as actual rules, on a par with free association, which instead of being the golden rule, is considered a prerequisite on equal footing with all others. The setting is also strictly defined:

> Precise definition of the number, frequency and length of sessions (a set time): nothing patients are led to say, in compliance with the main rule, shall in any way increase or lessen their set time for speech or silence. (Donnet, 1988)

Through this kind of Big Brother interference, institutions play the role of the analyst's Other and actually infringe the inviolate privacy of the analyst's office by requiring periodical reports from its members on the "progress" of their patients. Furthermore, imposing these rules on the setting's conditions deforms the analytical act and the experience of the unconscious. Sessions cannot be regulated and controlled by any institutional handbook.

Anchoring myself on Lacan's teachings, I now want to examine the lynchpins of the four conditions laid down by Freud. Analytical experience has widely confirmed how deeply they are determined and shaped by the very core concepts and ethics of psychoanalysis.

The highest standards in analysis will not be found by turning these conditions into rules, but rather by effectively performing the analysis of which the analyst must be knowledgeable. Hence, Lacan's demand for the need of preliminary interviews before accepting a patient for analysis, and in this time establishing diagnosis, symptom, and transference functions. These interviews match what Freud called the experimental or trial period of analysis. The use of the couch too cannot be made into a general rule. I will attempt in this part to pinpoint the reasons for use of the couch and how it fits into the field of jouissance and is linked with the analytical process, transference and the scopic drive. Furthermore, in analytical experience, time and money are dissociated and need not heed the logic of the capitalist catchphrase "time is money". Rather, the clock and the wallet are conditions that correspond to and are aligned with the logic and ethics of our profession.

If not by artificially turning Freud's prerequisites into statutes, then what makes a psychoanalyst qualified? Kafka's "Lacanian" aphorism gives us the answer: "Beyond a certain point, there is no return, this point has to be reached" (Kafka, 1973. p. 80). This matches our own experience as analysands where we cross a threshold and go beyond to that place where we become our own analysts. This (*la passe*) is that crossing-through-and-over which is the correlate of the end of analysis. The only *sine qua non* condition for performing analysis is the analyst's own analysis taken to the ultimate edge. Once we accept this assumption is essential and unassailable, we can then examine the technical conditions during analysis.

Starting

This chapter deals with the nuts and bolts of preliminary interviews. Among Freud's papers on analytical technique, "On Beginning the Treatment" mentions his habit of taking on the patient "at first provisionally, for a period of one or two weeks" which he calls "preliminary experiment" or "trial period" (Freud, 1913c, p. 124). His reasoning is the following: "If one breaks off within this period one spares the patient the distressing impression of an attempted cure having failed" (ibid, p. 124). Freud never explains why treatment could fail, however, as we shall soon see, continuing treatment depends on transference.

In the same paper Freud asserts that the analyst's first goal is to attract patients to treatment rather than to the analyst as a person. Although Freud does not thoroughly explore transference during the "experimental period", he hits the nail on the head regarding another of its tasks: diagnosis, and, especially, differential diagnosis for treating neurosis and psychosis.

We see how Lacan's expression "preliminary interviews" mirrors precisely Freud's "preliminary treatment". The expression indicates that there is a threshold, a gateway into analysis that is not the front door of the analyst's office. The period before analysis proper does not represent a continuity of this initial work but rather, as the term "experimental treatment" itself suggests, a break or change of course that signposts and determines a "before" and "after." This break corresponds to a crossing over into a new social bond, which in our case, is the AD.

In the everyday practice of analysis, it is not always easy to spot this turning point. Why? Because in both stages—"preliminary treatment" and then in analysis—free association is in charge working at full steam. "This preliminary experiment" says Freud, "is itself the beginning of psychoanalysis and must conform to its rules" (Freud, 1913c, p. 124). We might make a distinction, however, that during this initial stage you may allow patients to do nearly all the talking and explain nothing more than what is absolutely necessary to give free reign to their words. Thus, this is a clue that the analyst's task here is to keep the patient's discourse flowing. But we must not forget that according to Freud, "[…] there are also diagnostic reasons for beginning with a 'trial period'" (ibid, p. 124). Hence, the stakes are high because analysts at this stage begin their diagnosis.

Although the "preliminary treatment" may share the same structure as analysis, it is not quite identical. From the very beginning there is a paradox which we may express as follows:

$$PT = A \leftrightarrow PT \neq A$$

We may read this as: "preliminary treatment (PT) equals (=) analysis (A)" and also imply that it is different (≠) from analysis". From this we conclude either that paradoxically:

1. Free association may require identical preliminary treatment and analysis (PT = A).
2. This diagnosis period may require different preliminary treatment and analysis (PT ≠ A).

At this stage, analysts must surrender to this paradox: it will be their personal decision to accept or decline the patient's demand for analysis. From the analyst's point of view, preliminary interviews may be split into two periods: the first to understand what is going on and the second to reach a conclusion and make a decision. The conclusion and decision are analytical acts of evaluating the patient's demand, the conditions for analysis and taking on or declining of a commitment that transforms preliminary interviews into analysis proper.

The change of course is also part of the same analytical act whereby the analyst asks the analysand to lie down on the couch. This is the gesture symbolising the analyst's acceptance of the analysand for treatment. The gesture is noteworthy since accepting patients into the office does not mean they have been accepted for analysis. Subjects are aware they are "applying for the position" of analysand and hope the analyst they have chosen will in turn choose them for analysis. Through this hope for reciprocity, the subject's demand for analysis represents, in practice, the hystericisation factor ($\cancel{S} \rightarrow S_1$) in the production of the analytical symptom.

Preliminary interviews have a three-fold structure according to their purpose and follow a logical rather than a chronological order:

1. Symptomatic function
2. Diagnostic function
3. Transference function

Symptomatic function

A patient's demand for analysis should not be accepted unconditionally; it must be questioned. The analyst's reply to someone who arrives with an explicit demand for analysis cannot be envisioned, for example, simply in terms of a contract and a fee. Lacan reminds us there is only one true demand which leads to the start of analysis—the demand to rid oneself of a symptom. Lacan's straightforward answer to anyone approaching an analyst for greater self-knowledge is a lesson in itself: "I send him off" (Lacan, 1976, p. 33). He does not consider this "wanting to know oneself better" as a demand worthy of an answer.

A demand for analysis is correlated with the presentation of the "analytical symptom" as such. What is at stake during the preliminary interviews is not the subject's analysability or his or her strong or weak ego to undergo the hardships of the analytical process. Analysability is a function of the symptom not the subject. The symptom's "analysability" is not some personality trait or a feature of the subject's character: the analyst must determine beforehand the subject's "analysability" for treatment to begin, by transforming the subject's complaint into an analytical symptom.

It does not suffice for subjects to show up at the analyst's office, voice their complaint or even ask to be rid of it. This grievance must become a demand addressed to the analyst and formulated as a question (rather than an answer) that will encourage the subject to decipher it. In preliminary work, the analyst must question the symptom and attempt to pinpoint the specific jouissance the symptom seeks to answer or fulfil. In Freudian terms, this problem may be set down as follows: why did repression fail and bring on the symptom that resurrected the repressed element?

Freud's "Rat Man" and the latter's imaginary debt provide an example of a symptom which comes as an answer—an emerging jouissance—to the subject after the "Rat Man" hears the cruel captain's tale of the punishment. (Freud, 1909d, pp. 153–318) The entire issue of the subject's debt and the impossibility of paying it off revolves around the revealed jouissance.

In the case of a patient who shows up at the analyst's office with a painful obsession, it is necessary that this symptom—signified for the subject in some shape or form—unveil the dimension of the signifier, entailing both the subject and his or her desire. The symptom appears as the Other's signified s(A) along the signifier chain, and is addressed to the analyst who stands in the place of the Other (A) as in the vector s(A) → (A) in the Graph of Desire. The analyst must turn the symptom into the question "*Che vuoi*?" or "What do you want?" in Italian and slam the ball back to the analysand. The analysand's question called desire is translated as "*Che voglio*?" or "What do I want?" Desire is, thus, an element which the analyst must graft onto the analysand's symptom.

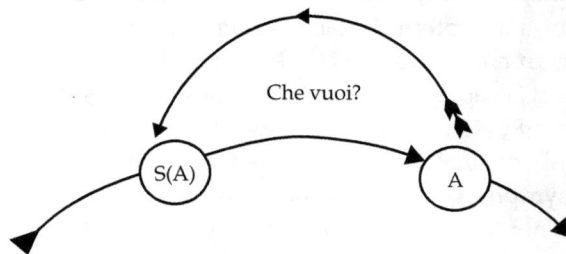

The make-up of the analytical symptom is correlated to the transference that reveals the subject-supposed-to-know, the main player in that process. It is during this moment of hystericisation that the symptom becomes an enigma and comes to represent the subject's division ($). As long as the symptom is part of the subject's life before meeting the analyst, it can be considered a sign that represents something to someone. But when the symptom is turned into a question it evinces the subject's division. At this stage of the game, when the symptom reaches the right address—the analyst—*voilá* it becomes explicitly analytical. So, the analyst (as S_1) completes the symptom (in the place of $\varnothing$) slotted into the HD.

$$\frac{\varnothing}{a} \rightarrow \frac{S_1}{S_2}$$

With this symptom, the subject asks the analyst: "What does this mean? What is this a sign of?" This stance encompasses knowledge because the patient assumes the analyst knows the truth about the symptom as a part of some corpus of knowledge. Thus, the hysteric corners the master (S_1) and makes a plea for knowledge (S_2) about the truth of the jouissance (a) the symptom is concealing. But this ploy is destined to fail because the assumed knowledge is powerless to explain the truth of the symptom's jouissance (a).

The enigma ($\varnothing$) is addressed to the supposedly knowledgeable analyst (S_1) and this entangles the analyst with the patient's symptom to complete it. Therefore, preliminary interviews aim at bringing on the subject's hystericisation, since "hysteric" is the term given to the split subject and the "working Unconscious" (Lacan, 1970, p. 89). Hysteria is the unconscious at work.

Diagnostic function

Differential diagnosis in psychoanalysis concerns the direction of the analytical treatment: *diagnosis* and *treatment* share a logical relationship with each other, namely, that of implying something: $D \rightarrow T$ (if D, then T). Psychoanalytical diagnosis only makes sense if it guides the analysis. Hence, a diagnosis can only be based on the Symbolic, where the subject's crucial questions (sex, mortality, reproduction, paternity, etc.) are conjoined and related to crossing the Oedipus complex. In the Symbolic order, branding the Name-of-the-Father (NF) on the Other of language produces phallic signification which assigns subjects their place among the sexes.

The differential structural diagnosis is thus based on the Symbolic through three forms of Oedipal denial—denial of the Other's castration—corresponding to the three clinical structures (neurosis, perversion, psychosis). Two kinds of denial reject and simultaneously retain castration.

One denies and simultaneously retains it—the neurotic's repression (*Verdrängung*) that refuses the repressed element but tucks it away in the unconscious—and the perverse denial (*Verleugung*) that denies the element but holds on to it as a fetish. Finally, the psychotic's forclusion (*Verwerfung*) is also a form of denial which leaves no trace or residue: it wipes out and erases the element. The first two forms of denial retain traces that imply Oedipus in the Symbolic, which is not the case in psychotic forclusion.

Each form of denial corresponds to the return of the denied element. In repression (*Verdrängung*), the element in the Symbolic returns on that same level as a symptom—the neurotic's symptom. In disavowal (*Verleugnung*), the same element is concomitantly asserted on the Symbolic level and makes a return trip as the pervert's fetish. Finally, in psychosis (*Verwerfung*) the foreclosure element in the Symbolic returns and shows up in the Real as some kind of mental automatism, mostly expressed through hallucinations. The term "forclusion" as a form of denial indicates the place where the return of the denied element occurs; an "inclusion" outside the Symbolic order. The table below offers us a handy summary:

Clinical Structure	Form of Denial	Return Register	Phenomenon
Neurosis	Repression (*Verdrängung*)	Symbolic	Symptom
Perversion	Disavowal (*Verleugnung*)	*Symbolic*	Fetish
Psychosis	Forclusion (*Verwerfung*)	Real	Hallucination

How does this differential structural diagnosis reveal itself in practice? Freud tells us that in neurosis, the Oedipus complex is the victim of a shipwreck which corresponds to hysteric amnesia. The neurotic does not remember what happened during childhood, but the symptom shares the structure of the Oedipus complex. We have the example of the "Rat Man": "[…] if I see a nude woman my father must die" (Freud, 1909d, p. 163). The repression of the representation of his death-wish for his father returns as a symptom in the Symbolic. The obsessional thought expressed by the "Rat Man's" utterance denotes his Oedipal structure of the paternally linked prohibition—seeing a nude woman. The symptom thus opens the gateway to the subject's unique organisation of the Symbolic.

In perversion, castration is admitted alongside denial in the Symbolic. This mechanism, as well as other forms of denial, concerns the female sex: whereas the absence of a penis is inscribed on the woman and is, therefore, a biological difference between the sexes, that same inscription is denied. The return of this brand of denial in the pervert appears as a fetish, in the Symbolic and can be apprehended through language structure as we see in Freud's initial example in "On Fetishism".

It is noteworthy that Freud does not use classical examples of a fetish such as feet, panties or other commonly recognisable everyday objects. Rather, Freud describes the case of a patient whose condition for desire was linked to a certain "shine on the nose". Analysis revealed trans-linguistic wordplay which allowed Freud to understand the patient's obsession since "shine" in German is *"glanze"*, a homophone of "glance" which in English means "look". The secret of the fetish was to be pinpointed in the early years of childhood, which the subject had spent in an English-speaking country. Hence, the Symbolic coordinates provided Freud with the clue for grasping the reason for the fetish in the subject's life story, a fetish which, like all others, denotes the drive object gaze.

In psychosis, however, the signifier returns in the Real in the external relationship between the subject and the signifier, which can be seen generally through speech disturbances—the psychotic paradigm represented by those auditory hallucinations clinicians report in their encounters with these kinds of patients. Psychosis also includes:

1. Delusional intuitions wherein subjects lend a certain event enigmatic signification and simultaneously are unable to precisely define that signification;
2. Thought echoes subjects repeatedly hear in their mind and whose resonance they actually attribute to someone else and;
3. Imposed thoughts subjects fail to recognise as their own chain of signifiers that thus acquire an autonomous status granted to another agent.

In brief, these phenomena are a kind of parade that Clérambault termed "mental automatism". These ideas are not subject to dialectics, to doubting or questioning since they force themselves on the subject as monolithic blocks of absolute certainty. Whereas doubts are a feature of the neurotic because they evince the split subject caught between a "yes or no", in psychosis, unbending certainty is already a sign of disruption in language. The forclusion of the Name-of-the-Father (NF_0) implies "zeroing" the phallic signifier ($NF_0 \rightarrow \varphi_0$), rendering it impossible for the subject to assume the role of man or woman among the sexes. This is an effect with myriad phenomena that span the range from the sense of real castration to the delirious transformation of man into woman as in Freud's Schreber case.

Freud describes the diagnosis function in "On Beginning the Treatment", precisely regarding treatment of psychotics:

> I am aware that there are psychiatrists who hesitate less often in their differential diagnosis, but l have become convinced that just as often they make mistakes. To err, moreover, is of far greater moment for the psychoanalyst than it is for the clinical psychiatrist, as he is called. [...] Where the psychoanalyst is concerned, however, if the case is unfavourable he has committed a practical error; he has been responsible for wasted expenditure and has discredited his method of treatment. [...] He cannot fulfil his promise of cure if the patient is suffering, not from hysteria, but from paraphrenia, and he therefore has particularly strong motives for avoiding error in diagnosis. (Freud, 1913c, pp. 124–125)

We agree with Lacan who says there is no subject that can be cured, for nobody can be cured of the unconscious (Lacan, 1984, p. 18). No matter how much analysis neurotic subjects undergo—even crossing beyond their fantasy and reaching the terminus of analysis—the unconscious will never cease to manifest itself, because its divisions appear in the subject's slips of the tongue, dreams and jokes: our own subjectivity has no cure This holds true for "neurotics", "psychotics" and all subjects: we are all incurable.

Nonetheless, which promise of cure is the analyst unable to keep regarding psychosis? How can analysts interpret Freud's admonition? I offer the following answer: the analyst cannot promise to insert psychotics in the phallic norm, or make them "normal" by slotting them in the male norm (*la norme mâle*). This norm, ruled by the Oedipus and castration complex, bestows phallic signifier primacy on the sexes. The forclusion of the Name-of-the-Father (NF_0) excludes the subject from the phallic norm and so makes it impossible to turn psychotics into neurotics. This, alas, is what we deduce from Freud's admonition and also confirm in Lacan's further teachings and the analytical experience itself.

It is important the analyst know if the subject is psychotic, the direction of the treatment cannot have the Name-of-the-Father (NF) and castration as references. Consequently, we see how essential preliminary interviews are for detecting the subject's clinical structure.

Another reading (which I do not share) of the Freudian text holds that psychoanalysis is not intended for psychotics. Lacan makes recommendations underlying the need for caution, although he leaves the final decision of accepting psychotics for analysis up to each analyst. "We happen to accept pre-psychotics for analysis, and we know what the outcome will be—psychotics" (Lacan, 1955–1956, p. 285). Since analysis is the *locus* where speech and language are unravelled, it may end up bringing out concealed psychosis. Nevertheless, Lacan makes further recommendations: "Paranoia, or rather psychosis, is absolutely fundamental to Freud. Psychosis is that which the analyst must not shy away from, under any condition" (Lacan, 1977, p. 12). In such cases, we may interpret Lacan's words to mean that when analysts encounter psychosis already triggered, there is no reason for them not to accept the subject's demand. Lacan offers additional advice concerning psychotic transference structure and this at least shows that he never ruled out analysis for such patients. Among Freud's papers, we find many cases of psychoanalytic treatment for psychotics.

Regarding general direction of the treatment during preliminary interviews, it is important to distinguish the two clinical types of neurosis (hysteria and obsessional neurosis). Henceforward, *cum grano salis*: a cautious analyst must lay down a strategy to ensure analysis does not run amok. The bedrock of the analyst's strategy in the direction of the treatment will always be transference correlated with diagnosis.

Since analysts are called upon to occupy the place of the subject's Other to whom his or her demands are addressed, it is important during preliminary interviews to have a clear idea of the kind of relationship the subject has with the Other.

For the obsessional neurotic, the Other indulges in a terrifying and deadening jouissance as we see in the tale of the "Rat Man's" cruel captain who uses rodents to inflict horrendous anal punishment on the victim.

The hysteric's Other is an Other that desires and is marked by lack, thus rendering the hysteric subject powerless to achieve jouissance. This was seen in Freud's case study about Dora and her fantasy about her impotent father who only engaged in oral sex with his lover (Freud, 1905, pp. 3–124). This was Dora's fellatio fantasy and her aphonia was the symptom of her condition:

$$\text{\st{S}} \lozenge a \rightarrow s(A)$$

This connotation of the hysteric's sexual jouissance of dwindled pleasure and of the obsessive analysand's heightened pleasure can be traced back to Freud's notes in *Draft K* in his letters with Fleiss. There, in search of an etiology for neurosis, Freud attempts to initially differentiate hysteria, obsessional neurosis, and paranoia, through the mode of jouissance experienced during the mythical first sexual encounter and the representational vicissitudes linked to it. During preliminary interviews, we should therefore not disregard this question of jouissance and its manifested symptoms as diagnostic criteria determined by the subject's fundamental fantasy.

Transference function

"In the beginning of psychoanalysis is transference", says Lacan and its lynchpin is the subject-supposed-to-know (Lacan, 2001, p. 247).

The appearance of this subject during transference marks the plunge into analysis. This is what we gather from Frau Emmy Von N's rule of free association when she asks Freud to just listen: there is knowledge for her in her utterances during analysis.

The decision to seek out an analyst is based on a hypothesis about real knowledge embedded in the symptom or in whatever mental malaise the person wants to be freed from. That a subject's symptom might provide knowledge is a pre-interpretation formulated by patients themselves.

Transference must occur for analysis to start—this is what I call the transference function of preliminary interviews. But transference is neither conditioned nor motivated by the analyst. "It is there in 'the Proposition', accorded by the analysand. We do not have to present reasons for what conditions its existence. Here it is, right from the start" (ibid, p. 247). Transference is the function that belongs to the analysand

and not the analyst. The analyst's function is knowing how to deal with it and use it during analysis. Transference proceeds from the analysand but it is the analyst who manoeuvres it.

Lacan's article "The Function and Field of Speech and Language" provide us with the first formulation of this issue when he refers to "knowledge transference". This latter is an illusion in which subjects believe their truth is to be found in the analyst who knows it beforehand. Actually, analysands end up transferring unconscious knowledge they do not know they have to the analyst. This "subjective error" is inherent in the start of analysis. The same subjectivity is still a correlate of the formative effects of transference, albeit the effects are now different from all previous ones. The correlation between knowledge and this emerging subjectivity as a constituent effect of transference is, in Lacanian terms, the subject-supposed-to-know. "Each time, that for the subject this function of the subject-supposed-to-know is incarnated by someone, whether analyst or not, this means that a transference has already been established" (Lacan, 1964, p. 211).

The subject-supposed-to-know is defined in Lacan's early teaching as, "the one who is constituted by the analysand in the figure of his or her analyst" and later equated with God the Father (Lacan, 1968, p. 39). Analysts must beware of occupying this omniscient vantage point because they run the risk of turning analysis into a practice based on a theory (or theology) which in lieu of the concept of lack posits an absolute, albeit non-existent someone, a big Other.

The clear distinction between the function of the subject-supposed-to-know and that of the analyst as a person appears in Lacan's formula for the start of analysis as a transference algorithm expressed in the matheme:

$$\frac{S}{S\,(S_1, S_2, \ldots, S_n)} \rightarrow Sq$$

S in the fraction's numerator is called the transference signifier or the analysand's signifier addressed to any other signifier (Sq—*signifiant quelconque*) represented by the analyst. This latter is constructed by the analysand and it will lead him to seek out a specific analyst for any number of reasons. Lacan formulates this choice of the analyst as a coupling of two signifiers (S and Sq) corresponding to establishing transference.

The effect of this signifier transference is an emerging subject, represented by s (signified), related to the signifiers of unconscious knowledge $(S_1, S_2, \ldots, S_n)$ chain-linked together represent the set of unconscious-knowledge signifiers. The union between symbolic transference with the analysand's "any signifier" for the analyst produces the subject: that which one signifier represents for another signifier.

$$\left(\frac{S_1}{\cancel{S}} \rightarrow S_2 \right)$$

This subject is not real but rather the product of transference, a signified (S) based on the patient's unconscious knowledge. What we have here is a subject instituted through initial free association made possible by the patient's signifier pair (S $\rightarrow$ Sq), the same subject of the unconscious whose fantasy is represented by the formula ($\cancel{S}$ ◊ a). It is this artificial subject which will be discarded when the transference relation ends. This is Lacan's "subjective destitution" at the end of the game that we evoked earlier: the very keys—handed over by the analysand to the analyst—that opened the doors of analysis are thrown away when the curtains close.

Lacan's mathemes follow Freud's initial postulates in "On Beginning the Treatment" where he makes the well-known comparison between psychoanalysis and chess.

> Anyone who hopes to learn the noble game of chess from books will soon discover that only the openings and end end-games admit of an exhaustive systematic presentation and that the infinite variety of moves which develop after the opening defy any such description. (Freud, 1913c, p. 123)

Freud says he only sets down a few basic conditions for beginning treatment. In the same spirit, Lacan's transference algorithm represents an attempt to succinctly summarise those essential guidelines, regardless of the unique structure of each analysis session.

The analysand does not necessarily impose this subject-supposed-to-know, represented by the fraction's denominator, on the analyst. What is crucial here is the relationship the analysand sets up between the analyst and the subject-supposed-to-know. Based on transference, the subject-supposed-to-know does not give the analysand any certainty the analyst is very knowledgeable. However, this assumption of the subject-supposed-to-know is quite compatible with the fact that the analyst's knowledge for the analysand may possibly be dubious (Lacan, 1971–1972).

Analysts evidently know nothing of the analysand's unconscious at the outset of treatment. We can see this clearly in the algorithm where "any signifier" (Sq)—representing the analyst—is not (or not known) to be related to any unconscious knowledge. This is a laconic Lacanian formalisation of Freud's statement that psychoanalysis is born anew and tailor-made to fit the needs of each new patient: knowledge of other cases can only go so far, but it is ultimately worthless since it cannot be neatly fitted into other cases. Each case is, therefore, as unique as a snowflake, and the analyst must approach each analysand with this in mind.

The transference algorithm is assembled through another algorithm found at its base: Saussure's S/s, which implies the linguistic sign's referent or that which it points to; that element in the world designated by the sign.

In the transference algorithm, the signification of unconscious knowledge corresponds to the place occupied by the referent in the Saussurean sign, insomuch as such signification of knowledge, albeit latent, is always referential. Furthermore, Lacan conjoins the subject's referential knowledge in all its uniqueness with textual knowledge, since psychoanalysis owes its consistency to Freud's texts. Lacan links "psychoanalysis in its intension to psychoanalysis in its extension" using the transference algorithm, for he relies on the conveyance of particular knowledge and its linkage with Freudian texts (Lacan, 2001, p. 246).

What is the effect of establishing this subject-supposed-to-know? Love. When love appears, we witness the shift from the transitive—the patient always demands something (time, attention, diagnosis, care, interpretation, freedom from the symptom, etc.) to the intransitive—"Just give me … love."

Love is the effect of transference as resistance. Love is the analysand's form of resistance to the manifested desire of the Other. Once this desire has appeared, as a question (*Che vuoi?*), the analysand answers it with love; it is up to the analyst to show in shining colours the dimension of desire in this demand, a desire related to the subject-supposed-to-know. Furthermore, it corresponds to the subject-supposed-to-desire in the patient. All of this is linked to the function of the symptom.

Consequently, the analyst is able to reveal the essence of desire and show how it appears as the Other's desire (belonging to the Other and not the subject) and thus reveal the symptom as an enigma. The analyst does so through the implicit link between desire and knowledge which becomes a desire for knowledge.

It does not suffice for a patient to demand to be freed of a symptom; it must appear to the him or her first as an enigma that, through the dynamics of transference, can be deciphered.

What does this transference love seek? Knowledge. Transference itself is defined by Lacan as knowledge-seeking love. Nevertheless, its finality, as it is for all love, is not knowledge itself but to know that object cause of desire. This object (*object a*) is what makes transference real: the Real of sex. This is that part of transference which can be equated with enacting the sexual reality of the unconscious. Opposing transference as the replay where the demand signifiers are addressed to the Other of Love represented by the analyst, is transference as an encounter with the Real of sex. It is *object a* that, upon filling the constitutive lack inherent in desire, becomes the marvellous object which Socrates seemingly represents, as we saw in Part 1, to Alcibiades in the *Symposium*: the *agalma*:

$$\frac{a}{-\varphi}$$

Transference, as a means of flushing out the sexual reality in the unconscious, is based upon *agalma*, the cause of desire "pinpointed" by analysands through their analysts. *Agalma* is the very core of desire and it correlated with the subject-supposed-to-know. Consequently, in the transference function during preliminary interviews, analysts should know what they represent as the patient's *agalma* to those same patients and assume it during interpretation (*faire semblant*) to ensure transference and perform analysis in the truest sense of the word.

Couch

From what place are they looking at me?
What things unable to look are looking at me?
Who spies from everything?

The corners stare at me.
The smooth walls are truly smiling.

Sensation of being only my spine.

The swords.

—"The Mummy", Fernando Pessoa[1]

The couch—the actual piece of furniture—is the main symbol of psychoanalysis. For the social Other, the couch is a signifier representing the Freudian psychoanalyst who asks analysands to lie down. For the IPA (International Psychoanalytical Association), use of the couch is a rule included in the standards set down for treatment. The Association's other current rule covers the forty-five-minute analytical duration of the session according to a pre-determined regularity.

Although Lacan did not do away with the couch, he disregarded these standards and insisted on shattering this emblematical image of a session by recommending analysts work with patients through free association. Free association is the one and only *sine qua non* rule.

Nonetheless, Lacan advocates the use of the couch and preliminary interviews since both conditions are interconnected. Pointing the patient to the couch signals the end of the preliminary interviews and the start of analysis proper. Is this act merely a technical procedure? Absolutely not. From Lacan's return to Freud, we clearly see that ethics have always guided psychoanalysis. Consequently, Lacan had always been searching for the ethical principle behind every technical procedure, and examining its structure. Certainly, the couch is another ethical player in this game.

In "Problems of Psychoanalytic Technique" (1951), Otto Fenichel's justification for using the couch as a "practical detail", neatly summarises a common-sense idea: the couch allows the analysand to relax and sets the analyst at ease from being stared at. Furthermore, Fenichel also mentions the procedure's ceremonial character and the sort of magical mood the analysand may feel. This explains Lacan's more ethical and theoretical approach towards technique and his statement that "everything is permitted once you know the reason why". According to Fenichel, the psychoanalyst may relinquish the couch whenever analysands either refuse to lie down or are extremely anxious about doing so (Fenichel, 1951, pp. 159–161).

The PIP

In 1963, this issue once again was brought up at a congress where the IPA European psychoanalysts from Romance-speaking countries convened and blatantly imitated their American peers to create the PIP (Psychoanalytical Inspired Psychotherapies) (Held, 1963, pp. 64–65). The congress greenlighted a set of "standard-treatment variations" which not only got a "free pass" from the European community but were also standardised in the form of a rule book.

Lacan totally opposed the PIP. "Variations on the Standard Treatment", was the title of Lacan's 1955 article especially for *The Encyclopédie médico-chirurgicale* (EMC). Lacan would later repudiate the title of his article as "abject". The article assails standardisation and variations of psychoanalysis because the sole treatment expected from a psychoanalyst, is precisely "a psychoanalysis", namely, an unconscious experience representing a speech function that is a tributary of the river of language.

In psychoanalytic theory, the PIP are actually a product of the privilege granted to the "I" (ego), since this type of therapy is mostly recommended for "those with a weak ego". According to the author of the PIP report, promoting these therapies is the result of the constant evolution of psychoanalysis, i.e., the discovery of the *I* (the ego) that takes over the driver's seat from the unconscious and a sign the Oedipus complex, has been eclipsed by the mother–child relationship. In short, new cures for new diseases. The report assumes that:

> [...] qualification of an authentic psychoanalytically-inspired psychotherapy could only happen if we consider the uniqueness of this double spatial and temporal movement that took the patient from the chair to the couch as a result of the first evolution concerning the face-to-face technique and the visual isolation. Secondly, this movement took the patient back from the couch to the chair and to the face-to-face. From then on, the following pattern has been set: for standard treatments and simple psychotherapy, the pair "couch-chair" and "chair-chair" and for psychoanalytically-inspired psychotherapies, the pair "chair-chair". [...] the dialectics between couch-chair and armchair-armchair. (Held, 1963, pp. 64–65)

Furthermore, we are warned of the dangers of forcing patients to lie down where they might feel uncomfortable with the analyst gazing at the back of their necks. Such a situation could drag up age-old fears concerning both the animalistic need for security (food, shelter, etc.) as well as more elaborate fears (being eaten, etc.) of being "found out' and "judged" regarding matters of pleasure/displeasure and love/loss of love. In the case of a weak ego, the patient may fear depersonalisation, dismemberment or even death when regression has led the patient to the pre-verbal borders. In sum, these are the supposed dangers that justify the PIP technique.

According to a paper published by the Société Psychanalytique de Paris (SPI), "The Presentation of the SPT for the Use of a Lay Reader" (Donnet, 1988), the standard-treatment analytic setting must follow the guidelines set down, above all, for the "couch-chair arrangement", and adhere to "the strict rule concerning the number, frequency and length of sessions" (ibid., pp. 687–700).

For these practitioners, the Freudian arrangement is not defined by free association but rather by the furniture, namely, the couch-chair pair. Nevertheless, a few original minds among them proposed some variations for the analytic setting at the *Congress of French-Speaking Psychoanalysts of the Romance Countries* held in Paris in May 1989. Paulette Letarte, for example, placed her couch in a comfortable position for the analysand so that the latter's gaze and that of the analyst could both converge at the same point in an imagined scene wherein the analyst refers to the characters with hand gestures underlying her interpretation. As we shall see later, the justification for this kind of imagined psychodrama is totally at odds with Freud's discussion on the use of the couch specifically related to the relationship between speech and the images that parade before the analysand during the session. This sort of make-believe stage is:

> [...] a place where we can offer our plea to avoid mutual devoration, and act out the passage of the fantasy to act and interpret it in beforehand instead of forbidding it in a way that dissipates the shadows of the past and turns them into visible images and allows us to negotiate transference tensions of transference. We are giving back, in an enhanced way, to the patient what he/she has projected in us. (Letarte, 1989)

Here the author loses her footing because she is not aware of the Symbolic that relocates the analytical experience to the field of language. That knowledge would have empowered her to deal more effectively with the concept of transference. Unfortunately, a mere technical procedure such as changing the position of the couch will not do the trick.

Freud shatters the mirror

In "On Beginning the Treatment", the use of the couch has, above all, a historical significance for Freud: it is the leftover from the era of hypnosis. His insistence on the lying-down position during analysis is so that the analyst who sits behind the analysand is "not to be stared at". Freud gives further reasons for sticking to the couch. First, no analyst could stand being stared at over eight hours a day. I certainly do not wish to analyse Freud here, but I could evoke his own modalities of the scopic drive and his dreams such as "Please close one eye", "*Non vixit*"—where we find Brücke's annihilating eyes—or "Count of Thun" as the representation of Freud's father who had glaucoma, etc. Rather than Freud's dreams and fantasies, which certainly provide a field day for anyone wishing to justify the use of the couch in the analytic experience, what interests me more are Freud's comments about the structure of this arrangement.

Regardless of his unique case, this is a sort of experience most of us analysts have been through. Beyond merely personal reasons, Freud explains he does not want his facial expressions to provide the analysands with any sort of sensitive information that might lead them to be influenced or even reflect on his speech. As he says: "I insist on this procedure for its purpose and result are to prevent transference from mingling with the patient's associations imperceptibly, to isolate the transference and to allow it to come forward in due course sharply defined as resistance" (Freud, 1913c, p. 134). Therefore, the main reason for retaining the couch during analysis is neither historical nor personal but rather related to the structure of transference itself.

The recommendation for using the couch at the onset of each treatment is an analytical act because psychoanalysis is recreated in each process. The goal of the Freudian tactic is to dissolve the Imaginary register in transference, to enable the analyst to distinguish when symbolic transference occurs during treatment. *Shauplatz* is not the analyst's office; it is the signifier's Other. Analysts are the agents that work under the effect of transference but they are not in show business performing. "Making" the *semblant* (*faire semblant*) of *object a* is altogether different as I explain in Chapter 3. They should not do any acting-out. By this I mean they should not stage their fantasies. The measure of the analyst's act is the Real, not to be seen but to bring on desire. Upon unveiling the scene of the Other through speech, Freud refuses the show put on by hysterics. Lying down on the couch is a favourable condition for isolating transference in signifiers and assailing the narcissistic wall (represented by the axis a—a') in the L Scheme so that analysis occurs along the symbolic axis between S and A, exactly in that area where the object circulates:

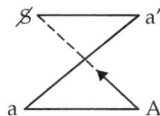

Couch tactics aim at undermining imaginary transference to catalyse transference in the signifying chain, which we can approximate to the transference algorithm which only contains signifiers. Bringing speech functions to centre stage means reducing eye contact, which Lacan designates as the outstanding field for desire's deception since desire is shielded by an image [i(a)] through visual contact. In the subject's relationship with the imaginary other, vision does not perceive the desiring being ensconced behind the desirable subject. The Lacanian function, known as "the analyst's desire", works against the deceptiveness inherent in visual contact and enables the analysand to question his or her own position regarding the Other's desire, now represented by the analyst. Freud's couch arrangement for the analysand thus erases the image of the other, i(a), which would be otherwise represented by the *persona* of the analyst, replacing it with the I(A) or the Other's ideal.

The first time a hysteric male analysand of mine lay down on the couch (it was his first analysis), he became dizzy and had an anxiety attack that made him feel like "a boat with no oars adrift at sea". My refusal to help the patient back on his feet to recover his poise is an example of an analyst who does not act like a little other and actually encourages the patient to drift in his own ocean of signifiers. Unable to see the effect of his words on my facial expressions withdrew the supportive anchor the analysand would ordinarily have sought through visual contact. The patient was in a daze and this was a transitory symptom from being stunned (*étourdit*[2]) by his own utterances. Such symptoms could be likened to a message from the Other [s(A)], and its deciphering allowed me to make the connection between the patient's lack of paternal support and his complaint addressed to his father through the utterance "Father, can't you see me?" in his transference with me. This symbolic transference was possible because I shattered the imaginary reciprocity (*a-a'*) in the mirror while the patient lay on the couch.

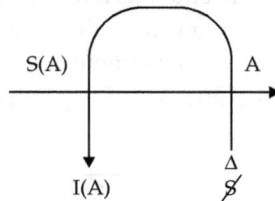

S(A)—symptom: sensation of being in a daze. I(A)—place of the analyst as the absent father.

This personal case study involving a hysteric patient and the analyst (myself) shows the correlation between the couch position and free association. I deliberately avoided any visual contact with the patient and then sent him out in those deep waters to fend for himself. This process actually encouraged the analysand to examine himself and his position regarding the Other's desire. Nevertheless, this is not sufficient, since the main rule in psychoanalysis (free association) is the one that really matters. The couch position introduces, however, the difference between "the vacant place for the subject to fit in but which he or she does not really occupy" and "the Ego that is coming here to stay" (Lacan, 2001, p. 668). The correlation inferred in this case study between the hysteric that lies down on the couch and free association involves the removal of the analyst from the analysand's line of sight. Thus, the Freudian patient felt as if Freud were telling him to switch off the lights to see the unconscious movie better.

Freud uses a railway metaphor to formulate a fundamental rule: "Act as though, for instance, you were a traveller sitting next to the window of a railway carriage and describing to someone inside the carriage the changing views which you see outside" (Freud, 1913c, p. 135). This colourful comparison tells us much more about the importance of dressing images in words during analysis than about inner vision or insight: in Lacanian parlance, translating images into signifiers. *The Interpretation of Dreams* highlights the importance of understanding the way signifiers translate the Imaginary and words convey dream images through storytelling that can bring on insight like a flash in the mirror. Freud puts speech acts and utterances—the speaking subject—on centre stage rather than the insightful subject, which can be equated with the understanding subject of the understanding ego.

Shaulust *deprivation*

According to Freud, the analysand generally considers:

> [...] this lying position as a privation and protests against it, especially when the scopic drive plays an important role in his neurosis. [...] A particularly large number of patients object to being asked to lie down while the doctor sits out of sight, behind them. They ask to be allowed to go through the treatment in some other position, as most of them feel anxious to be deprived of the view of the doctor. (Freud, 1913c, p. 138–139)

And he resoundingly adds: "Permission is usually refused". No concessions should be made to *Schautrieb* (the scopic drive) or *Schaulust* (scopic drive satisfaction). The scopic drive offers us a paradigm for dealing with jouissance during the analytic experience: analysts must deprive themselves of it and delete it. Thus, the use of the couch is also a kind of abstinence rule for analysts and analysands: they must say No to jouissance since "[…] as far as possible, the analytic treatment should be conducted in a state of frustration, neutrality" (Freud, 1981, p. 735). Lacan raises this issue briefly in *Seminar* XI where he regards the scopic drive and the gaze as *object a*. Lacan points out:

> […] the reciprocity plan concerning being "gazed upon" and "gazing upon" is more likely to work as an alibi for the subject. […] Therefore, it would be appropriate, through our interventions in the session, not to let him/her settle in that plan. It would be necessary, however, to take him/her away from this ultimate point regarding the *gaze* as the latter is illusory […]. We do not usually say to the patient:—*Wow! You look awful! Or—the first button on your waistcoat is unbuttoned!* That is why the analysis is not face-to-face. (Lacan, 1973, p. 74)

This explains why the couch represents a breaking away from the prior eye-to-eye contact between patient and analyst during preliminary inter-views. Severing all ties in imaginary reciprocity implies an ethical position for the analyst who aims at eliminating any symmetry between the subject and the other and targeting the relationship between the subject and the Other (the unconscious). This is an attempt to erase a geometrical plane of perception in favour of the logic of the signifier in the inter-utterances that will unmask the unconscious. Analysis is not two-body psychology or a *tête-à-tête* between two parties. Erasing the analyst–analysand reciprocity swaps the "gazing-upon-me" effect for the "it-has-me-now-gazing-upon-it" effect which occurs at the scopic level of sexual drive activity.

The logic of the analytic process places the analyst as a watchman and, therefore, in a spot which could be misconstrued as the vantage point of the ego ideal from where subjects perceive themselves as lovable beings. This is due to transference where subjects regard themselves as the *beloved ones*. Lying on the couch does not guarantee patients will not try to "show-off" because, when their ego ideal governs their speech acts, they feel they must prove they deserve being loved by the Other.

Transference, according to Lacan, is love addressed to knowledge, that is why it brings the subject-supposed-to-know into the place of the ego ideal. The subject thus sees himself or herself as having love and being able to be loved and assumes the Other knows "everything" about him or her. This analogy regarding structure allows the love in transference as a corollary of the subject-supposed-to-know. This love phenomena in transference cheats and covers up the "the analyst-is-looking-at-me" sensation, which is anguish brought on by the Other's gaze (maintained by the analyst) through *semblant* strategy.

There is a sort of ping-pong movement between the vigilant Other, with its penetrating gaze (a), and the Other of Love [I(A)] because the ego ideal and the watchdog superego are overlapping. Thus, this ongoing surveillance relentlessly gazes upon and evaluates the subject according to the ego ideal, "[…] as if it were the ultimate gaze from which the subject should separate" (Lacan, 1973, p. 74). During early stages of analysis, *object a* is latent and analysts must clearly pinpoint it, sever it from the ego ideal and empty out its jouissance. Hence, by telling analysands to lie down on the couch, analysts are already saying No to any misleading or equivocal identification between I(A) and (a). This disjunction should always be a target during analysis (ibid, p. 245).

We can find the paradigm of the ego ideal overlapping *object a* in the hypnotist's gaze. Hypnosis gets its power of suggestion through the conjunction of S_1 (the leader supporting the ego ideal in this twosome) and his or her mesmerising gaze. Telling the patient to lie down on the couch is an upgrade from hypnosis to analysis: the latter works quite differently from the former since it brings on the disjunction between the ego ideal and the surplus jouissance of the gaze, the object of the scopic drive.

I was inspired to think of the dovetailing of the gaze and the ego ideal during the case of a woman who came to me and told me her marriage was on the rocks. Once she had managed to calm down after a few interviews, I decided to refer her to a colleague, as she was relocating to another city, and I was unwilling to sign her on for further analysis. The next day, she called to tell me I had hypnotised her, "touched her subconscious" (her own words) because, I had supposedly stared at her to make her think she was a lesbian. "Doctor", the ideal signifier she addressed me with, occupied the same place as the object of her jouissance, the gaze. She had supposedly projected onto me the powers of clairvoyance and the ability to manipulate her "cranium" (her words) which empowered my gaze to suck out some hidden secret in her skull. I had these amazing powers because I was a "Lacranian shrink" (her words). This case dramatically illustrates how the Other can overlap with the object, the latter which is indeed the analyst's role (*semblant*). The major difference is that, in this case of psychosis, the gaze object was not latent but out in the open.

The scarlet shame

During my psychoanalytic practice, I have noticed that patients often ask to lie down on the couch when they feel ashamed of something. This usually occurs at the end of some preliminary interviews. The feeling of shame is usually associated with sex scenes and fantasies of desire, which are particularly intimate and secret, desire fantasies.

In "Creative writers and Day-dreaming", Freud stresses that "[…] adults are ashamed of their fantasies and usually try to disguise them in the presence of others. By treating such fantasies as something intimate, adults would rather confess their faults than reveal their fantasies" (Freud, 1908e [1907], p. 145). Shame, says Lévi-Strauss regarding the misfortune that befell the rivals of Quesalid, is a social feeling *par excellence* (Lévi-Strauss, 1958/1974, p. 207).

Shame is the feeling a person may have when a scrutinising gaze seems to beam out from the Other's radius towards the subject. Freud neatly illustrates this when examining dreams related to nudity in *The Interpretation of Dreams* (Freud, 1900a, p. 213). The sign of the presence of this invisible gaze is the feeling of shame. The subjects behave like an ostrich: they close their eyes thinking this will prevent them from being seen. There is "[…] no outrage more flagrant than to forbid the culprit to hide his face for shame", writes Nathaniel Hawthorne in *The Scarlet Letter* (Hawthorne, 1991, p. 46).

In Hawthorne's novel, the letter "A" embroidered on Hester Prynne's garment makes a public show to the world of her adulterous jouissance and magnificently illustrates how shame may attach itself to the subject's being like a leech. The patient's demand to lie on the couch out of shame is an attempt to avoid the analyst's gaze. Patients are afraid of this and want to sidestep the gaze of a critical eye. They erase the analyst's gaze from their visual radius to "hide away" on the couch.

The real feeling of shame expresses transference since the analyst is viewed as an audience. It is a sign the analyst represents the *semblant* of *object a*. However paradoxical it may sound, the demand to lie down in this case is only expressed when the Other (manifested through the analysand's utterances) is separated or distanced from the analyst as a person. Neurotics only perceive this distance because they somehow know that transference as a repetition mistakes the analyst for someone else. Moreover, neurotics also uncannily know that the Other does not exist because their lack acts upon their subjectivity. With psychotics, the blending together of the analyst as a person and the figure of the Other implies a kind of transference, as opposed to neurosis, in which there is no mistaken identity but rather a real encounter.

The feeling of shame belongs typically to the neurotic: it is both a sign of drive satisfaction and a barrier to it, as it splits a subject simultaneously prevented from showing himself or herself and also commanded to "strip naked". The couch enables and empowers free association by allowing analysands to "hide away like ostriches" and overcome the feelings of exposing themselves. But rather than hindering, them, the couch actually helps analysands bring on the Other's "gaze upon them". Shame is the sign of drive activity expressed at the scopic level.

The image and the spot

What is the connection between the gaze and the image in the mirror? We know Freud's metaphor of the "mirror analyst": the analyst must behave like a mirror that reflects what is shown (Freud, 1981, p. 69). Concerning this metaphor, Lacan points out that analysts are not reflective mirrors although they do indeed supply the fixed image—i(a)—namely, the mirror image the subject sees in the Other. Nevertheless, the real secret of the narcissistic snapshot concerns the gaze object. The mirror is still a veil because the image (i) therein represents *object a* while at the same time conceals it; that is what the matheme i(a) means. Indeed, for Lacan, the problematical obstacle between *object a* and the subject's *Spaltung* is the mirror image itself. This obstacle arises because the gaze operates uniquely as an invisible object. Instead of placing themselves in the mirror where i(a) is reflected, analysts should preferably reduce themselves to a blurred spot that can represent the gaze (*cf. Seminar* XII), where the *tyché* function lies in the scopic field. A blind spot suffices to destroy any illusions in the visual *eidos* (form/shape). When analysts interpret as *semblant* of *object a*, they also put a blot on the mirror images of the analysand's myriad representations.

The spot works like the fabric covering the *agalmata* or jewel box that analysands think is the analyst's property and thus reveals a certain ambiguity about the jewellery inside: the fabric both conceals and reveals the "wonder of wonders", i.e., the *agalma* or precious goods Alcibiades so desperately wanted from Socrates in the *Symposium*. This ambiguity is duplicated in the transference situation. The reason for this is that a stain immediately attracts our attention. Likewise, the analyst catches the analysand's attention since the former has something, albeit hidden, the latter finds desirable. *Agalma* is the bright gem that lends its nature to the idea of Beauty or that charming thing the analysand's eyes make the analyst into. But such charm is an inconvenience to the analyst who must avoid falling prey to the tricks, traps and enticing gaze of the *agalma*. However, the analyst shall make use of it (*agalma*) in his or her *semblant* strategy. The treasured *agalma* awakens and stirs desire: it is *object a* and the castration (–φ) inherent therein. It is an object that serves as a cork to stop up the gaping hole of the lack it conceals. *Agalma* is a trap sprung by the gaze.

According to Freud in *Three Essays on Sexuality*, charm (*Reize*) is the quality the eye (as an erogenous zone) conveys to the sexual object and that which "gives us the sense of beauty" (Freud, 1905d, p. 209). Thus, whenever and however the analysand sends the analyst some sort of erotic scopic message, the latter acts as if he or her were saying: "you don't see me from where I see you", which opens up the dimension of the Other's desire. What does the Other want? "To get some jouissance from me", the superego replies, but this answer can only appear with the downfall of *agalma*, when (a) is separated from (–φ). It is an a-morally obscene kind of answer that the analyst's desire makes impossible for the analysand to sidestep. Undoubtedly, the couch is a part of the analyst's ethical principles since it can be used as a tool to nip in the bud any fascination the analysand may have for the analyst and divorce (a) from (–φ) so that the desired object appears in its full "glory" as junk or surplus jouissance. The strategic use of the couch allows subjects to fully experience themselves as lacking beings during analysis.

The couch: satisfaction out!

Although I have tried to point out some general features about using the couch, there are no set standards for any part of analysis we can fall back on. Each new case is unique and presents challenges that the analyst must rise up to meet in order to catalyse and foreground free association. I offer a personal case to wrap up this chapter.

A patient (we will call her Joan), came to my office to talk about her marital troubles. After the first preliminary interviews during which she "spewed out" an unbearable chapter in her life story, Joan lost her voice and consequently missed the second interview. The aphonia soon became an analytical symptom whose common denominator was connected to her request to see her father who had died when she was a child. The terrible episode in her past was also her way of calling out to her father: when she was a child, she jumped out of a fire and her dress caught fire. She became a living torch, but luckily the fire was swiftly put out. The singed fabric of the garment stuck to her skin, and while her mother tried to take off Joan's dress, she accidently ripped off some strips of skin that had become glued to the tatters.

To make matters even worse, while struggling for her life with her mother, Joan's father was absent. After the incident, Joan's father was the only person she would allow to change the bandages. He was also the only one with whom she would eat something during the anorexia that ensued after the wounds healed. Furthermore, he was the sole person who cared during her many bouts of angina, which caused her to lose her voice when she was a child.

The aphonia symptom re-enacted during the preliminary interviews exemplifies how I had become the father surrogate for Joan's demand. This was a clear sign of emergent transference. Moreover, Joan confessed she felt very inhibited facing me while speaking and suggested she could lie on the couch, but I held off. Henceforward, Joan overtly avoided my gaze. One day she was very embarrassed and said she was undergoing that thing called transference. Then, with great difficulty, she reported a childhood memory in which she recollected having engaged in a sexual game with her brother—it was something concerning voyeurism or exhibitionism in a kind of a striptease act. She also told me that once, during the game, he put his penis into her vagina. There she suddenly halted her report to talk about the difficulty of telling this story while looking at me. I then pointed to the couch and told her to lie down, but she refused despite my insistence and her previous demand.

I let her continue her story. She then started telling me that at her father's funeral she could not stand looking at her brother, as the sexual game would pop up in her mind as an embarrassing memory throughout the burial. In the following interviews, I kept repeating she lie on the couch, but alas, to no avail. My insistence only showed me to be powerless. "I cannot", she said and added she would nevertheless do anything to please a man except that (!). I decided to abandon the role of the "master" that she had projected onto me with her teasing behaviour and continue with the face-to-face meetings during the following sessions.

When we met again, she told me that the previous week she had gone to bed with five different men—all of them sexually impotent (!),—and further added that the men always resembled her father. There I interrupted the session and said to her, "Okay, but I'm not your father". During the next session, she told me she felt sexually excited by my presence, and finally managed to lie down on the couch.

This short narrative illustrates an obvious point: that the couch is the bed where analysands make love—transference love. But as a bed, there is no satisfaction to be had on the couch. The couch is the bed for the moaning and groaning and sighing for the One ... I love. It is on the couch that longings and the worst expectations are re-enacted. Fathers are all powerless to quell the desires that will arise on the couch-bed.

In analysis, the couch is not intended for relaxation or naps: it is a *locus* representing the very opposite of the numbness and trance-like state of hypnosis. "The clinic is always related to the bed", Lacan says, "[…] and we have found nothing better than to tell the ones seeking out psychoanalysis to lie down […] It is lying down that people do many things, love in particular and love leads to all kinds of statements" (Lacan, 1977, p. 8).

Regarding Joan's case, we can say that the gaze object as the latent object of desire finally remerged on the couch. It first appeared in the mirror image, which I was underpinning as an analyst and then in the mutual sexual game Joan had played with her brother during childhood. Then the gaze became deadly as *object a* in the scene where her mother's morbid jouissance tore off the tatters of the dress fabric together with parts of her daughter's flesh. According to Joan's interpretation, she could see that jouissance in her "m-Other's" eyes as her mother furiously ripped off Joan's dress and the clinging charred flesh.

If, as in this case, jouissance permeates some inhuman and ghastly horror, the fundamental rule—"to say anything that comes to one's mind"—prevents the love couch from becoming a death bed. That does not mean the couch cannot be represented by death or any other morbid signifier, such as the one in Delacroix's painting *The Death of*

Sardanapulus where the deathbed of the Assyrian ruler is surrounded by the treasure of his regal jouissance and pleasure: necklaces, jewellery, ewer and basin, lavish fabrics, slaves, horses, and semi-clad women. Or John Everett Millais's painting *Ophelia*, whose character lies peacefully in a deadly watery bed strewn with flowers. Corpses are always lying down.

If the couch can be represented by funereal signifiers that convey a fatal end, it is because it is the place where the subject is once again mortified by the signifiers that have shackled his or her own life and whose psychic "leftover" still throbs with the silence of the death drive.

In the French literary movement *Les Précieuses*, there was a kind of shame to name *le divan* (the couch) according to its function, as it is considered a place just to sleep, as we find in the *Great Dictionary of Les Précieuses* (Ribson, 1600) or *The Key Language of the Streets* such as the "Old Dreamer" or "Morpheus's Empire". If the bed is for us to sleep on, the analytical couch is not made for patients to lie down on peacefully to indulge their regressions of childish libido. The analytical couch is not a bed for sleeping and dreaming, but rather the place of awakenings through the re-enactment of life narratives. The Persian word "divan" or "couch" effectively designates a place of discourse and speech: a room furnished with pillows and cushions where the Sultan's council assembled to talk business regarding the great Ottoman Empire. We should also recall the meaning of "couch" as a verb: to express one's feelings through words and phrases. Thus, the analytical and ethical couch is "like a bridge over troubled waters" where the subject lies down to awaken all the unconscious creatures submerged below in the river of language.

Time

How many minutes do we spend on that game? Only heaven's clocks will have marked this time both infinite and brief. Eternity has its pendulum; although it is endless it always wants to know how long our happiness and pain last.

—Dom Casmurro, Machado de Assis

L et us consider Five Propositions for psychoanalysis about time during analysis for our not-so-new millennium:

1. Time in psychoanalysis must correspond to the structure of the Freudian field. This is thus not merely a technical or empirical issue, because time matches the core concepts of psychoanalysis.
2. The logic of the unconscious and ethics rather than bureaucratic planning determine the length of psychoanalytical sessions.
3. The logic of psychoanalytical sessions without a pre-set time is grounded on two distinct definitions of structure that take into account two aspects of the subject.
4. Time in analysis opposes the neurotic's sense of time.
5. Session time must entail the end of analysis. Therefore, the end of the analysis is always implicit in that time.

Two considerations regarding Proposition 3:

A) The structure of the psychoanalytical field matches the structure of language. The subject is defined and determined by signifiers according to the Lacanian formulation of the unconscious structured as a language.

B) Structure is not only defined by language ("if everything is structure", says Lacan, "not everything is language") but it is also related to *object a*—something real and external to language and beyond the signifying chains. The structure of the psychoanalytical act is at stake: "an act that I base", says Lacan, "on a paradoxical structure wherein the object is active and the subject is subverted: (a ◊ $\cancel{S}$)" (Lacan, 1968, p. 34).

What does time mean in analysis? How long should a session or treatment last? "Walk!" is Freud's answer based on Aesop's *Fables* in "On Beginning the Treatment" (Freud, 1913c, p. 128). This answer is a correlate to the one given by Lacan upon beginning his teaching (1953–1954) in *Seminar* I on psychoanalytical technique where he describes the Zen Buddhist Master who answers the students with silence, sarcasm, a kick in the pants or a thump of his staff (Lacan, 1975a). This is the way of Zen for dealing with inquisitive students searching for clear-cut answers or meanings and I will further examine it in Chapter 3.1. Like the Zen students, Lacanian analysands must find the answers to their questions on their own.

Time has always been a controversial issue in psychoanalysis for two reasons:

• First, regarding the length of treatment, which aims at the end of analysis when analysands become their own analysts.
• Second, the length of each session.

Lacan examined the length of sessions and opposed the IPA standard fifty-minute period in an attempt to make time correspond to the function of speech in the field of language. This is what Lacan termed "short sessions" or "working within logical time" in a 1945 article ("*Le temps logique et l'assertion de certitude antecipée*"). Lacan never gave up the short sessions and stated that "they are not devoid of meaning" (Lacan, 1966, p. 315).

According to Lacan's proposed concept regarding analysis, session length is an analytical function insomuch as analysis heads towards a *terminus*. It is equally significant here that Freud also examined the problematical feature of the end of the analysis in "On Beginning the Treatment": "In the early days of my psychoanalytical practice, I used to have the greatest difficulty in prevailing on my patients to continue their analysis. This difficulty has long since been shifted, and I now have to take the greatest pains to induce them to give it up" (Freud, 1913c, p. 130).

Freud revisits the issue in 1937 in "Terminable and Interminable Analysis" because of the difficulty he noticed analysands experienced about ending treatment. As we can see, after the problem was first formulated in 1913, it became increasingly more vital and crucial for Freud towards the end of his life. Nowadays, the ripples of Freud's examination of the problem of time are still being felt in the entire global analytical community.

What is Freud's position regarding time in "On Beginning the Treatment"? He states he would plan sessions by scheduling the number (regularity, i.e., six times a week, except Sundays or holidays) and setting the length (one hour). Therefore, analysands would have a one-hour daily session to use regardless of cancelations.

Although Freud stressed that those norms were best suited to him, the IPA took them as a standard and added some convenient amendments, such as setting the minimum number of sessions to three times a week (instead of Freud's six) and decreasing session length from sixty to fifty minutes. However, no justifications I know of were ever offered for these changes. Consequently, many analysts have become "functionaries" of the institutions which oversee their practice.

In his teaching, Lacan had denounced this obsessive policy as early as 1953. In opposition to an institutional default setting, he proposed analysts should allow the analysand's words to guide them during analysis, which is essentially a speaking experience in the field of language. Today, this seems very clear since Lacanian teaching has become widespread, but back in 1953, the situation was quite different because the psychoanalytical debate centred on techniques dealing with resistance during analysis.

So, just what is this time, which is not the standard one set by the IPA clock, but one related to the unconscious? If the unconscious is timeless, as Freud says, how can the length of a session be based on it?

We cannot answer this conundrum without considering the first innovation introduced by Lacan when he began his teaching based on his axiom that the unconscious is structured as a language. Lacan states that the unconscious is neither inside nor outside the analysand but in his or her own speech, so it is the analyst's task to underscore the unconscious. How? Through the analytical act.

Punctuation and retroaction

Lacan's first proposes punctuation. The analyst brings out the unconscious by punctuating the analysand's speech. Through punctuation, regular speech acts manifest the unconscious. This is the opposite of techniques which try to raise awareness with a question such as: "Are you aware of what you are saying?" or hermeneutics-based interpretations based upon the Oedipal or Pre-Oedipal phase, or about the "good" or "bad" object. It is the break or pause in the plot of the analysand's storytelling rather than chronological time that ends a session. This follows a Lacanian communication scheme found not only in the analysis but also in ordinary daily experiences and verbal intercourse.

To understand a sentence we must listen to it until the end. For example, if I say "Now, I will ..." nobody will understand what I mean. Only when listeners have heard the complete sentence—"Now, I will ... go to the blackboard to write what I'm saying"—do they grasp the meaning of "Now, I will ...". If we consider the sentence as a chain of signifiers, only the complete sentence makes the meaning of the beginning of sentence clear. This is what Lacan calls retroaction (*après-coup*).

This communication schema here corresponds to the Freudian *Nachträglich*, in other words, retroaction, afterwardness, *aprés-coup* or the *a posteriori* attribution of meaning. Only hearing a sentence from beginning to end can the listener understand its full meaning. And only the period at the end of the sentence makes the latter meaningful.

COMMUNICATION SCHEME

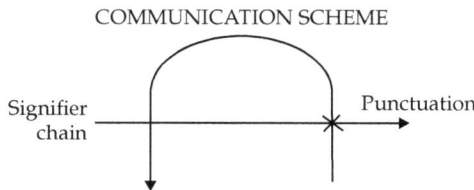

Signifier chain   Punctuation

This retroaction schema is fundamental in psychoanalysis, because it corresponds to the constitution of trauma and the structure of signification.

For traumas to occur, two moments in time are necessary. If we take castration as the emblematic trauma, we have: at the very onset of childhood masturbation, the boy hears real castration threats. The menacing words will only bring on the boy's anguish when he confronts the lack of penis in women (his mother), in other words, when he confronts the Other's castration. The effect of the threat gains its meaning through retroaction by re-signifying the boy's initial experience.

Lacan goes on to consider the retroaction schema as a fundamental Oedipal schema; it will be the matrix of the future "graph of desire", called *point de capiton* or "quilting" or "anchoring point".[3] The French expression is used in cushion-making: it is stitch which defines the cushion's specific design. The *point de capiton* allows, in terms of structure, the very making of meaning—which, according to Freud will always be sexual.

We can describe the *point de capiton* according to the Oedipus complex and based on the Lacanian paternal metaphor: the inclusion of the Name-of-the Father (NF) in the Other corresponds to the advent of the phallic signifier, which gives meaning a sexual connotation:

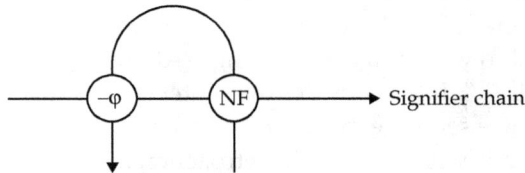

We can imagine this simple graph as a representation of the psychoanalytical experience. The life story of every person has some condensed enigmatic points indicative of specific points of jouissance recurrent in his or her speech acts and utterances. The enigmatic point returns as compulsive repetition and appears in the subject's utterances addressed to the Other as the place the analysand has chosen for the analyst. This point, apparently meaningless to the analysand, is a meaning-laden enigma like all other riddles. The subject gives an event a meaning (or interpretation) and then later, another meaning and then even a further meaning and so on and so forth. The same event acquires different meanings throughout analysis.

As a re-signifying experience, analysis allows leeway for multiple interpretations of the same event, since many other signifiers can also come into play to signify the same event, since every psychic event is structured by signifiers:

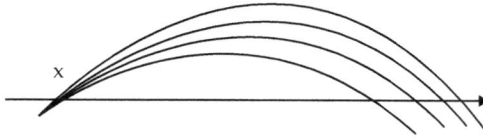

x = Enigmatic point in the subject's life story re-signified through different interpretations.

The two Lacanian terms employed for interpreting psychic events are resubjectification (subjective destitution) and restructuring (Lacan, 1966, p. 256).

Lacan's example of the structure of the *après-coup* or Freudian retro-action is seen in his analysis of Freud's "Wolf Man", who retroactively re-structures a fundamental event in his (The Wolf Man's) life story: the primal sex scene. Analysis allows different significations of the same event, which is re-signified *a posteriori* or *après-coup*.

The session's "cut" is already an interpretative act of that determines meaning. It is wordless interpretation in action, that decides a meaning. "The session's cut", states Lacan, "cannot be indifferent to the discourse's plot and will play the role of scansion in the session, which is worth as much as an intervention to bring on the concluding moments" (ibid, p. 252). In 3.1 I examine other features of the cut as an interpretative act.

This form of scansion, however, need not match the session's inter-ruption. In poetry, scansion is a literary term defined as punctuating, underlining, rhyming, and pronouncing words or sentences by stressing syllables or groups of words. We will later see just how important it is that the session's interruption shares the scansion-structure of poetry.

As the agent responsible for interrupting the session at any given moment (i.e., the one who will place the full stop at the end of the "sen-tence"), the analyst determines the meaning, which always belongs to the Other. Hence, from this standpoint, the analyst "holds the truth" and dispels the common myth of assumed neutrality:

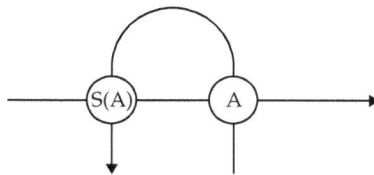

A—Analyst in the place of the Other; session "cut". S(A)—The Other's meaning.

In this sense, the analysts cut can be the concluding moment for a sentence, a session or line of thought. But it can also be used to adjourn a session aimed not at reaching a conclusion but rather creating an enigma as we will see later. Based on this schema, analysts who give a key role to the unconscious are unconcerned about the time ticking away on the clock because they will interrupt the session according to the punctuation in the analysand's discourse. Time in analysis is not chronological time. Nevertheless, analysts must not disregard the temporal dimension during analysis due to the two key factors I will now examine.

Of time and language

The first factor is the successive temporal dimension in the signifying chain since speech implies linearity in time. Notwithstanding this, it is only possible to conceive time starting from language as it exists at the grammatical level of verb tenses (past/present/future) in all modes (indicative, subjunctive, imperative, etc.). That said, not only is the signifying chain subject to temporality in diachronic terms, but time itself also implies language. Concurrently, the simplest time frame will always require and reflect a language structure in Lacanian analysis.

What else does Lacan do when he borrows from linguistics except introduce temporality using Saussure's algorithm of the linguistic sign? In this linear chain of signifiers (S), every S is linked to a chain of signifieds (s):

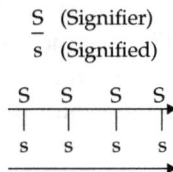

$$\frac{S}{s} \quad \begin{array}{l} \text{(Signifier)} \\ \text{(Signified)} \end{array}$$

$$\begin{array}{cccc} S & S & S & S \\ | & | & | & | \end{array} \longrightarrow$$
$$\begin{array}{cccc} s & s & s & s \end{array}$$
$$\longrightarrow$$

Lacan includes the unconscious time dimension in the linguistic sign coupled to the *après-coup* or retroaction structure by representing it with intercommunicating vectors: the chain of meaning crosses the chain of signifiers:

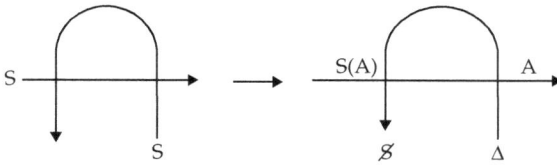

Lacan introduces time into Saussure's algorithm for the graph matrix: a time swerve that represents the Lacanian concept of the subject in which the notion of time is embedded. It is a signifying chain—corresponding to resubjectification during analysis—that shapes the subject. We can thus equate analytical resubjectification with the re-signification of an event in the subject's life story.

Downsizing this schema further allows us to see that the signifying chain—represented by a simple a signifier pair matrix (S_1 and S_2)—will, retroactively, *après-coup* style, engender the subject:

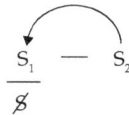

The subject—always refusing any ultimate or definite signifier to represent him or herself—is created as the signifying chains unrolls. Punctuation here will produce the subject. The subject is an effect of time acting retroactively upon the signifying chain and is ever being moulded over time because another signification, rather than the previous one, is always possible.

In "The Subversion of the Subject and the Dialectic of Desire", Lacan equates the primary matrix of the graph of desire with individual submission to the signifier "[…] produced in the circuit that goes from s(A) to A and returns from A to s(A)" (Lacan, 1966, pp. 806–815). He insists on the dissymmetry of these two intersecting points: A (the Other) is a place (the place of the treasure of the signifier) and s(A) is a moment or scansion—a punctuation in which "the signification becomes the final product" (Lacan, 1966, p. 806). In this matrix, the Other, defined as the *locus* of the treasure of the signifier is the full battery of signifiers installed in A. This, of course, is impossible because the Other is incomplete and lacks the signifier that would grant it the character of absolute truth.

Lacan then defines this Other no longer as the location of the code but as "the previous site to the pure subject of the signifier", the place of the analysand's speech acts and utterances (Lacan, 1966, p. 807). The place wherein is uttered the first dictum that decrees and legislates and thus grants the Other (i.e., the mother) its enigmatical and mysterious authority and incarnates the Other's omnipotent albeit hollow "phantom" (*fantôme*) around which the subject's signifiers swing to the tune of desire and demand.

The unary trait of the subject is the alienating sign through the subject's first identification to form the ego ideal [I(A)]. This is an *après-coup* effect of the analyst's answer given to the analysand from the *locus* of the Other as we can see in Lacan's graph of desire. In the graph below we reproduce the lower part of the graph of desire in which we notice a shift in the subject's place in relation to the previous graph:

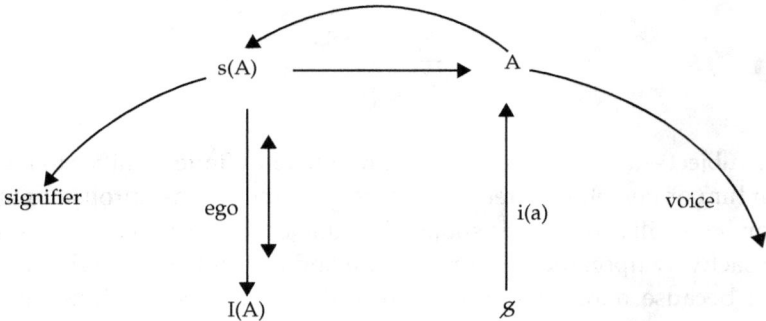

The analyst "naturally" occupies the Other's place as we see when the analysand targets his utterances at the analyst when transference takes place. Analysands will address their demands to the analyst as an Other of love and knowledge.

If analysts answer from this vantage point, they will reinforce the subject's submission to his or her first identifications and lead him or her to a false self-idealisation stemming from I(A) and away from the awareness that this Ideal conceals a blatant lack-of-being like the hole in a doughnut.

We might think that in an effort to prevent the analyst from occupying this structural *locus* of the Other's omnipotence, the IPA uselessly attempted to propose an analyst–analysand contract with timed sessions.

Session length cannot be external to the analytical experience—which is linguistic in nature. No person or institution can represent the Other as an outside guarantee for analysands against the analyst's whims and moods.

If we assume the analyst should be submitted to a set time we also assume there is the Other's Other. So, just as the analysand has his or her Other in the person of the analyst, the latter would have his or her Other in the form of an institution: the Psychoanalytical Society This is more appropriate to a police state than to the analytical setting. It would be tantamount to assuming an ultimate and absolute dimension of meaning equivalent to something like God. But there is no final meaning or absolute meaning, nor that which, from a Hegelian viewpoint, is called Absolute Knowledge. Therefore, there is no warrant for assuming the existence or reality of this Other: this is what the $S(\cancel{A})$ means because the Other lacks $(\cancel{A})$, it is inconsistent, in other words, its lack is the very sign of its non-existence. By the same token, there is no signifier capable of answering the question: *who am I?* It is, at the very least, hypocritical for an analyst to assume this all-knowing-guru-like place of the Other, because the Other is a *locus* not a person. At the linguistic level, there is no signifier capable of representing an attribute that sums up the subject in definite terms, nor one to represent the whole of the subject's being and jouissance. There is no *status-quo* established Other that guarantees the analyst to whom the analysand addresses demands and desires. Nor is there any guarantee of the Other in transference with the analyst (Lacan, 1984).

Let us therefore dispel, once and for all, any nonsensical ideas about the Other's Other, or Time's Time. If such entities indeed existed or had reality, what would they be like? Such thinking only adds to the garbage heap of useless speculative metaphysics.

However, returning to the analytical experience of measured time, chronological time could indeed be considered "Time's Time" or the "Other's Other". Granted the Other's inconsistency and dreamlike essence, analytic time, strictly speaking, can only be intrinsic to and quantified by the analytical act itself.

The scansion of signifiers through session cuts must attempt to sever the subject's identification with that Other and unyoke him or her from the dependence on that signifier scanned during the session.

The subject verbally addresses the Other. The analyst's answer as a "non-answer" to the demand which this speech act implies will arouse the dimension of desire that always appears as an enigma or a question about desire that unveils itself as the Other's desire.

At the phenomenological level of the experience, the patient could indeed ask: *Why did he cut me off there? Why did he stop me when I brought that up? What was so important about what I said* or even *Was I being annoying or talking nonsense?* It is after the session that desire is empowered to appear. This is expressed in Lacan's famous question *Che vuoi?* (What do you want?) in his graph of desire:

The Graph of Desire

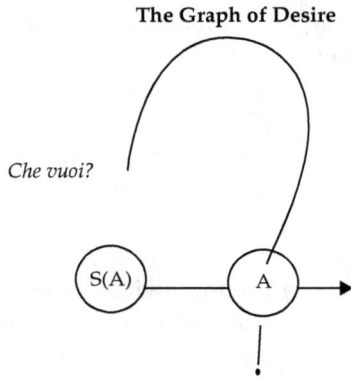

Che vuoi?

S(A) —— A →

According to the graph, session cuts introduce the dimension of unconscious desire, which is highlighted as an enigma: this is exactly the function of the analyst's desire, which appears as an x, *like a riddle to be deciphered*. I have found in clinical practice that the last phrase or word immediately before the session cut continues to echo in the analysand's mind afterwards and can spark further associations. This technique allows signifiers to be deployed beyond the analytical setting and continue the analytical process outside the consulting room. Hence, the session cut has an interpretative function as a signifier-engendering riddle in the patient's mind.

"Everything has to refer", says Lacan, "to the cut of speech, the strongest one being the one that produces the bar between the signifier and the signified. This is where we surprise the subject who interests us" (Lacan, 1966, p. 801). Wrapping up the session with a cut aims at inhibiting the usual signifier-signified links and bringing out the subject caught in the signifying chain that is shaping and alienating that person. The cut consequently produces an effect of "de-alienation" and brings out the subject of desire.

Of time and logic

The time issue gives psychoanalysis its rigor as a conjectural science and reveals a perspective capable of accurately portraying the complexity of human psychic life.

Analytical time is described in "The Sophism of the Three Prisoners" found in Lacan's article on logical time (ibid, pp. 197–213). Here, Lacan introduces the haste function introduced into analysis. I paraphrase the story and Lacan's commentary:

The prison warden chooses three prisoners and tells them he will free one of them. The winner of a guessing game/riddle he proposes to them will be the lucky one. The warden tells them that there are five disks: three white ones (o) and two black ones (•) and that they will be randomly attached to the back of the prisoners. The warden then attaches three white disks to the back of the three prisoners, who, without knowing their own colour, can see the other disks placed on the back of their cell mates.

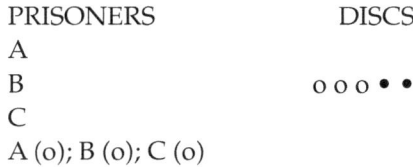

PRISONERS	DISCS
A	
B	o o o • •
C	
A (o); B (o); C (o)	

The warden then tells them that the first one to leave the cell and logically demonstrate how he guessed the colour of his disk wins the prize of freedom. Let us say that prisoner A is the first one to leave the cell to give his answer and demonstrates his logic:

> *I am white and here is my answer: I am white and I know that because I can see that B and C are white.*
>
> *I thought, if I (A) were black, putting myself in the shoes of B and C and thinking as I believe they would, they would conclude that they were white and both would come out. As they did not, I came to the conclusion that I am not black, but white.*

A then breaks down his reasoning:

1) *If I (A) were black (•) and putting myself in B's place, I would think: if I were black, C would see two black disks and would leave the cell, concluding B is white:*

B (?)   A (•)
            C (o)

2) *If I (A) were black (•) putting myself in C's place, I would think if I were black, B would see two black disks (•), concluding he is white (o) and he would leave.*

C (?)   A (•)
            B (o)

As none of them left, I (A) can only be white.

A deciphered the sophism and was made a free man. Lacan says A is a person of pure logical thinking; what determines the judgment of the subject is the non-action of the other two; the time that has stopped for B and C.

Lacan then splits the sophism into three moments in which time appears differently to each prisoner as a way of showing us the discontinuity of these three logical moments.

First proof of reasoning

Facing two black disks, one knows he is white (• • → o): this is exclusive logic which immediately delivers valuable evidence. Lacan describes this moment with a very interesting expression: it is a mental flash where time equals zero. This is the instant of seeing.

Second proof of reasoning

This second moment delivers a hypothesis regarding an attribute unknown to the subject (in the sophism: I am white). This hypothesis is formulated thus: if I were black, the two white disks I see would soon be recognised as white ones. Lacan calls this the time for understanding, which implies a time lapse for thinking things over: this is A's reasoning who puts himself in the place of the others and thinks about the situation. Therefore, the time for understanding belongs to the others. According to Lacan, time thus objectified is immeasurable and can be downsized to the instant of seeing: "the objectivity of this moment wobbles within its limits" (Lacan, 1966, p. 205).

Third proof of reasoning

A says:

> I rush to affirm/present myself as a white one so that the other white disks I see do not overtake me since I recognise them for what they are.

This is the *id* moment Lacan describes as the moment of conclusion, which is actually the continuation of the time for understanding. This "click" which appears after he has thought about the situation can be equated with the Freudian "insight" of a purely logical subject. It subjectively pops up as if it were a delay in relation to the others prisoners, which explains the rush. Prisoner A must hurry otherwise or the others will beat him to the finish line. It can be seen as urgency during the moment of conclusion. Lacan describes this moment as a sudden brainstorm that eclipses the objectivity of the time for understanding.

In the sophism, this is the time for the prisoner's conclusion and immediate action. If he does not swiftly conclude he is white, he runs the risk of losing to the others. If the others leave the cell first, his time will have run out. It is, therefore, the pressing nature of the logical movement that kicks the prisoner's judgment and action into high gear. This is the function of haste. In a subjective assertion (I am white), subjects ascertain the truth of a fundamental attribute granted to them for their freedom.

How can this assertion be checked? It can only be verified through certainty, because if the subject is in doubt (am I black or white?) he will never manage to check it. That is why Lacan calls it anticipated certainty. It is something that can only be verified through action.

We see that anguish motivates the prisoner's quick conclusion (anguish = conclusion): if I rush to reach a conclusion it is because I fear the delay may lead me to make a mistake, most probably a fatal for me (= a long prison term). Anguish, an emotion you can always rely on in time of trouble, carries with it an intrinsic certainty. What is at stake in the act is extracting certainty from anguish. Haste is the mother off all conclusions.

Lacan's 1945 text posits a different kind of subject for each moment:

1. In the instant of seeing, the subject is noetic (i.e., he knows) and impersonal. The assertive subject simply *is*: it is known that there are two black disks, so one of them must be black. There is an impersonal agent (it is known) during this instance of seeing.
2. During the time for understanding, what is at stake (we see how time started A's thinking process as he puts himself in the shoes of B and C) is the reciprocal indefinite subject who appears on equal footing with the other two (the white disks I see). Here, the Imaginary of otherness is introduced—this other as pure reciprocity because one who recognises himself in it. Thus, we have an indefinite subject who belongs to an imaginary ego (I) that mirrors itself in the other.
3. At the moment of conclusion; the articulated subject (I am white) overlaps with the articulating subject that chooses its identity (because of that, I am this).

Lacan's proposes these moments of logic in action as the logical moment of the subject's genesis: "I rush to present myself as a white one"—this is the crucial moment shaping the subject.

What is relevant to the time issue is the structure of this anticipated certainty present in the subject's assertion wherein the prisoner declares who or what he is. The conclusion's uniqueness in the subjective assertion is the prisoner's certain foreknowledge because the clock is ticking and time is running out. The function of haste speeds up the prisoner's statement regarding his identity.

Prisoner A seizes the moment and concludes he is white while facing the subjective evidence of a delay which pushes him to the cell's exit to win the prize of freedom. If A does not strike while the iron is hot, he will have to face the objective evidence of the others making for the door and mistakenly conclude he is black. In this make-believe sophism, all three prisoners eventually exit the cell and gain their freedom since we are dealing with a fiction based on logical motives, in which there is actually only one real subject who reaches his conclusion at different times.

Shorter sessions, as Lacan theorises, aim at nothing less than speeding up the subject's moment of conclusion, to exit the prison and gain freedom. Truly, analysis fully supports our adage that "haste is the mother of all conclusions."

Of time and neurotics and their hasty conclusions

During sessions, introducing the time structure of anticipated certainty defines analytic time as the counterpoint of the neurotic's time. It is not without reason that neurotics whine so much about short sessions. Hamlet's drama reveals the neurotic's difficulty for action: it is always too late or the time is not right.

For neurotics, the time issue can be associated with the structure of their desire, since the latter is always hindered by its own impasse: unsatisfied desire, in the case of hysteria, and impossible desire in the case of obsessional neurosis. Hysterics always anticipate everything, arrive too early and miss the point while obsessional neurotics postpone everything and wind up arriving too late.

For neurotics, the hour of their desire's "moment of truth" never arrives: they find a way out, escape, hesitate, scurry away or procrastinate. Neurotics are always losing track of time because they are suspended in the Other's time—which is a correlate of their desire to be suspended in the Other's desire: neurotics take their desires from the Other's desires.

According to Lacan, all things in the order of creation take place in discontinuity and are linked more to urgency. Consequently, although there is a time for everything under the sun, modern society undervalues the time to understand and values the moment of conclusion. This latter is the moment time has run out for understanding. Thus, in the hustle and bustle in the fast lane of modern life, the time for understanding is roughly on equal footing with the instant of seeing: it must be instant like our coffee and fast like McDonald's because there is no time to waste.

In the hysteric's trauma fantasy, the Other seduced the subject, taking advantage of his or her immaturity and preventing him or her from reacting: the subject is the victim of the Other's desire. Hysteric subjects seduces but when the time has come for the "moment of truth"—they are the teaser-object who scurry off but keep desire burning through dissatisfaction. The relationship of the subject to the Other's desire brings his or her unique difficulties in time.

Lacan says, "In the case of the neurotic, the Other's demand takes on the function of the object in his fantasy" (ibid, p. 823). During analysis, the neurotic defines time as part of demand. Session cuts are thus interpreted as a resounding No to their demand—always for love, presence, and attention that dovetail with the time and love they feel the Other has denied them. But there is never enough time or love for the neurotic.

Whereas hysterics use delays and absences to make the Other miss them, obsessional analysands refine their work during analysis to closely follow the Other's time and rise up against this Other who supposedly disrespects uniform time and whose whims and tyranny appear in the father-figure of jouissance Freud describes in *Totem and Taboo*.

During the analysis, I have noticed that this complaint ceases when patients achieve the release that comes from cutting all ties with that imaginary Other, since the session cut always points to a lack of something: the subject's lack-of-being or the lacking signifier that would tell them what and who they are, which is always never enough. It is the tension in life's rush that makes us perform our duties and put off the task off until the last minute. It is the final minute that drives us to act.

Lacan's tale of the three prisoners shows the action of the interdependence of individuals. The action of one of them is linked to the action of the other and thus reveals the very logic and essence of mass psychology. Since neurotics are floating in the Other's time zone, it is the action of the analyst as *semblant* of *object a* that will lead patients to open up the floodgates of their signifiers through anticipated certainty. The crucial point for Lacan is how analysts effectively manoeuvre transference, reduce the subject's hesitancy and, speed up the analysand's encounter with the cause of desire made present by the analytical act.

Money

> He (the analyst) can point out that money matters are treated by civilized people in the same way as sexual matters—with the same inconsistency, prudishness and hypocrisy.
>
> —"On Beginning the Treatment", Sigmund Freud

Marilyn Monroe's iconic performance as the showgirl Lorelei Lee singing *Diamonds are a Girl's Best Friend*[4] in 20th Century Fox's blockbuster *Gentlemen Prefer Blondes* (1953) is a prime pop-culture example that shows how libido and capital are swappable. But what do blondes prefer? Why, diamonds!

The musical number takes place on a crimson stage. The voluptuous pink-clad blond bombshell (Marilyn herself) is wearing a sumptuous diamond necklace and oversized diamond bracelets surrounded by a host of mesmerised beaus donning tuxedos and holding flimsy red cardboard heart symbols. Marilyn's glaring shades of pink on red stage evoke sex, but despite her teasing dance, she wants diamonds rather than any form of love. Unlike Marilyn, wagging her talent across the stage, the other women in black are paralysed like statues holding up phallic-like candlesticks.

Lorelei does not give a hoot for the French who would duel and kill for love. Nor do kisses on the hand "*... pay the rent*". She knows the volatility of carnal desire ("*men grow cold*") and is also acutely aware of the impermanence of her own mesmerising beauty: "*As girls grow old.*" But diamonds are forever!

"*But get that ice, or else no dice*" is Lorelei's philosophy of life: there is a price tag on the goods she is flaunting. As the performance progresses, Lorelei's admirers appear, much to her delight, with diamonds to offer her and the scene ends when she tosses a diamond bracelet back at an unhappy man in the audience, a suitor whose diamond bracelet was not big enough for her. So, Lorelei gets her diamonds and the biggest bidders will get her favours. Close curtain (red, of course).

This Hollywood kitsch classic is firmly predicated on capitalistic ideology and also civilisation's discontents. The diamond as the subject's best partner and the desired object appear as nothing more than a prime investment opportunity for that individual. The made-in-Hollywood Marilyn Monroe shows, like the psychoanalytical experience, that libido is cashable. Psychoanalysis demonstrates that capital can be equated with the subject's libido. However, capital is only libido if it can be translated into euros, pounds, dollars and cents which, as we shall see, is indeed the case.

Freud defined libido as a primordial vital energy: that quantitative albeit immeasurable power of the drives which fall under the heading of everything we understand as love (Freud, 1981, p. 151). Furthermore, love is the "[...] dynamic manifestation in the psychic life of the sex drive" (Freud, 1923b, p. 297).

Freud posits that only the *Vorstellungrepräsentantz* of the drive can be pinpointed, namely, the drive's representative *representation*, which is a signifier. This is the one ($) that could be read in the drive's matheme ($ ◊ D) where (D) refers to the signifiers of the oral and anal demands etc. Lacan would later point out the impossibility of any representation of the unconscious in the libido's wide-ranging quantitative power. Hence, the drive's essence is twofold:

$$\text{DRIVE} \begin{cases} \text{Signifier (representative of the } \textit{represention)} \\ \\ \text{Libido (quantitative power)} \end{cases}$$

The libido is that which is understood by its "dynamic manifestation" as *Befriedigung* or the satisfaction present in dreams, symptoms, and hallucinatory states after which the subject's pleasure is paradoxically followed by displeasure: this is jouissance in Lacanian lingo. The sexual drive's satisfaction—I refer to that fulfilment which extinguishes itself on attaining its goal—is impossible since the very object capable of such gratification is forever lost from the very start. Sex only satisfies the drive partially, and due to this impossibility, the drive finds those specific signifier-network derivations (Freud calls them vicissitudes or destinies) that constitute the set of *representations* in the unconscious. Thereafter, the drive seeks its fulfilment in symptoms, dreams and sublimations, and, last but not least, certainty in sexual activity! In Lacanian parlance, this feature of the drive's plasticity is known as "drift". An apt term insomuch as it is akin both to something that has drifted in from another direction after direct sexual satisfaction and also something that is adrift. Thus, Lacanian jouissance semantically enlarges the Freudian concepts of libido and *Befriedigung* that lacks unconscious representation.

Drive signifiers are those which constitute the oral demand for the Other (i.e., "baby-wants-mommy's-breast") and the anal demand from the Other (i.e., "mommy-wants-to-see-baby's-poo-poo"). In transference, the "mommy-baby" relationship characteristic of these same drives is re-enacted under a different guise: the demand for love and interpretation (analysand) and payment (analyst).

What is actually sexual in human beings is something marked by phallic signification. The missing phallus or symbolic castration lends the oral and anal drives etc., their sexual characteristic. But not all of the drive is conjoined with the signifier. Nonetheless, if whatever receives the phallic signification can be represented in the unconscious as a signifier, there still remains the unfathomable jouissance—with all its pain and pleasure—that initial vital (Freud's "quantitative power") driving force that permeates all human activity and actions.

The sex drive is therefore twofold: its unconscious representation (signifiers) and its dynamic manifestation, the very libido which Freud, much to Jung's dismay, always deemed sexual (jouissance). There is a part of the object-cause of desire which the drive aims its guns at but misses. The drive can only dance around this unknown but can never attain or own it. This is Lacan's *object a*: something the sex drive cannot reach or grasp since this object lacks any psychic representation and is only implicitly perceived. *Object a* is the object condenser of jouissance.

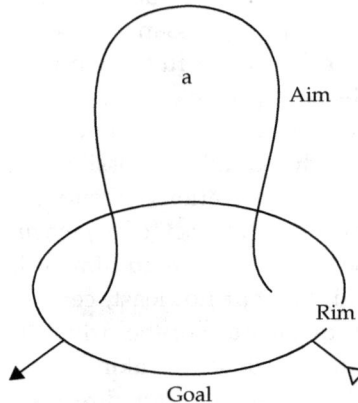

Drive Circuit.

The demand signifiers representative of the drive are the ones unconsciously repressed and ciphered. In analysis, ciphering is equated with putting things into words or signifiers. In the unconscious, the cipher is the business world's equivalent of the final amount after all operations have been tallied up. Drawing a parallel, we can say that the amount as well as the currency sign = the total amount of libidinal operations.

If we analysts attempt to decipher something, we assume the prior reality of something ciphered that can be pinpointed. This feature of the drive is exactly what makes a symptom analysable, since it belongs to the order of language and, as such, a formation of the unconscious.

The libido (the unrepresented part of the drive) is what a symptom seeks to fulfil and what constitutes its twofold resistance: first, to analytical deciphering and second, to being dissolved, because it persists and as jouissance a symptom is a hard to crack.

Therefore, the idea of money and price in analysis brings us to a crossroads where we attempt to decipher signifiers while dealing with the subject's priceless unmeasurable energy which Freud labels libido. The fees analysts charge allows them to calculate the subject's libido in purely monetary terms. If, on the unconscious level, what belongs to the process of ciphering tallies up with the figures of a business transaction, capitalism equates the amount and the currency sign with the total value libido at work in the subject. Is this true?

Capital, value, and money

According to the *Dictionnaire Littré* capital "[...] is the fruit of labour". A handy definition of capital which I can paraphrase as the set of fulfilment means gained from previous work. Current usage defines capital as the wealth we own and, figuratively, as the set of goods (intellectual, spiritual or moral) belonging to any person or country.

The very thing whose excellence stems from its universal exchange value—money—can be accumulated or dispersed. Furthermore, money can also serve as a metonym for the type of capital (as part of it) I am discussing herein or as a metaphor, i.e., the thing which substitutes this capital by representing it. In a nutshell, money is libido. Money circulates according to the laws of language.

"Capital appears as a mysterious source; as the creator of profit and source of its own growth. The thing (money, good, value) in itself is already capital, and capital shows itself to be a simple thing" (Marx, 1984, pp. 293–294). That is what Marx, for whom almighty capital is the *primum movens* of work, says. Our philosopher posits a relationship between capital and work that links money—the object-fruit-of-one's labours—and its ownership: "All the productive forces of social work appear as capital, in the same way that the social form of work generally appears in money as the property of a thing." Whatever bestows value to an object is the work "quantum" or the "[...] time of work needed, in a given society, for the production of an article" (Marx, K. Quoted in: Martin, 1984). "Time is money" has an aptly Marxist ring to it.

The difference between value attributed to abstract work and the use value corresponding to concrete work is what we can call the exploitation of work. It is the surplus value employees generate for the boss without getting paid for it. In our system, it is precisely this value—sucked out of the worker—that is left over from the equation, time = money. Just like a magician and his bag of tricks, capitalism's time-as-money ideology performs a disappearing act with surplus value by cleverly hiding time that could be accountable in any bookkeeping system.

Marx showed that this surplus value—"the great secret of modern society"—governs the capitalist-proletariat relationship and which is irreducible to the value = time-of-work equation:

> Surplus value production is, therefore, only the production of value prolonged beyond a certain point. If the work process only

> continues up to the point where a new equivalent is exchanged for
> the value capital pays the work-force then there is merely a simple
> production of value, but when it oversteps this boundary, surplus
> value is produced. (Marx, 1969, p. 51)

For Marx, we exchange money for the sum total of nature and our objective world. Money can be swapped for everything and anything under the sun: it can not only buy all things, it can appropriate them as well. Ownership's privileged object is a four-letter word: c-a-s-h.

But what is really exchanged is the lack-of-jouissance. The exchange object has a twofold characteristic: first, it is something which an individual can enjoy but does not want to since he or she is not satisfied by it use value and wishes to get rid of it and, second, something which he or she wants but cannot enjoy because he or she does not own it or its use value. For both parties, the exchange value of goods is actually the lack-of-jouissance (Naveau, 1988, pp. 112–114).

All goods can be exchanged. But the one thing—Money—excluded from the set of goods, becomes their "general equivalent" and is an exception that represents the rest.

Surplus value produced by extended proletarian work shifts is the Other's surplus jouissance. It is the "[…] cause of desire whereof an economy—one of extensive and thus insatiable production—of the lack-of-jouissance" (Lacan, 1970, p. 87).

Money is a representation of libido, because like the latter, there's never enough of it. This is why Lacan says, perhaps tongue-in-cheek, that the rich cannot be analysed since they lack nothing and can get everything.

Surplus value in analysis

In psychoanalysis, dream interpretation represents the signifier's work on jouissance, namely, the casting of jouissance into a linguistic mould. This is "significantisation": the way of ciphering jouissance through language. But just what product does this work end up producing? *Object a*, that is to say, the leftover jouissance after this operation: the remainder, the left-over dregs and trash. This ciphering could be summed up like this:

$$\frac{\text{Language}}{\text{Jouissance}} \rightarrow \textit{object a}$$

Object a is language's effect on jouissance. In other words, the metaphorisation of jouissance has a leftover which is *object a*. When the signifier ciphers the jouissance, a surplus value pops up: *object a* or that object which is surplus-jouissance. Besides deciphering, analysis should take ciphering to the brink and "[...] push jouissance into the Unconscious, namely, that dimension where it can be accounted for [...]" (Lacan, 1970, p. 72). Beyond all possible utterances during the analytical experience, there remains a leftover that resists any ciphering: *object a*, an object lacking any substance, albeit quite real. This is the final product of the analytical process. Lacan considered *object a* an object, but only when imagined in an object-subject relationship. Just because *object a* is the product of language does not mean it is inside language: *object a* is to language what the inside hole is to the doughnut (this is the topological figure of the torus). The locus of *object a* is the "inside outsideness" of language. Moreover, as soon as the subject gets a glimpse of *object a*, the latter has already evaporated like a drop of water in the hot desert.

Picture your everyday worker exerting himself on raw materials and producing an object for someone else. From our perspective as analysts, we ask: "what is the thing that only the subject him or herself can enjoy without ownership?" The answer is *object a*: the product of the signifier's exertion on an irretrievably lost object of jouissance. If we imagine the worker model and the Master–Slave dialectic, *object a* represents the surrendering of jouissance, a function that stems from the order of discourse rather than the orders of the Master. In my attempt to map out the money issue, let us take again the structure of the four discourses:

$$\frac{[agent] \rightarrow [other]}{[truth] \quad [production]}$$

Let us picture an agent who, following some principles he or she considers right or true, acts on another person (the other) to obtain something (the production). Following the MD we represent this agent as S_1 or the Boss who acts over the employee (S_2) performing the work. The product of this relationship is *object a* whose surplus or left-over value must be relinquished by S_1 for S_2's jouissance. According to the MD, this relationship can be expressed as:

$$\frac{S_1}{\cancel{S}} \rightarrow \frac{S_2}{a}$$

Here Lacan conflates the MD with that of the unconscious, which is itself a maze of signifiers whose existence we only perceive through its multifarious formations (jokes, word play, dreams, symptoms, etc.). These formations are the host of invisible witnesses of the desiring subject who inhabits the unconscious. The surplus product of these unconscious formations is Freud's *Wunscherfüllung*. The unconscious is the around-the-clock, full-time, non-stop employee that every boss dreams about. No holidays, vacations or complaints: all work and no play.

The unconscious is that tireless workaholic on the graveyard shift who burns the midnight oil even while we sleep. The unconscious is capitalism's ideal worker since it does not think, judge, nor tally up figures: it just works ... and keeps on ticking like the Timex watch. The unconscious produces surplus or left-over jouissance.

In analysis, this *object a* (*plus-de-jouir*) is granted agency that causes $\cancel{S}$ to produce those primordial signifiers (S_1) which alienate the subject. Hence the AD matheme:

$$\frac{a}{S_2} \rightarrow \frac{\cancel{S}}{S_1} \downarrow$$

Lacan translated the Marxist market-place-surplus value function as the surrender of jouissance and this act of giving something up will appear likewise in *object a*'s surplus jouissance function. In the marketplace of the Other, someone will always grab the surplus jouissance. However, one agent gains ownership of the jouissance because many others have surrendered it.

As surplus jouissance (*plus-de-jouir*) *object a* is produced for but is not owned by the Other. Someone who wants something but cannot have it is bound to fantasise about it. These fantasies involve the subject's relationship to this object ($S \lozenge a$) in the form of an answer to yearnings and desire for the Other. Somehow *object a*—the drive's target—always belongs to the Other the way the subject imagines it to. Analysis aims at making subjects aware that the Other does not have or own anything either. The Other is hollow.

This quick overview maps our initial approach to the subject of money. Since my thesis here is to see capital as libido and vice-versa, we shall recognise how powerful a cipher money becomes in its role as a representational construct of jouissance. Let us now examine capitalist discourse.

Capitalistic discourse

Like Freud in *Civilization and its Discontents*, Lacan expresses in "Television" his own discontent with civilisation, equating it with capitalist discourse. In 1970, Lacan declared that modern MD belonged to the UD, but four years later proposed capitalism's discourse as the source of society's discontent. I believe this has all become much clearer after the 1989 fall of the Berlin Wall and the collapse of non-capitalist societies and ensuing globalisation. According to Jean Baudrillard in *The Consumer Society: Myths and Structure* (1970), nowadays we exist as witnesses to the feverish and rampant consumerism and the abundance of multiplying objects in which the wealthy no longer surround themselves with other individuals as a sign of rank and distinction, but prefer consumable objects (planes, yachts, mansions, cell phones, gadgets, etc.). Our social relationships are no longer based on social bonds with others, but instead on how we receive and consume goods and information. "I consume, therefore I am" could be an apt catchphrase for our age and society.

Capitalist discourse does not bond individuals together, but rather proposes an interactive relationship between a gadget—a quick consumable thing like a Big Mac—and the subject reduced to a consumer. Indeed, this discourse induces a kind of autism and incitement to self-gratification by short-circuiting the desire of the Other and supplying an illusion of completeness—instead of a love partner, you have a partner you can switch on and off with your hand like in the film *Her* (2013) where a troubled man falls in love with a computer programme that simulates a love life for him. Lacan formulates capitalist discourse as a shift from the MD. He only wrote it on the blackboard once (in Milan, 1974), inverting S_1 and $\cancel{S}$ and introducing a new arrow:

$$\left\downarrow \frac{\cancel{S}}{S_1} \diagdown\!\!\!\!\diagup \frac{S_2}{a} \downarrow\right.$$

Here it is possible to see how *object a* as a gadget, linked to the subject ($\cancel{S}$) is the actual cause of the individual's desire. The consumables (all that stuff money can buy) are the squatters on *object a*'s property and are produced by scientific-technological knowledge (S_2), financed by capital (S_1), which is the Master signifier in this discourse and social bond. Capital is the bigwig and alienating "truth" and instead of split subjects we have insatiable consumers who cannot decide on the brand or product to purchase.

$$\left|\frac{\text{Consumer}}{\text{Capital}}\right. \quad \times \quad \left.\frac{\text{Techno-Science}}{\text{Gadgets}}\right|$$

In this network, consumers earn wages—probably the sole motivation for facing the daily rigmarole—and their money enters the market and, like venture capital, finances the knowledge that cranks out the latest most popular gadgets that become the subject's objects of desire. This capitalist subject/object complementary pairing expresses something specific to this discourse: a kind of social bond that forecloses (*forclusion*) castration. In other words, a bond that radically denies the desired object's structural lack.

Capitalistic discourse eggs you on to own and enjoy these objects, yet at the same time, you are a Johnny-come-lately because you will never have the latest, fanciest or most awesome gadget, since as each day passes, a newer, better and more powerful one is invented and released on the market. A society ruled by capitalistic discourse will fatally feature a lack of jouissance because mass production of countless gadgets also produces hordes of insatiable subjects wanting those same things. This is the economy whose capital is its libido. Furthermore, surplus value tacked onto the consumerist cause of desire can potentially turn each individual into his fellow man's exploiter since unpaid work can generate profit. The popular American expression—"You have to watch out for Number One"—sums up narcissistic capitalism wherein the only pronouns are "I", "Me", and "Mine."

In this cycle, surplus value coincides with the objects of surplus jouissance which, says Lacan, is the cause of desire found at the root of an economy ruled by capitalistic social bonds. But it is a jouissance which, albeit promised, is structurally unattainable. The result is the dog-eat-dog world with its rampant deception, unbearable sadness, depression, boredom, annoyance, and nostalgia for the One promised in vain. Not to mention all those varieties of substance abuse and addiction. These are diseases (or illnesses) brought on by capitalist discourse. When a social bond produces a subject driven by capitalist desire, the Master signifier will soon appear in the form of the love of money. This subject lacking being is transformed into a subject lacking money and the lack of jouissance can equated with the lack of money. Thus, capitalist discourse produces the money-crazed, but actually miserably de-capitalised, impoverished and bankrupt subject.

Capitalism's discourse differs from that of the MD because the latter establishes a bond between the one giving the orders and other obeying and working, as Hegel accurately demonstrates in the master-and-slave dialectic. There the desire of the master is coupled with the other's desire in a social bond that encompasses life and death, work and the production of objects/labour. In the Hegelian dialectic, the transforming knowledge is the slave's work. In capitalistic discourse, however, the bond between the post-modern Master (the capitalist) and the proletarian is severed. The figure of the capitalist tends to fade and be replaced by the impersonal figure of globalised capital: the absolute post-modern taskmaster who replaces the Hegelian figure. In this society, Lacan theorises, we are all proletarians. The great equaliser nowadays is no longer death itself but capital. To have is to live, to lack is to die even before your time.

Capitalist discourse overshadows our age, superimposes the market onto society, for there is no more society except the market, which according to Adam Smith, is an invisible but all-pervading hand. This invisible grasp that regulates the market is regulation-less, for there is no law, only imperatives which are the signs of upcoming castration. Market regulation is so impossible, that even a mega-investor and market-shaker like George Soros himself is left aghast by the highs and lows he brought on. Rather than mirroring reality, financial markets actively create a reality they later end up reflecting. This is a nightmarish example of how discourses actually structure reality. Soros describes the impersonal face of capitalism as an immense circulatory system that sucks in capital for financial markets and central institutions and regurgitates this money—nowadays quite virtual—again under the guise of investment portfolios, credit, and multinationals (Soros, 1998).

Capitalist discourse is therefore *not* a social bond that regulates or institutionalises anything: its politics are neoliberal and everyone looks out for number one and fights all comers for a piece of the pie. In such a scenario, there is no place for everyone under the sun. Capitalist discourse is "segregationist"—I use the term here in a capitalist and not racial sense—rather than regulatory. Lumping everyone under the heading of consumer and promoting market-driven segregation is the sole way capitalist discourse can paradoxically treat diversity and difference in our consumer-oriented and scientific society. You either have access to the products of science or you do not; it is therefore not a discourse which exactly implies a social bond. Hence, the proliferation of the "haves" and the masses of "have nots": the something-or-other (land-, job-, home-, etc.) less people in our society. The "in crowd" of capitalistic discourse is actually "out", for capitalism produces a blatant lack through the illusion of abundance and consumers unable to gauge the depths of their impoverishment.

The AD is the flip-side of capitalist discourse because it shows consumable gadgets are fake *objects a* and "capital" a poor surrogate for the subject's truth. Furthermore, the AD stresses that the subject's lack is structural and aims at "de-alienating" the analysand from those primordial signifiers. As such, it brings its main focus to bear on lack and castration and encourage subjects to engender their own uniqueness through the "de-alienating" process aimed at severing the bonds with the Other's Master signifier. Now it is time to go back to Freud's conditions to begin analysis.

Necessity, demand, and desire

In "On Beginning the Treatment", Freud broaches the topic of money—the fourth condition of analysis:

> The next point that must be decided at the beginning of treatment is the one of money, of the doctor's fee. An analyst does not dispute that money is to be regarded, in the first instance as a medium for self-preservation and for obtaining power; but he maintains that, besides this, powerful sexual factors are involved in the value set upon it. (Freud, 1913c, p. 131)

This tidbit of wisdom aptly condenses the money issue and serves as our compass here.

Regarding this monetary prerequisite for analysis, Freud mentions self-preservation—which I translate as something belonging to the order of necessity as an incarnation of power and, concomitantly, a manifestation of sex. Here we must bear in mind that for Freud sex is split into desire (d) and demand (D) to/from the Other (A):

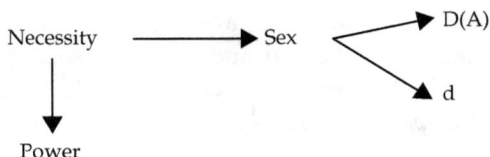

$$\text{Necessity} \longrightarrow \text{Sex} \begin{cases} \longrightarrow D(A) \\ \longrightarrow d \end{cases}$$
$$\downarrow$$
$$\text{Power}$$

Here we divide capital into five functions: necessity, power, demand (for love), desire (sexual and unconscious) and the all-pervading, ever-present jouissance. Let us see how money has all of them.

1) Necessity or *primum vivere* (or "I gotta pay the bills").

 If you want to live, you have to give ... money. We all have bills to pay: rent, gas, food, clothes, education, entertainment, etc. Everything in our life requires money. If hugs, kisses, poetry, and music sufficed, analysis too would follow suit. But capitalism dances to the tune of money for its show to go on.

2) Money as a sign of power (or "I wanna sugar-daddy").

 The sign (the linguistic element) represents *something to someone*. But money is also a sign of power and status since the phallic mark is written all over it. As such, money—as well as the things that give you purchasing power—is the phallic symbol representing the ownership of jouissance. Yet, it also conceals a blatant gap (*manqué-à-avoir*, a lack of being) in that ownership hides the castration through the illusion that if you have money, you can get anything. The wealthy use their luxurious yachts, oversized mansions, glittering rings, flashy watches, stream-lined sports cars, flamboyant wardrobes, etc., as powerful phallic symbols of privileged and differentiated being. They do not call it the jet set for nothing. Like characters in a trashy Jackie Collins novel, the ostentatious swagger of the *nouveau riche*, the not-so-handsome old millionaire alongside his twenty-year-old "knock-out" wife, and the attitude of the beautiful woman who treats men as exchange objects—exactly as Marilyn Monroe does in her Hollywood number—all illustrate capital's undeniable and penetrating phallic power in our society.

3) Money as the sign of love (or "love and money go together").

 Money can be a token of love when we give and ask for it. This we see in the prototypical "mommy-wants-to-see-baby's-poo-poo" situation. But the "gorgeous-sweetheart-wants-diamonds" situation is not so much a sign of love because love is a "giving what one does not have" according to Lacan. That lack is ably symbolised by diamonds—those most precious of stones. But there is a love which is also the giving of money we ourselves may need to a loved one. Furthermore, you can also give gifts as a demand for love—"How about giving daddy here something in exchange for those glitzy diamonds, sugar lips?" Giving means so many things: it can be a demand someone makes to be acknowledged as a generous, kind, and helpful person. Here, the very open-handed giver actually wants love in return. A kind of "scratch-my-back-I'll-scratch-yours" *modus operandi*. To cut a long story short: money appears under the guise of one of our demand objects and is therefore equated with and conveyed as love.

What specifies money in this register is not the demand but the delivery of money. Money plays the role of one of those objects we can ask for: a demanded object that acquires a value conveyed as a sign of love.

4) Money as a signifier (or "money-talks").

Money pops up as a signifier in the subject's associative chain as we shall see later. As a signifier, money also represents so many different things that it cannot be represented by any single signifier. Money signifies no one thing and paradoxically everything under the sun at the same time. For each person, money comes to mean a different thing: for some it represents independence from drudgery for the pursuit of higher aims, for others a time to party and rock and roll, and for others, like Donald Duck's old skinflint Uncle Scrooge, an endless quest of mean-spirited hoarding of sacks of gold coins that are not doing anyone any good.

5) The jouissance of money (or "money makes me feel so good").

Money jouissance—the *plus-de-jour* or surplus value of cash—is the true libidinisation of capital for the speaking subject—the "sexual factor" proper which belongs to the drive.

Everything we view as necessity oozes with demand and desire. A prototypical image would be to picture ourselves starving. Through language, hunger—a basic necessity—blows up to the proportion of a desperate pursuit of food (oral drive). The statement "I'm starving" is an utterance masked as a demand for the Other as well as an expression of our own basic necessity. Humans transcend the mere biological urges of animals that, when hungry, eat and satisfy their bodily needs. But humans can be hungry and they can also be grotesquely gluttonous as the Roman vomitoriums show us.

Freud never denies the manifold registers of human necessity and carefully examines our "self-preservation drives." However, the imperative nature of basic necessity (if you do not eat, you die) passes through other registers of demand and desire. If every necessity has a specific correlating object (breathing/oxygen, appetite/food, fatigue/sleep, etc.), in the speaking being, the signification of necessity and its coupling to the drive distort the specific correlate object as it is transformed by language into voracious desire or demand. Unlike animals, we do not have a perfect object that can satisfy us. The object is lost and entirely non-existent and, in its place, our lack and castration take centre stage.

Culture implies that, in our psychic life, language semantically broadens the range of human necessity, and thus money for us goes beyond mere immediate physical survival or basic needs. The very idea of money already denotes a symbolic transaction of objects and goods: language is, therefore money is (the thing). Asserting that the financially impoverished cannot do analysis is to treat them like animals and to reduce the money issue to mere necessity. The wealthy—if we consider those who lack none of the finer things this world has to offer—are far less suitable subjects for analysis than the poor.

While necessity spotlights the subject's dimension of absence and lack of having, demand and desire unveil another feature in the subject: lack of being. The object complementing the Other, the object of the Other's desire, lacks being. My desired object is lost and that is why all the surrogates of this object do not give me any satisfaction. The same process occurs with love.

Money desired and demanded is a globe trotter carrying its gaping lack-of-being everywhere. Indeed, we see money as a key entry in Freud's catalogue of symbolic equivalences which conflate lack with objects such as breasts, penises, children, gifts, and, of course, the baby's poo-poo for mommy, among others. As residents in the city of castration, these objects must inevitably be listed in the Freudian phallic *Yellow Pages*.

Money too plays an important role in ciphering jouissance. This is what allows Freud's "Rat Man" to conflate money and rodents—"[…] so many Florins, so many rats" (Freud, 1909d, p. 213). is the formula of the Rat Man's obsessional neurosis. The "rats" are creatures ciphered by money and this link is made possible by the homophony between the words in German *ratten* (rats) and *raten* (instalment payments). This is what lies beneath the Rat Man's difficulty in paying off his debt, which is his symptom.

The Rat Man's big hang-up and obsession is centred on the gruesome tale of torture told by the "cruel captain" who ties up the victim, shoves a funnel up the latter's anus and then drops in some rats that bore their way through and pierce his intestines. The Rat Man's obsession was the thought that one of his loved ones was undergoing this torture. Freud pinpointed the symptom's jouissance in the expression the patient used in his description—which translated the "[...] horror of something he was unaware of"—and also during analysis revealing the patient's childhood anal eroticism, whose fundamental role was reinforced by prolonged bouts of intestinal worms (Freud, 1909d, p. 167).

Analysis here allowed Freud to decipher the link between the terrifying torture image and the symptom of having to pay an impossible debt. From the signifying equation, rat = debt payments, Freud made the link rat-money-paternal inheritance. Moreover, analysis uncovered a further signifying chain: rat-syphilis infection-father-penis-worms. This final chain, according to Freud, is a phallic series since it shows the rat's phallic significance. Nevertheless, Freud insisted on deciphering the chain's jouissance as a form of anal eroticism (Freud, 1909). The "money complex" takes on an obsessive character through implied anal jouissance: money thus becomes a drive.

Therefore, as the surrogate for the object representing lack—castration (–φ)—money forms part of the series of objects detached from the body:

$$\frac{\text{Breast}}{-\varphi}, \frac{\text{Faeces}}{-\varphi}, \frac{\text{Penis}}{-\varphi}, \frac{\text{Money}}{-\varphi}$$

The lack (φ) here is represented by its object-metaphors: money being yet one more among the many possible metaphors to represent desire's implied lack.

Another variation could be desire as a metonym for capital, where the relentless desire for something else is endless. In the capitalist mode, this is desire's relentless pursuit, moving from one consumable to the next, *ad infinitum, ad nauseum* ...

We kid ourselves if we think that desirable consumer goods are unrelated to *object a*. We do not have to go to Amsterdam's red light district to see showcased prostitutes to grasp the relationship between "eye candy" in a shop window and *object a*. This can also be seen in the endless ads that attempt to titillate our senses and tease us in such a way that we feel we must have the latest gizmo. Consumable goods can be imaginary-object surrogates for *object a*, or: $\frac{i(a)}{-\varphi}$ where *i* stands for any available marketable commodity desired and *a* the lack. Money as capital's metonym always appears as a substitute for *object a.*

The prostitution fantasy

Freud's statement—"money involves powerful sexual factors"—simply means that money and libido make good bedfellows.

It has always been possible to swap money for sex: in the noble courts of ancient Rome, on a shady street corner or some out-of-the way massage parlour in London or on Rio de Janeiro's tropical and sunny boardwalk known as Avenida Atlântica. In this line of business, love is not at stake: relations of this kind are in fact devoid of love and marked by the "if-you-want-to play-you've-got-to-pay" (prostitute) and "I'm-picking-up-the-bill-so-I'd-better-get-my-fill" (customer) attitude. Customers dish out their cash not only to keep love at bay, but above all, to rent a body to indulge their fantasies: the body they purchase to fulfil their desire is not driven by the same desire for the customer's body, but for something else: money.

Sex professionals have many games and tools to help enact the customer's fantasy and enable phallic jouissance. And customers pay for that jouissance. Money can help fulfil a fantasy and to sidestep the enigmatic nature of the desire of the Other. Some analysands harbour the fantasy that paying their analyst is like a prostitute-customer transaction. The analysand may fall prey to this fantasy because he or she feels that paying grants him or her the right to avoid the analyst's desire—that act that aims at drawing out of the analysand the manifestation of the desire of the Other. Analysts oppose this idea from the start of analysis and do not succumb to the analysand's fantasy. Rather, they draw out the enigmatic dimension of the desire of/for the Other. In other words, analysts bring into play the x of the equation of desire. The analyst's desire opposes fantasy jouissance by revealing the hollowness and structural lack inherent in desire.

In no way can analysts and prostitutes be lumped together. The latter know and should have all the know-how necessary for customer jouissance. The analyst, however, working against the grain of the fantasy and jouissance, attempts to enable the analysand to catch a glimpse of a hidden landscape of unflagging desire and lack.

By charging, analysts show their act is not aimed at making the analysand an object of their own jouissance, their research project or a means of gaining prestige in some prestigious psychoanalytical society. Payment shows that something of the analyst's own desire as an individual is cashable; after all we live and work in a capitalist society. Both the analyst and analysand have desires which can be partially fulfilled through a financial transaction. We are paid not to give satisfaction but to point out a lack.

When analysts charge, they are working towards undoing the subject's problematical jouissance in two ways: first, by refusing to give in to the analysand's fantasy and second by not enjoying the analysand as an object of the jouissance of their private lives (i.e., as sexually desirable objects or subjects for scientific curiosity). Money in analysis serves as a deterrent for the patient's jouissance in order to make desire prevail. Like a parachute that softens the impact without completely breaking it, it is a para-jouissance. And like a "stopgap", it exists for lack of anything else: it is a stop-jouissance.

Division of the subject and the analyst's ethics

According to Freud "[...] He (the analyst) can point out that money matters are treated by civilized people in the same way as sexual matters—with the same inconsistency, prudishness and hypocrisy" (Freud, 1913c, p. 131).

The Standard Edition translates *Wiespaltigkeit* as "inconsistency" but a more accurate translation would be "duplicity" and the connotations of ambiguity of a two-faced or split being, since Lacan translates the root of *Spaltung* as the subject's division. Duplicity is inherent to the split subject: the "I-want-it/I-don't-want-it" dialectics are inherent in ambitions and desiring things such as trips, marriages and are a feature and translation of desire and its accompanying lack. And so is ambiguity: the "I'm-rich/I'm-poor" related to the fear of not having or losing money. Freud spotted this split in his "Rat Man", whose doubt about marrying a rich woman or a poor one is a classic case study of psychic cleavage in the personality.

Questions of money and those of sex actually divide the subject. In both cases, as we saw previously regarding the meaning of money for different individuals, the same holds true for sex: each person's relationship with sex is unique. From our standpoint as analysts, Freud offers some wisdom for the analyst:

> The analyst is therefore determined from the first not to fall in with this attitude, but in his dealings with his patients to treat money matters with the same matter-of course frankness to which he wishes to educate them in things relating to sexual life. He shows them that he himself has cast off false shame on these topics, by voluntarily telling them the price at which he values his time. (Freud, 1913c, p. 131).

Regarding hypocrisy, Freud rejects the stance of the disinterested philanthropist, since such a position would actually be damaging to the analyst since it puts the analysand in the role of persecutor, that is, one who exploits an analyst who imagines the analysand as someone in need of a hand-out or a favour.

Freud further develops arguments against free analysis and stresses the harm it would cause: "[...] nothing in life is so expensive as sickness and stupidity" (Freud, 1913c, p. 133). This witticism clearly equates sickness and analysis in monetary terms because both are cashable.

Sickness and stupidity—the latter as a stubborn refusal to want to know—fall in the domain of psychoanalysis: all symptoms are in fact cashable. Like the diamonds for the character played by Marilyn Monroe in the movie, symptoms are a neurotic's best friends.

Benefits gained from symptoms

Symptoms are the diamonds of the neurotic's unconscious display case. And neurotics love them with the passion of a fervent lover. They are the neurotic's juicy investment opportunity and the accruing saving account at the First National Bank of Libido. This is what Freud calls the "prime benefit" of the symptom and Lacan, its jouissance.

Neurotics gain a twofold benefit (profit) from this libidinal economy. The primary perk is that symptoms deliver libidinal satisfaction: subjects are going to invest their libidinal venture capital in that terrific start-up company that provides the best dividends: Symptoms Ltd. No wonder Freud says that getting sick entails an economy of psychic force. Sickness is the path of least resistance and the cheapest and most convenient solution when mental conflict arises. One inevitably gains some kind of edge and advantage from mental sickness. Sickness and symptoms are the easiest way of dealing with libidinal conflict, but they are, psychically speaking, too expensive because they take their toll through suffering and pain.

The secondary bonus can be seen in the subject's relationship with others. Initially, the symptom is felt as the intrusion of a foreign body or Freud's "undesirable guest". Afterwards, subjects find ways of exploiting to their full advantage the symptom beyond its drive fulfilment.

Freud's metaphor for the secondary benefit is expressed precisely as a monetary benefit. As a case study, he describes someone who, as a result of some mishap, is crippled and becomes a beggar. On first impulse, the beggar refuses corrective surgery because he would lose the benefits of begging for a living. The symptom then moves its luggage into an intersubjective zone and finds a comfortable place where the beggar may continue his profitable panhandling. Thus, the amputated legs for the legless beggar come to represent the same subject in relation to the social Other. Any corrective measure for restoring his ability to walk again would cancel out the very thing that represents the subject's $\left(\dfrac{S_1}{\cancel{S}} \right)$ new-found mobility. Freud very straightforwardly links the secondary benefit to financial gain.

The transference of money

In analysis, capital transference takes place from the symptom to an object: the analyst. Instead of "being paid" for his symptom, the analysand must pay for it and transfer capital to the analyst. Furthermore, the transference of money entails a libido transference in which the analysand comes to "fall in love" with the analyst.

The first effect during the analytical cure is a break, a chokehold on the formerly thriving economy of jouissance by demanding payment from the subject. We all know how difficult it is for analysands to increase the number of sessions, which would mean more money for the analyst. Although this stubbornness can be related to the urgency of everyday necessity, it is certainly entangled at the level of the libido and the symptom's jouissance. Freud attributes his initial concept of resistance to the subject's conscious stance against analytical deciphering of the unconscious and then proceeds to uncover that its mainspring is no longer in the ego. Later, he discovers that most powerful resistance flows forth from the Id in the form of a refusal to give up the jouissance embedded in sickness. This powerful attitude can easily impede the beneficial effects of analysis and can even shatter the analytical bond.

In analysis, subjects pay to transfer capital from their own solid and trustworthy First National Bank of Symptoms to a totally unknown institution called the analyst. What guarantees do they have? No matter how skilled, renowned, humane and empathetic the analyst is, the Other cannot guarantee, promise or indeed, ensure even the slightest thing in analysis. No wonder subjects are recalcitrant against paying the analysts with money because they already have a safe haven for their capital invested in the symptom.

Although money works well enough to cash in the capital of a subject's libido, the price for treatment (beyond the basic level of necessity) cannot be lowered. It is only when the price is high for subjects that they can equate it with the price of their symptoms (as Freud so aptly stated). Analysts cannot have a fixed price for each analysand since this would shift their practice from the level of the libido—in the strictest Freudian sense—to that of mere services where one hour of this means one hour of that.

Paying the price

If symptoms are the subject's easiest and most immediate investment for libido capital, why set up an appointment with an analyst?

At the first stage, subjects become aware that they are paying an exorbitant price for their symptom in terms of cost/benefit. Symptoms are, in fact, commitments and formations of the unconscious. The symptom's jouissance is paradoxical: it brings both pleasure and pain (it is the satisfaction of an impossible desire). But there comes a point when the commitment is broken and pain brings on an imbalance in libidinal economy that can lead the subject to seek out (but not always) professional help. This first stage alone, however, will not suffice to do the trick.

A second stage becomes necessary: subjects chose to try to decipher the hang-up and assume there is indeed a ciphered meaning embedded in the symptom which is now afflicting them. Finally, the third stage: subjects become aware their problem is not physiological or religious but purely subjective.

I cannot stress enough the importance of the subject's awareness of the need of deciphering the symptom's problems and understanding the nature of ciphers about his or her own position in life as a subject, about sex, desire, demand, etc. This assumption will lead subjects to make their own choices about meaning(s). This stage can be equated with that causal operation Lacan calls alienation in *Seminar* XI. Thus, the subject chooses to decipher his or her own alienation caused by the signifier from the Other. It begins with questions like: "What is happening to me?" or "Why am I hurting so much inside?" With this should come the awareness of the pain and, consequently, the individual's acceptance of the idea of paying an analyst to address his or her personal issues.

Initial beneficial effects at the clinic may be Imaginary, Symbolic or Real or a combination thereof. Certainly, one of the positive effects is the analysand's sensation of relief during analysis. Let us see how all this works:

- The Imaginary level expresses itself in terms of transference love— reciprocity, the act of loving and being loved—in which subjects love and feel that their grievances are being heard and their pain empathetically understood.
- The Symbolic level spans the signifying chain through free association where the analyst is equated with the Other and becomes the target for the subject's signifiers.
- The Real level is the rearranging of libido. The effect of the real transfers the pain of the symptom to the pain of payment. Here, the subject pays—and money is the means thereof—for an object—the analyst—to be "produced" and "consumed". Subjects pays for an analyst as they would pay for some nice thing they want to enjoy. And analysts also sell themselves initially as an object with a price tag and a cashable commodity/service on a price-per-session basis.

The analyst thus becomes a libidinally endowed consumer object and agrees to accept cash for such status. From a capitalist standpoint, this all makes sense and it is also the same perspective of the economic function of the unconscious and the libido network. Through transference, analysts are something to be bought or hired. They provide the ride for the subjects who are their passengers. There is no room for being thrifty, stingy or miserly here, since the cheaper the product, the cheaper the jouissance. That means that a petty skinflint mentality can be equated with a kind of retention that breaks the golden law of free association: if we hold something back we clip the wings of free association.

The only way to perform analysis is by investing your all. Nothing can remain outside the realm of analysis without making it self-defeating. Expenditures of time and money reflect those of the libido corresponding to the symptom's haemorrhage of jouissance and its simultaneous transference to the analyst. In conclusion, besides being a transference of signifiers, analysis is also a libido transference in terms of capital and money.

Why do analysts charge?

"If we didn't charge, we could enter into the drama of Atreus and Thyestes which is that of all subjects who come to us to confide their truth" (Lacan, 1964, p. 257). Not charging gives us a free pass into the tragedy of the analysands; it is as if we kept a stolen letter we wanted to throw away. But charging a fee allows analysts to step out of this game and still deal with the tragedies (Lacan, 1964, p. 267).

Crebillon's eighteenth century tragedy *Atreus and Thyestes* showcases a particular theme contained in the verse: "A destiny so tragic, if not worthy of Atreus, is worthy of Thyestes." In the play, Atreus is first betrayed by his own brother and later murdered by his putative son. As for Thyestes, he eats his own sons.

This ancient legend tells the story of two brothers at odds with each other because each is vying for the throne of Mycenae. They are fratricidal brothers, egged on by a cunning and bloodthirsty mother to slay their half-brother, the offspring of their father's adulterous infatuation with a nymph.

When the throne was made vacant in ancient Mycenae, an oracle exhorted the people to choose one the two siblings as King. Both of them issued a wager: Thyestes proposed that the one who could deliver a golden fleece be made King. Atreus immediately accepted, since in his flock he owned a golden-fleeced sheep that he commanded to be slain and placed in safe-keeping. Atreus was not aware that his wife was having an affair with Thyestes and had purloined the prize (the sheep) and given it to her lover. When Thyestes triumphantly shows up with it, Atreus loses the wager but still suspects nothing about his wife's hanky-panky.

As gods often do, Zeus takes pity on Atreus and whispers to him that he should propose his own wager: that the true King should be the one who can change the path of the sun. Well, Zeus performs his supernatural legerdemain and thanks to this big pal from on high, Atreus becomes King and Thyestes is banished.

It is only later when Atreus realises his brother's betrayal, and, under the false pretence of a letting bygones be bygones, he summons Thyestes to the Royal Court. Meanwhile on the sly, Atreus kills Thyestes's three sons, chops them up like a butcher, and prepares a banquet in honour of his prodigal brother. After Thyestes had his fill at what he thinks must be the best steak house in Mycenae, Atreus pulls out the amputated heads of the three slain sons and banishes his double-crossing brother again.

Crebillon's tragedy ends there, but according to the legend, Thyestes makes it to Cyane and, hopping into the sack with Pelopia—who is not aware she is his daughter—gets her pregnant and has a son named Egistus (!). The incest increases when Pelopia then marries her uncle Atreus, who entrusts Egisto to bump off Thyestes. Luckily, Egistus finds out soon enough that his real father is Thyestes so he returns to Mycenae, where he slays Atreus and delivers the throne to Thyestes. This is the kind of real hard-core ancient Greek soap opera that makes our family dramas look like kids' stuff.

Why this gruesome story? If the analyst does not charge, he enters the drama of Atreus and Thyestes as a depositor of a valuable secret without being able to circulate it. Mandatory payment allows the analysand to turn something which belongs to destiny into an object of exchange, since analysts allow their analysands to decipher this jouissance through repeated and necessary storytelling of the tragedy's horror. Destiny is represented here by a bloody orgy of incestuous jouissance, which is, at least, how tellers of these kinds of stories experienced them.

Subjects narrate their crimes and make those utterances cashable as a way to start removing the debris of the symbolic debt. The fees charged are also the ride the analyst sells that brings subjects into the Symbolic.

Demand for payment shows analysts are not there for a joy ride. Analysts are not working on behalf of some vague altruistic ideal. Analysts are not there for a quick chuckle or to be flabbergasted by the patient's blood-guts-and-sex stories. The jouissance of listening to subject's tragedy is for a theatre audience rather than the analyst. By charging for the act, analysts show they are not there out of love, altruism, "a worthy cause" or any kind of jouissance.

This is a key point regarding love transference in which—as seen in the love clinic—loving is wanting to be loved. When love transference takes place it is also met by the demand for love. Beyond love transference, what is actually at stake is the very kernel of love that pops up in the question "What am I as an object for the Other?" It is there that the analyst is called to the *locus* of the Other who enjoys the subject as an object. Payment as a signifier means the analyst is not interested in the subject as an object but is there as the trustee of the subject's highly valuable psychic narratology. Analysts accept money so they can exercise the same freedom of choosing their own objects as their patients.

The analyst becomes the trustee who does not suddenly find stolen letters on his desk, but rather a precious life story that has been entrusted to him with the strictest terms of confidentiality and disclosure. The burden of responsibility that comes with the delivery of these letters is partially offset by the fees we receive, since mandatory payment neutralises the otherwise one-sided responsibility of this intimate transference and conflates it with that signifier—money—empowered to annihilate almost all significance.

The analysand should pay the money up front and deliver it personally to the analysand: this is the price exacted for having the analysand as the safe wherein the patient's sickness and goods are stored and safeguarded. The price "[…] has a function of deadening something infinitely more dangerous than paying with money, which consists of owing something to someone" (Lacan, 1964, p. 267).

What do the analysand and the analyst bestow on each other? The analysand gives his or her love—transference love. In the dynamic of love and the dialectics of giving, love means giving what you do not have: giving, for example, your time when there is no time to give or giving eternity like André Gide to his Madeleine. Love transference is the effect of the intransitive demand the analysand addresses towards the analyst: "Just give your presence!" or "I don't want anything but you".

And the analyst? In "The Direction of the Treatment and the Principles of its Power" Lacan shows how analysts pay at three different levels: the Symbolic (S), the Imaginary (I) and the Real (R):

- S—with words—the analytical interpretation/ciphering/deciphering.
- I—with personhood—upon submitting themselves to the transference phenomena, analysts surrender their unique personality, their "I", "ME" or "MINE."
- R—with being—in an act of self-effacement, analysts empty themselves as subjects with a unique personal history, desires, pains and pleasures to interpret the *semblant* of *object a* (Lacan, 1966, p. 597).

In analysis, love is not requited with love. If love is giving what you do not have, then the analyst has nothing to give. Yet, Lacan says "[…] even this nothing he gives not". Paradoxically, analysts must charge for this "nothing", otherwise analysands would not deem them valuable or seek them out (Lacan, 1966, p. 610). As the Other of love to whom analysands directs their demands, analysts are cherished since they supposedly have the precious object cause of the analysand's desire (a). It is this priceless object—*agalma*—that the analyst supposedly owns, but this misapprehension stems from ignorance: the object is something that neither the analyst nor indeed anyone else can own or can give to another. The analysand pays for a non-existent object: the analyst's act aims at unveiling its overwhelming reality. The "doughnut" matheme below is a torus that expresses this as:

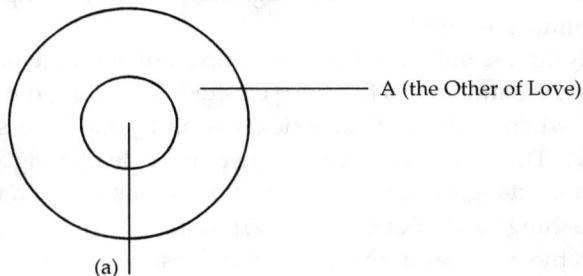

A (the Other of Love)

(a)

In *Seminar* XI, Lacan summarises this overwhelming reality: "I love you, but as I inexplicably love something in you that is more than you—*object a*—I mutilate you" (Lacan, 1973, p. 241). The analysand is truly interested in this priceless *object a* he or she located in the person of the analyst.

The analyst's desire and act lead the analysand to glimpse the object-cause of desire. Such a glimpse of this causality of desire can serve as a watershed in the analysand's life. This is what the analyst gives the analysand: a ticket to board that streetcar named desire. Surely such a ticket is worth more than all the capital, diamonds, money, and gadgets under the sun. This ticket has a name: a still unnameable but always priceless *object a*.

III

THE ART OF THE ANALYST

C linical Lacanian technique entailed the handling of transference and a strategy of interpretation, first, in the field of language (since 1958) and then in the field of jouissance (since 1970). From his earliest days, Lacan separated psychoanalysis as a domain from science, psychology, and medicine. The analyst's task must be elevated to the status of art. Freud often compared psychoanalysis with art and proposed that analysts follow in the artist's footsteps, because the latter has always been a pioneer in unveiling the mysteries of subjectivity. In this part of book, I want to link the handling of transference and the strategy of interpretation with theatre and poetry.

Lacan approaches the field of language for analytical technique in "Direction of the Treatment and the Principles of its Power" regarding power, tactics, strategy, and policy. In the 1940s and 1950s, psychoanalysis had turned into ego psychology and even "human engineering". Lacan's task was highlighting speech in analysis and developing these two acts (transference handling and interpretation) within his framework of the linguistically structured unconscious. The first thing analysts must do is relinquish power—that power created by the analysand's transference.

The "[…] exercise of power is a correlate of the impotence to authentically maintain a praxis" (Lacan, 1966, p. 586). Here is the thesis that informs Lacan's thorough examination of psychoanalytical literature regarding how analysts should act. Analysts, who have having lost their way in this regard are unable to maintain the ethical standards of our practice, fall into the snare of having to display some form of power over the analysand.

The art of war

The issue of power—regardless of how the "impotent analyst" attempts to wield it—is structurally inherent to analytical praxis. As an initial approach to the subject, I use the wartime parlance of politics, strategy, and tactics since these terms and concepts underpin Lacan's description of the direction of analytical treatment.

In *On War*, Prussian general and military theorist Carl von Clauswicz (1780–1831) holds that the political end of a war is the latter's original cause and that war is merely a continuation of politics through other means: "War is not merely a political act, but also a real political instrument, a continuation of political commerce, a carrying out of the same by other means" (Clausewitz, 1918, Sec. 24).

The twofold logic of war is defined through tactics and strategy. If tactics correspond to every battle whose "[…] means are the disciplined armed forces which are to carry on the contest" (ibid, 1918, Sec. 29), each analytical session corresponds to a tactical procedure. Within this framework then where tactics represent short-term goals, strategy is "[…] military action […] for the political object" (ibid, 1918, Sec. 11). Strategy is a higher aim of analysis with its own tactics.

According to Lacan, analytical tactics are present in interpretation—whatever happens to circumstantially appear in any given session—and the analytical strategy in handling transference. Interpretation sums up the analyst's tactics while transference sums up the analysand's strategy. As a strategy, properly speaking, transference belongs to the analysand and it is counterpoised by the analyst's strategy *that opposes any transference that invests power in the analyst.*

The analyst's tactics and strategy are based on *the politics of the lack*, that of the psychoanalytical experience. In that very domain where analysts could brandish their power—a power transference grants them—they choose to represent lack instead. This is why, regarding politics and the analyst, the analyst "[…] would do better placing himself in his lack of being rather than his being" (Lacan, 1966, p. 589). The lack-of-being politics are the antidote for the potential of transference power in the analyst.

The power and the analyst

The scope of the demand made upon the analyst during transference allows us to examine power in its twofold sense: as the capability of acting on someone, and as the potential and possibility of answering a plea. Here power are the means and possibility of being able to respond to the patient's SOS. This is related to transference and the concepts of the Other and ego ideal. Let us now examine these structures based on Lacan's Graph of Desire:

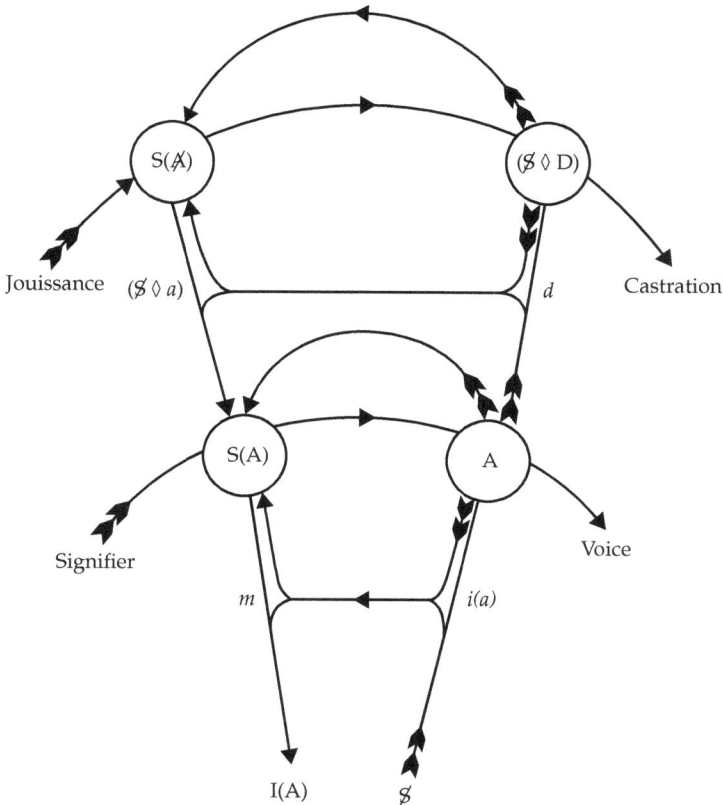

The Graph of Desire.

The Other's omnipotence or potential power is relative to the demand a subject addresses to an Other empowered to answer and give. This Other is not marked by a lack; it is a non-barred Other (A) through which subjects identify and alienate themselves so they may see themselves as loveable and worthy of love: it is expressed as [I(A)] corresponding to Freud's ego ideal. Hence the reason why the Other's feature (omnipotence) is a unitary feature of the ego ideal (actually the Other's Ideal [I(A)]) that lead the subject to believe this Other is complete and therefore all powerful. It is the subject that indeed lends this omnipotence to the Other by identifying it as ego ideal. And it is exactly because the Other is invested with this supremacy that subjects target their demand at it. The demand for love—unconditional love—enchains the subject to the Other. The subject's fantasy structurally supports the Other's non-existent omnipotence. Treatment proceeding in this fashion is reduced to a psychotherapy represented by the bottom half of the graph [$\emptyset \rightarrow A \rightarrow S(A) \rightarrow I(A)$].

Since love is always reciprocal, transference love is a love demand made on the analyst called upon to incarnate not only the subject-supposed-to-know but also the subject-supposed-to-be-empowered. If the subject-supposed-to-know is the outcome of the signified through the signifying chain—the product of free association unleashed through the symbolic coupling of transference—the subject-supposed-to-be-empowered is the outcome of love. We all know the story: the patient "hooked" on the analyst, always dependent on a sign of love or affection for the patient.

The subject-supposed-to-know appears when the patient locates in the Other something that conceals the latter's structural lack; knowledge about a gap glimpsed by the subject such as Socrates for Alcebiades or the analyst for the analysand. The analysand suppresses the Other's lack in the analyst and locates in that Other Ideal, power and other features of illusory omnipotence.

Thus, the analysand locates in the analyst the Master signifier of power (S_1) and of knowledge (S_2) and assumes the analyst is in the place of this powerful Other through the signifying chain (S_1–S_2) that makes the analyst's chair fountainhead of knowledge and power. Lacan differs from Foucault who equates power with knowledge. For Lacan, the power signifier (S_1) is different from the knowledge signifier (S_2) despite their coupling, as we see in the discourses, as social bonds.

Although transference locates analysts in the place of power and knowledge, they respond from neither position: the *semblant* of *object a* rather than S_2 or S_1.

The cornerstone of the politics of the direction of treatment is precisely this absence of power in the Other, which corresponds structurally to the inherent lack in the Other, namely, the Other's own castration. The sole power is summed up by Hamlet (Act 2, Scene 2): "Words! Words! Words!" This is Lacan's conclusion in 1958.

The function of the act in the field of jouissance

I intend to update Lacan's triad regarding the direction of psychoanalytic treatment entailing tactics, strategy and politics. My personal take is not from the perspective in "The Function and Field of Speech and Language" (1966), but rather from an angle I will call here "the function of the act in the field of jouissance".

The Lacanian triad (following Clausewitz) for psychoanalytical technique regarding the field of language is:

1. Tactics of Interpretation.
2. Strategy of Handling of Transference.
3. Politics of Lack-of-Being.

I propose the following triad for the analyst's *savoir-faire* for the field of jouissance:

1. Tactics of the Act.
2. Strategy of *Semblant.*
3. Politics of Surplus Jouissance.

The table below breaks down these components according to their correspondences in the two fields (language and *jouissance*):

Function	Speech	Act
Field	Language	Jouissance
Tactics	Interpretation	Act
Strategy	Transference handling	*Semblant*
Politics	Subject's lack-of-being	Surplus-jouissance

My proposal is that analytical interpretation is granted the same status as an act aimed at transforming the subject. The strategy of handling transference depends on how analysts handle and work with the *semblant*. While the politics of surplus jouissance is based on *object a*'s twofold feature: a) desire's cause and; b) episodic substance of jouissance, since *object a* lacks any substance capable of turning psychoanalysis into an ontology and, like *tyché*, we only encounter *object a* as a fleeting jouissance.

The *semblant* is an artistic act analysts perform for analysands and interpretation is a creative way of using language based on the analysand's free association. Analysts must be up to par with the true artist they will be dealing with: the unconscious.

Cut!

The session cut is a kind of act that Lacan proposes as a way of terminating the session. It's an act whose purpose is interpretation. Analysts are concerned about how to start (See 2.1) and carry out analysis, but they should also focus on the end of analysis and on the most effective way to cut the session.

On the first page of *Seminar I* Lacan evokes the Zen Buddhist Master and describes an analytical act he fully incorporates decades later in his thoughts on the *semblant*—the interpretation or the analyst performing the role of the analysand's *object a*. The unorthodox approach of the Zen Master and theatrical interpretation are acts aimed at causing the effect of splitting the subject. Both the Zen approach and the theatrical interpretation I propose herein are acts that subvert conventional dialogue that merely exchanges information and ordinary everyday communication. Whereas analytical interpretation works with words, the Zen act is silent like the cut, like an analytical act.

Zen and the art of the analyst

Lacan compares the use of "logical time" (See 2.3) in analysis with the technique of Zen Buddhism. According to him, the procedure of short sessions has:

> [...] an exact dialectical sense. And we were not the only ones to observe that it (the dialectical sense) meets up, at the brink, with that technique known as Zen used as way of revelation for the subject in the traditional askesis of certain Far-East schools. (Lacan, 1966, p. 315)

Zen technique aims at bringing the subject to the state of *satori*: a spiritual experience of revelation or enlightenment. *Satori* is a sudden experience where the subject's mind is first "turned upside-down and inside-out" to achieve a sense of total liberation. Zen Master Allan Watts (1915–1973) has cautioned that where there is the least uncertainty or feeling that it is all too good to be true, *satori* has only been partially achieved since there still remains an implicit attachment in the subject. Until this attachment is totally severed, the *satori* experience is not complete (Watts, 1994).

Master Hui-neng describes the Zen experience as a peek into one's own nature which, being "no thing", is not. (Suzuki, 1949) In Lacanian terms, this is the very view of hollowness and it can be equated with the instant of seeing: the view of "no thing" or hollowness or something characterised by a total lack of representation (The Zen doctrine of "no-mind") rather than any action.

The *satori* experience is always described in terms of suddenness or abruptness in which subjects find themselves aware of some sort of void. Suzuki states such experiences are not the product of thought or rational thinking. Rather, subjects abandon their normal forms of thinking and discourse and, in the process, exhaust their will power (ibid). *Satori* therefore aims at something located outside the signifying chain in both conscious and unconscious thought. This sudden enlightenment or flash of understanding is inseparable from Zen technique and is used by the master to lead the student to attempt (through the practice of meditation) to cast off and be free of the enslaving signifying chain. Watts also refers to the liberating effect of *satori* as a release from a state of socially induced hypnosis ("I must be this or that/I want this or that"). This can be equated with *la passe* which is also a release from the bonds of the state of lack-of-being. The analysand sees the Other as essentially hollow and this realisation removes the enormous burden of the ego ideal or the relentless pursuit of the unattainable *object a*. In other words, the spell the Other casts on the subject has been broken. Through *satori*, the student no longer relates to those signifiers responsible for shaping his or her identity. Likewise, at the end of analysis, the analysand no longer relates to those alienating signifiers.

What interests Lacan in Zen is less the experience of enlightenment (also called awakening) than the technique involved in achieving it. He compares this technique, rather than any mystical askesis, with the short-session. Lacan's examples highlight the master's interference during the encounter with the student: "The master interrupts the silence with anything, sarcasm, a kick" (Lacan, 1953–1954, p. 9). "The best to be found in Zen Buddhism consists of answering you, dear friend, with a bark" (Lacan, 1972–1973, p. 104).

Ancient Zen masters also developed an unexplainable method for conveying their teachings through the *koan*, a word meaning literally "official document." The *koan* is an absurd or paradoxical question the master asks the student to solve: "What is the sound of one hand clapping?" is among the more famous ones. Zen students are thus lead to meditate on the *koan's* riddles and attempt to find a meaning through all possible free associations. From time to time, the student meets with the master to check how the *koan* deciphering is coming along.

The main feature of these meetings is that they are brief exchanges during which the disciple, after deep thought, arrives at an extreme formulation of his or her current situation. The master's reply may bring on the flash of enlightenment when disciples notices that the absurd *koan* leaves them mentally discombobulated. According to Watts, this is where students lose their footing only to reach a higher plane of awareness (Watts, op cit). Although the disciple ends up realising the *koan* is devoid of meaning, in most cases, the master's teaching flabbergasts the student and makes him or her hesitant. Here the master intervenes, breaks the silence and cuts the meeting short perhaps even with a radical act like a bark, a kick in the behind or a thump of the staff (Suzuki, D.T., op cit).

Lacan recommended analysts to avoid these radical actions and chose "a discrete application" of the Zen technique in analysis since a "lighter approach" is "[…] more acceptable than certain modes proper to analysis of resistance insomuch as it (the 'lighter approach') runs no risk of alienating the subject" (Lacan, 1966, p. 316).

The Zen master's approach always emphasises the "no-sense", just as Lacan stresses that the analytical act brings into play that which is beyond signifiers: *object a*.

The analyst's presence

The analogy between the master-student exchange in Zen and the analytical session leads us see the cut as a modality wherein the analyst's *semblant* comes to represent *object a* to the analysand. The analyst acts within a paradoxical structure of the psychoanalytical act wherein the subject is subverted and the *object a* is an active part of that structure, albeit outside of language. Although it is beyond any possible representational forms, *object a* nevertheless shapes the signifying chain. It is the object which bedrocks the metonymy of discourse from signifier to signifier. It is the object that lends its feature to desire as "always being the desire for something else." It is the object that runs parallel to the signifier chain and can only correspond to the gap between signifier (i.e., that hollow thing floating between signifiers):

$$(a)$$
$$S - S' - S'' - S'''$$

Object a shares the structure of the cut; an object—as the breast or excrement—can only occupy *object a*'s function if it can be separated from the surface of the body and gain the value of a detached and lost object. Let us observe that the feature of the cut is not less prevalent in the object as analytical theory describes: nipple, faeces, gaze, voice, since all we see is a partial feature in each of these severed objects, behind which there is nothing else we can conceptualise. "One only sees the partial feature—here highlighted in each of these detached objects—not so much because these objects are part of a factual object that would be the body but because they only partially represent the function producing them" (Lacan, 1966, p. 877).

From his seminar on anguish, we learn how Lacan reduces *object a*'s modalities to four: oral object, anal object, gaze, and voice—this latter the real object beyond the signifying chain that lends the object the "sound" jouissance of hearing a human voice.

The cut in the signifying chain represented by the session cut implied in the analysand's "plot" of his or her story is equated with the analyst's presence as *semblant* of *object a*, that opaque thing which resists representation.

According to Freud, the relationship between the analyst's presence and the interruption of the analysand's discourse—shown in the example of the Zen master and the disciple—is transference's manifestation. This situation appears as analysts and analysands get closer to the patogenic core of the psychic problem whose resistance becomes ever more clear:

> When anything in the complexive material (in the subject matter of the complex) is suitable for being transferred on to the figure of the doctor, that transference is carried out; it produces the next association, and announces itself by indications of a resistance—by a stoppage, for instance. (Freud, 1912b, p. 103)

Lacan comments:

> We have much to say about this particular passage that highlights the transference performance as the reinstatement of the analyst's presence which the analysand joltingly perceives beyond his/her senses in a moment whose ensuing anguish and discomfort are the signs that *object a* has appeared. (Lacan, 1953–1954, pp. 51–54)

Clearly, the session cut belongs to the order of interpretation insomuch as it targets the desire-causing object (*object a*).

Analysts cuts the session short because their goal is this kind of transference—by definition, a failed encounter (*tyché*) with—*object a*—the patogenic core. This transference, and not the mere replay of signifiers (automaton) where the analyst occupies the role of the subject's Other, is what the analyst is aiming at, just like the Zen master who wants to lead the disciple to *satori*. Indeed, the analyst's physical presence enables and empowers analysis since, this latter, according to Freud, is impossible either *in absentia* or *in effigie* (Freud, 1912b, p. 108).

Through the session cut as an act of analytical interpretation, the analysand becomes the witness of *object a*'s function as the agent, like the prisoner in Lacan's tale, who is endowed with certainty in advance of logical time. In practice, the surprise effect or any other kind of perplexity, bafflement or reaction, shows nothing less than the subject's split: $(a \rightarrow \cancel{S})$.

The purpose of haste is "[…] that *little a* that 'thetifies' it", namely, that gives the haste of the three prisoners the urgency of a thetic judgement absolutely independent from other assertions about the situation. Lacan reinterprets the sophism of logical time (as we saw in 2.4) from the standpoint of *object a* rather than subjectivity:

> […] It is worth examining that what holds up each of the subjects is not his being one among the others, but rather his being in relation to the other two and to what is at stake in the mind of his cellmates. Each one intervenes according to *object a* which he perceives in the gaze of the others […]. In other words, although there are three, there are actually two other *objects a* that converge at the point of *a*, and are not reduced to two but One + *a* […]. Rushing to exit the cell is motivated by the little a, wherein the two are taken as One + *a*.
> (Lacan, 1975a, p. 67)

Lacan strives in *Seminar* XX to show how this One is not the Other but the autonomy of the signifier S_1 in relation to the set of signifiers (S_1, S_2) and its antinomy towards *object a* (according to the prisoner's reasoning, the Other's gaze). The One at hand is why the prisoner rushes because of *object a*.

The session cut is a way of performing the *semblant* for *object a*—an act dating from Lacan's analytical act concept in 1967/1968 representing the end of analysis. Analysands journey along the paths of the signifier in search of something that will tell them what they have been looking for and what they will never be able to find. They will seek their certainty not through their story as a subject, but at the other end of the structure: that point where their being has been defined through the fantasy object: ($\emptyset \lozenge a$).

The analysand crosses through and over in *la passe* the paths of the signifier to reach his or her final destination in analysis: the encounter with *object a* and the full view of its hollowness. There, the analysand becomes an analyst. I stress once again that analysts are only enabled and empowered to guide their patients to the same point beyond the realm of signifiers if they have experienced the same encounter with their *object a* during their own analysis.

The certainty implied in the analytical act is only possible after having witnessed *object a*; the analyst must bring the analysands to this point of certainty where they will encounter the hollow essence of their being whose consistency is only logical since psychoanalysis is not an ontology. The paradox in psychoanalysis consists in reaching this point of no return through language: it is here that the rest is silence and nothing more can be uttered because all words and signifiers have finally become exhausted.

The session cut—equated with a cut in the signifier chain—aims at revealing the dimension of this gap between signifiers and constitutes a scansion during analysis: in the very sense of underlining, stressing and cadencing not the signifier itself but its inherent gap and pointing towards the "ab-sense"—the absence of meaning (or the "non-mind" of the Zen Master)—and the lack inherent in the Other. The reference point is always the analyst during the interpretation of the *semblant* of the lacking object.

The session cut is indeed a paradox: whereas analysts, after punctuating the end of a session, appear as "masters of the truth", they also open a gap between the signifiers that points towards a leak—like a hole in a barrel—that empties out all meaning. This twofold paradoxical feature of analysis brings to light the dimension of the hollowness beyond the real of signifier, namely, the fleeting object around which the analysand's signifying representations orbit. The analyst's presence and the session cut halt the endless parade of the signifying chain, encapsulate the very structure and dynamics capable of bringing analysis to a swift conclusion and deny the analysand any sensation of infinite subjective time. The session cut anticipates and points toward the end of analysis.

Act and *semblant*

Through the Analyst's discourse (AD), Lacan shows us the structure of the analyst's act and interpretation: these are guidelines for the place the analyst occupies as an agent in relation to the analysand. This place is defined as the *semblant* of *object a* in *Seminar XVIII* ("A Discourse that would not be that of the *Semblant*") and later developed. In *Seminar XIX* ("… or worse") Lacan evokes Ancient Greek theatre to describe *semblant*. "The *semblant* has effects because it is manifested. When the actor uses a mask, his facial expressions do not change; it is not realistic" (Lacan, 1971–1972, p. 165). This is the key guideline for analysts to act; they cannot fake it but must rather use the *semblant* very blatantly and overtly. This is the specific way Lacan offers analysts to achieve the goals of analysis. Lacan continues "[…] this is to give voice to that thing which the analyst can demonstrate which makes the reference to Greek theatre so opportune" (ibid, p. 166).

Analysts use the *semblant* as *object a*'s mask to elicit the analysand's desire and turn the analysand into the analyst and interpreter of his or her own experiences and subjectivity. Thus, the analyst starts a process that in itself will rip analysands away from their personal tragedy, from the terror and horror of their desire, and their self-pity used as a defence against desire. Using Aristotle's definition of tragedy, Lacan stresses the importance of the analyst catalysing the same effects in the analysand as the Greek actors would do with their audiences. The reference to theatre and acting is a guideline for specifically applying the concept of *semblant* and defining the analyst's position during analysis.

Since the seventies, the meaning of *semblant* became increasingly more central in Lacan's teaching. During that time, he developed his concept of the field of jouissance or the Lacanian field—shaped and formatted by the social-bond discourses—as we saw in Part 1. These bonds have different elements acting as agents which represent all kinds of people as the *semblant*, i.e., bosses who think they have power, teachers claiming to have knowledge, hysterics provoking and teasing the other, and analysts in the role of *object a*.

During the 1970s, Lacan redefines the place of discourse. The *semblant* occupies the place of the agent; jouissance that of the other where the analysand is in the AD; and finally, surplus jouissance (*plus-de-jouir*) in the place of production. We can see this represented graphically as:

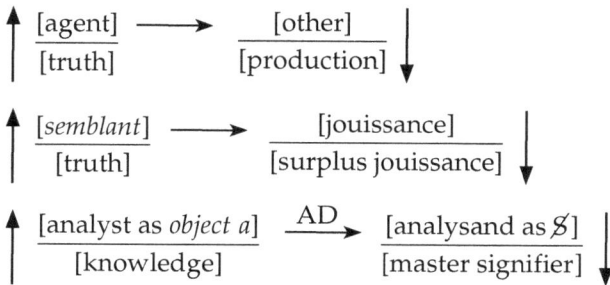

$$\uparrow \frac{[\text{agent}]}{[\text{truth}]} \longrightarrow \frac{[\text{other}]}{[\text{production}]} \downarrow$$

$$\uparrow \frac{[\textit{semblant}]}{[\text{truth}]} \longrightarrow \frac{[\text{jouissance}]}{[\text{surplus jouissance}]} \downarrow$$

$$\uparrow \frac{[\text{analyst as } \textit{object a}]}{[\text{knowledge}]} \xrightarrow{\text{AD}} \frac{[\text{analysand as } \cancel{S}]}{[\text{master signifier}]} \downarrow$$

Lacan relocates the analyst's act from the vantage point of the *semblant*. In the analytic act—a social bond invented by Freud—the analyst becomes and performs as the *semblant* (or representation) of the analysand's object. The analyst acts out the *semblant* to evoke, approach, and locate the analysand's jouissance. In *Seminar* XX, Lacan states that it is only possible to achieve the Real through the *semblant*: "[…] jouissance is only questioned, evoked, bedevilled, formulated from a *semblant*" (Lacan, 1972–1973, p. 85). This means the analyst uses the *semblant* as a strategy to operate on the analysand's jouissance that causes of latter's malaise and suffering, beyond the pleasure principle.

What we talk when we talk about semblant

The French word "*semblant*" comes from *similus*, which means "similar", "similitude", "simulacrum", "semblance" or "resemblance". "*Semblant*" is an ordinary everyday word in French related to the look or appearance of something. However, since the sixteenth and the seventeenth century, the word has acquired other meanings and nowadays, "*semblant*" is used in a negative sense to describe something illusory, fake or misleading more emphatically than the English word "semblance".[1] When a Frenchman says to me, "*c'est du semblant*", "*tu fais semblant*", he means I am faking something or engaged in some deception. This is not the meaning used by Lacan.

There is the "*semblant*" of the conman, and there is the *semblant* of Lacan, who resignifies the word into a concept related to appearance, performance and likeness. The Lacanian *semblant* is not opposed to what is true and "*faire semblant*" describes the analyst's acting, in a theatrical sense, to convey the likeness of something; it is related to unconscious representation (*Vorstellung*). A good translation of *faire semblant* would be make-believe or role-playing, that is, acting out something as if we were on stage in a theatre just as in a fictional drama where the actor performs a scene so convincingly and draws the audience into the reality of the fiction. The performance is true even if the story is made up.

Semblant *and mimesis*

We can equate Lacan's *semblant* with Aristotelian mimesis. In *Poetics*, mimesis (performance or representation rather than imitation as the term was so often mistranslated) is a fundamental concept for discourse on art: art is mimesis of nature. Such an idea is partly inherent in Aristotle's seminal definitions of both tragedy and man. Tragedy is the mimesis of an action performed by actors to bring on the cathartic experience of terror and pity in the audience. It is the performance of an action rather than the imitation of a character. And mimesis is role-playing inherent to any definition of a human being, as man is made and shaped by mimesis. As opposed to animals, man is the only living being capable of mimesis or role-playing that starts in early childhood. Often we see how kids playact roles in games with each other. Perhaps the origin of "to play" is related to role-playing itself. In their make-believe, children pretend to be doctors, nurses, cops, and robbers in roles they swap with their friends for fun. The very act of playing is what mimesis truly captures and conveys. When a painter depicts an apple on canvas, we know it is not an actual apple, but we do not say the depiction is not true. Hence, mimesis is an action which entails gathering and enacting things through scenes, where different roles are performed.

According to Lacan, *semblant* is related to representing or depicting something through action (in a social bond). Through language, we re-create the world around us since language is the highest symbolic function we have in our mental wiring. The very act of naming things in the worlds changes those things. This is what differentiates humans from animals since the latter (as far as we know) cannot enact or represent ideas. Animals cannot pretend to be hungry or fake emotions. Freud's *fort*-and-*da* game is the performance of a scene that is not false and is also a *semblant*, as the child make-believes the mother is leaving and returning (Freud, 1920g, pp. 14–15). If for Aristotle, man is a mimetic being, for Lacan, man is a *semblant* being. Every human being is a performer.

The act in theatre and analysis

Analytical technique draws its two main themes from the theatre: the act and interpretation. In a play, an act is assembled through a series of successful actions. Every act in a play implies character act-ion central to that part. For instance, in Act 1 of *Hamlet*, the action occurs when the father's ghost tells Hamlet: "Kill the King!" Interpretation refers to the way someone says something, reads a text and acts out a character.

But when can I say I am or am not acting or if I am or am not on stage performing a scene? Analysis is comparable to a long play split up in several acts. In fact, this is usually the way analysands organise the process during the crossing-through-and-going-over period (*la passe*) to the end of analysis where they become analysts. Analysands relate their acts and stress the ones representing a turning point in their life. They go on with their story and recall the important acts until the very end of analysis. The final act of this process represented by the *analytic act* is the moment analysands become analysts. We can also think about the analyst's acts that helped move this analytical play along.

The analyst's act in the direction of the treatment is only possible through the *semblant*. It is through the *semblant* and their acts that analysts bring out the analysand's subjective split: "[…] the only thing the analyst must do is to be in the actor's shoes, as an actor sufficient to support the scene" (Lacan, 2006, p. 350).

The analyst-actor

The analyst-actor is the author of the act because he or she has become an analyst during his or her analysis. Analysts are also permitted to perform their own acts and are only authorised by themselves through their own analysis and psychoanalytical training. They are free to develop their own tactics and carry out their own performance acts. Hence, the utterances of this kind of analyst are real interpretations in the psychoanalytic sense. These acts, however, must be underpinned by the *semblant* strategy analysts use during transference according to the politics of surplus-jouissance.

Since, according to Lacan, every agent of discourse is a *semblant*, he tells us that each social-bond act is related to the *semblant* itself. Therefore, there is no discourse that is not *semblant* and all social acts are related to it, including the one the analyst performs in the role of the object.

Semblant is the make-believe or the way each discourse agent seems to be or appear in any social bond. In the Master's act, a person plays the role of both the ruler and the embodiment of the law. In the University act, the teacher conveys the idea of knowledge. In the Hysteric's acting-outs, the patient is in the role of someone suffering from a split personality as if the he or she were performing before an audience. Finally, in the Analyst's act in psychoanalytic settings, the analyst plays the role of the desire-causing object. As a speech function based on the truth that governs each social bond, the analyst's act closely resembles a theatrical performance.

An act in a social bond, or rather, one that makes up the social bond, is performed by someone in the *semblant's* place or role aimed at the other's jouissance (the one ruled in the MD, the one taught in the UD, the doctor in the HD and the analysand in the AD) to make him or her produce *plus-de-jouir*, namely, the extraction of jouissance (a utility object in the MD, a split subject in the UD, a type of knowledge in the HD, a signifier that expresses the subject's uniqueness in the AD).

Lacan refers us to the analyst's theatrical performance and points out that the analyst pretends to be this paradoxical object, which is by its very nature, refractory to any sort of *semblant* since it is outside the realm of language and represents the surplus leftovers of the Master's discourse (MD). Whereas the analyst's practice as an act is an *acting cure*, the analysand's is a *talking cure*; whereas the former is not supposed to talk, the latter is not supposed to act out. When this rule broken, analysis becomes impossible since analysands usually respond to the talkative analyst by acting out some hang-up.

According to Lacan, the performance brings out the dimension of the unconscious. In *Seminar* VI, on *Hamlet,* Lacan states that "[…] the actor lends his limbs, his own presence, not simply as a puppet, but with his real *bel et bien* unconscious, that is to say, relating his own limbs to a certain history that belongs to him" (Lacan, 2013, p. 32). And what of analysts as actors? During analysis, they can only lend their body and voice to perform the role of the *semblant* of the object because they have uncovered unconscious knowledge (S_2) by having been analysands themselves. When transference takes place, the analyst is enabled to act according to the analysand's "script" whose unconscious knowledge becomes the truth that guides the analyst. We read this in the AD: knowledge appears in the place of truth (S_2). This knowledge is also related to the *savoir-faire* (know-how) regarding the analyst's own symptoms and represents the framework of psychoanalytical literature (Freud, Lacan, *et al.,*) based on other cases as well. Moreover, the uniqueness of every patient and every analysis adds to the analyst's body of knowledge.

The analyst's *semblant* as a theatrical performance will only do the trick if the analytical act is based on true knowledge (a [*semblant*]/S_2 [truth]). This knowledge (K) is three-fold:

K1: Knowledge gained from the analyst's own analysis.
K2: Knowledge gained from the patient's narrative.
K3: Knowledge gained from the Freudian canon (and others as well).

Failing to take this into account will turn the analyst's performance into mere mimicry. Without this knowledge of the *semblant* as the analysand's truth, any unanalysed actor could easily play the role of the analyst for the analysand.

Theatre cannot be reduced to the written play or text because it is related to the act that embodies the text on the stage. The theatrical text is never-ready—it is only complete and comes to life during the performance that is by definition ephemeral, instant and unique. The theatre's ephemeral essence is not because performances begin, end and then only leave a hazy dreamlike impression in our mind when the curtains close, but rather because we sense there is an eternal idea—always incomplete—at the moment we instantly experience its terminus.

(Badiou, 2002). A play's text can only fully exist when it is acted out. It can even be acted out without any words, as in Samuel Beckett's *Act without Words*, where the audience only watches scenes and feels the wordless enunciation.

Likewise, the analyst's interpretation exists only when it is uttered and performed. The text of analytic interpretation is only valid when interpreted in a theatrical sense, namely, during analysis. Thus, analytic interpretation is only likely to exist as an act, and the act must be related to a *semblant*.

The term "interpretation" that designates the analyst's acts may be confusing since it does not pertain to hermeneutics and meanings. We must stress that the analyst's words must not convey or aim at any hermeneutical or exegetical meaning. Consequently, we sidestep hermeneutics and semantics by understanding "interpretation" in the theatrical sense of acting and role-playing. The analyst interprets the analysand's text as an actor through the *semblant*. This text—"hanging in the air", so to speak—may or may not consist of words actually uttered by the analysand, since interpretation also takes into account the manner of the analysand's utterances and their silence. Analysts must pay special attention to the analysand's utterance as well because it evokes the real sound of the unconscious from its tone alone or accompanying body language.

The idea I posit herein sees the analyst as the *persona* who plays the role of *semblant* and whose analytic act is a make-believe of the very personal and real truth of the analysand represented by *object a*. My stance clearly counters the one of the "natural analyst" who effectively usurps the place of the Other through the power of transference. It also opposes the position of the myriad psychologists, therapists and new-age gurus who seek to transform the weaker egos of analysands into stronger ones.

Naturalism

In Western society, there are two basic approaches towards interpretation: identification and distancing. Identification or empathy with the character represents the naturalistic approach in which the actor "becomes" the character—he says, "I am Hamlet". The actor strives to embody the story, personality, conflicts, and emotions of the character. According to this school of thought, actors are a carbon copy of the fictional character. And their imitative art lends the character body and soul. This approach is linked willy-nilly by certain schools of theatre to the Stanislavsky method and falls under the heading of naturalism.

The analyst's naturalistic interpretation is grounded on authenticity as an ideal. From this perspective, analysts are human beings who understand the history, experience, and analysis of their patients. This kind of interpretation starts with counter-transference, namely, the effects the analysand's utterances and acts have on the analyst. The acts of "naturalistic" analysts are based on their ego, unconscious or their own symptoms. The more "authentic, sincere, and genuine" they are, the less they are able to fulfil the role of the *semblant* since these analysts are motivated by the desire to heal in the name of truth or any other ideal. This approach allows the analyst to preserve a certain "neutrality". Through transference and the desire for some presumed "authenticity" the therapist embodies the "nice father", or Winnicott's "good enough mother". The ending is predictable: transference is perpetuated and the analysand empathetically relates to the analyst through identification. Distancing, however, is a different matter entirely and it is what I propose herein: the analyst as the *semblant* of the *object little a*.

Acting as the *semblant* (*object little a*), the analyst keeps his or her ego, emotions, imagination, and subjectivity at bay. The stripping away of subjectivity in training analysis that transcends the therapeutic aspect is what empowers analysts to manage treatment. Through distancing, analysts cannot use their subjectivity but rather must follow the strategy of acting as *semblants*. By the end of their own analysis, analysts must know how to manage and keep their own symptoms at a distance. We will contrast naturalism and distancing later in this chapter, but first, we will take a short detour to examine some other features of the analyst-actor.

The analyst's stance

Analysts, I repeat, do not create the *semblant ex-nihilo*, but rather base their act on a specific form of unconscious knowledge, as we have seen.

In the AD, analysts perform this function legitimately, always in relation to the jouissance they grasp from the analysand's speech whose *semblant* they interpret to decipher his or her jouissance as the mathemes at the beginning of this chapter showed.

The analyst apprehends the jouissance through the analysand's utterances, gestures, and silences: this is the process that allows the analyst to understand how to perform the *semblant* because, as Lacan states in

Seminar XX, the Real can only be pursued and ascertained through the *semblant*.

I now propose to examine Lacan's thought on the mask: "The *semblant* should operate like a spokesperson once it functions just like a mask which is openly used, as on the Greek stage" (Lacan, 1971–1972, p. 165). Lacan further adds that "[…] the *semblant* has an effect because it is clearly shown. When the actor wears a mask, he does not make faces; it is not realistic […] so that the audience—the one belonging to the Ancient Greek stage—can find the surplus *jouissance* in it" (ibid, p. 165). You may ask what is the purpose of this mask for the analyst. The character's *semblant* is the "mask" the analyst puts on to interpret. The *semblant* need not be hidden—analysts need not pretend they are not performing but must make it clear they are grasping the effects of truth in the Real. At the theatre, we know we are watching actors performing as characters. Likewise, during sessions, analysts also display the *semblant* without needing to hide behind it. Analysts need not "pretend they are pretending", assume a naturalistic poise or behave as if they were playing the role of the father or mother in some soap opera. Using their body and voice, analysts openly represent—or better still, represent the real presence of the father and the mother by adopting a sort of *persona* that effectively re-enacts and embodies these figures. This can be seen during analysis with children—an easier task—where analysts can interpret by playing the role of the characters of a story or fairy tale.

In bringing together psychoanalysis and theatre, analysts are the agents (responsible for the analytical act) who are actors and the analysands are the audience. Whereas *object a* (surplus jouissance) is on the analyst's side through the *semblant* strategy, the subject of the unconscious as well as the *pathos* is on the analysand's side. Like actors in ancient Greek theatre, analysts cannot be affected by the analysand's utterances: pathos belongs to the chorus. Analysts should not relate to the patients, cry or be moved by them. Neither should the analyst be entangled emotionally with the *pathos* analysands attribute to their characters: dad, mom, brother and sis. In sum, analysts do not identify themselves with the big Other's characters.

The analyst's semblant

Analyst do not conceal their acting and performing. We know the actor in the theatre is not Hamlet and are aware he is performing the character's actions. Likewise, during treatment, analysts do not have to act like understanding fathers or "good enough mothers" but rather present themselves through a blatantly obvious *semblant*. Lacan says the *semblant* produces an effect because it is clearly unveiled and underlines "[...] that the actor is not realistic [...]" (Lacan, 1971–1972, p. 165). Likewise, the analyst's performance is not obliged to adhere to any form of realism since it aims at unrevealing something which does not belong to him/or her.

What is the purpose of standing in place of the *semblant*? Lacan answers: analysts must show the pitiful nature of the neurotic's conjured-up terror of desire. By doing so, the analyst employs in another fashion the two tragic effects described by Aristotle as part of any tragedy: pity and terror. In other words, the analyst-actor brings neurotics and other patients face-to-face with the desire they have tried to sidestep.

The actor — the hypocrite

In the ancient Greek theatre, the actor's performance is related to hypocrisy. In the *New Testament* the word takes on a pejorative connotation when Jesus rebukes the religious people of his time and calls them hypocrites because they were phonies. This is the meaning that has stuck with us, but examining the etymology will helps us understand the word's relationship with theatre. *Hypocrites* means "actor" and it comes from the verb *hypokrynein*—a word specific to Greek theatre—which means "to act out", "to play-act", or "to perform". It consists of the prefix—*hypo*—which means "underneath", and *krinein*, which means "to separate", "to decide", and "to criticise." Hence, the hypocrite is the actor who criticises from behind or "beneath" his mask. When theatre or movie critics decide what is good or bad, they sort out the parts of the play/movie they want to comment upon. As for the actor, once he is wearing his mask (or his character construction), he separates and chooses things to present to the audience and, as Brecht points out, may even criticise the character he plays. The character's action is the theatrical performance itself: the actor speaks and acts as if he were another person. It is precisely in this description that we find the relationship between Lacan's *semblant* and the theatre.

As *krinein* means both "to decide" and "to judge," a performance includes both a judgement and a decision on the way the actor will interpret his lines which, in the Greek theatre, were a poetic text. *Krinein* clearly shows the division between the actor as a subject and his performance.

The semblance on stage points towards the analytical *semblant*: actor-analysts decide and make a judgement on how to represent the patient's scripts (acts/utterances) using a "mask" (through the *semblant* strategy) that will be used during analysis. Analysts do not "put on" the *semblant* mask to act out their own emotions, symptoms or fantasies. Through a theatrical interpretation or a *semblant* performance whose only audience is the analysand, the analyst, gives voice and embodies something (*object little a*) the former has unconsciously revealed.

In a nutshell, this is how theatrical interpretation and psychoanalysis join forces during analysis through the *semblant*—interpretation is not only related to what is effectively uttered, but to the inflections, gestures, and silences of the analyst. Like a good private eye, the analyst knows how to pick up the clues to tailor-make a *semblant* for the specific patient. At any rate, this is not altogether merely a psychoanalytical issue: performance is always present in everyday verbal intercourse and all acts have their *semblant* even when unbeknownst to the parties involved. Notwithstanding this, Lacan, introduces the *semblant* into analytic practice and stresses that it is a make-believe situation based on something quite real and true that afflicts the patient. As an analytical act, the *semblant* aims at reaching, seizing and spotlighting something of the register of the Real.

Brecht advocates detached acting for the character in which an actor narrates rather than performs the lines of the fictitious entity. This is Brecht's distancing, an expression I borrow to show the analyst a way of treating the real jouissance of patients and their truth. Analysts acting out the *semblant* do not treat the truth in the same manner as the hysteric: rather, by distancing themselves from it they show how the patient's truth is a fiction of his or her making.

The *analyst*-semblant *of* object a

The analyst-actor plays the role of the *semblant* of the *object a* rather than as the subject of the truth. Through make-believe, the analyst-actor becomes the *semblant* because he or she must bring on the subject of the unconscious through the analysand's utterances and acts.

Object a is not a character, in a theatrical sense, but it must always be inferred in each analysis. The analyst must be a jack-of-all-trades when it comes to role-playing because of the uniqueness of each case he or she treats. In practice, analysts must make it clear this object does not concern them—the *semblant* must be crystal clear, as Lacan points out, and always detached from the analyst's own subjectivity.

"Do as I do, do not imitate me", Lacan says. He never hesitated to perform with his own quirks and antics in public or to purposely make a fool of himself. He played the buffoon, the clown, the wisecracker, the surrealist figure donning the most outlandish clothes and smoking a ridiculous twisted cigarillo. He even dared to say, "I am a clown, just watch me on Television". I am almost tempted to think that only those who are unafraid of being ridiculous are truly free and that is my impression of Lacan's public performances. We might translate Lacan's words thus: "Do as I do, wear your own *semblants* and do not imitate mine". Obviously, Lacan's performances displayed an ample repertoire of tactics and a political strategy *a la* Clauswicz aimed at deconstructing the infatuated analysts in his audience and in his private practice who would mistakenly perform the *semblant* of the "Analyst" and not of the analysand's *object little a*.

The *semblant* performance must make it clear that *semblant* is not the analyst, just as the actor is not the character. According to François Regnault, distancing refers to the actor's actions (body language, gestures, utterances, etc.) that specifically show his distance, as a human being, from the character he is representing. Likewise, distancing also allows analysts to present themselves as if they were someone else. This is theatre in a nutshell: to say something as if you were somebody else (Regnault, 2001).

Strangeness and defamiliarisation

Brecht's "defamiliarisation or distancing effect" (*Verfremdungseffekt*) is the opposite of naturalistic interpretation with its actor-character identification and, in this sense, it resembles Lacan's *semblant* quite closely. According to Brecht, distancing (or alienation effect) means, above all, depriving the character of all his or her obvious and well-known features in order to startle the audience and make it curious (Brecht, 1961). Brazilian philosopher and theatre critic Gerd Bornheim adds that "[…] if the actor does not disappear behind the character, it is because, besides showing himself as an actor, he also shows the character" (Bornheim, 1992, p. 259). The simplest way of producing the Brechtian distancing effect is through masks.

After having missed some sessions, a female analysand gets a phone call from Lacan whose tone of voice closely resembles that of an adult addressing a toddler. And in this sugary tone of voice, Lacan says: "When should I see you again, my little girl?" Although Lacan's attitude horrified his patient, she laughed at it because it reminded her of her mother's requests which always made the patient feel guilty as her mother was a poor penniless widow who relied entirely on her daughter (Didier-Weill, 2007, pp. 72–73). This anecdote illustrates the way Lacan blatantly acted out a *semblant* for a patient by impersonating the object voice of the big Other (the mother).

"It was my mom's voice", said the aforementioned female analysand after Lacan's phone call (Didier-Weill, 2007, p. 73). How would you feel if you got a phone call from your analyst and he or she sounded just like your mom?

The literal translation of *Verfremdungseffekt* is "the effect of making something or someone sound strange or like a stranger". This is similar to the defamiliarisation (*ostranenie/остранение*) of the Russian literary formalists where something commonplace is artistically depicted in an unfamiliar and unusual manner.[2] This has led some people to translate it as "estrangement", but I prefer the description American literary critic Harold Bloom offers when speaking of the weirdness or uncanniness of great works of literature that have a "[...] strangeness that we either never altogether assimilate, or that becomes such a given that we are blinded to its idiosyncrasies" (Bloom, 1994, p. 4).

Fremdung takes us back to ourselves as psychoanalysts, to the *Fremdeobjekt*, that "strange object", as weird or uncanny as anything we can imagine in our fictions. According to Freud in the "Project for a Scientific Psychology", this foreign object is regarded as *Das Ding* (The Thing) which belongs to the Complex of the Neighbour (Freud, 1895, p. 331). As we know, Lacan further conceptualised *Das Ding*, gave it dignity and based his theory of *object a* on it. This concept describes the effect of strangeness the analyst's act should bring on during analysis to uncover the analysand's surplus jouissance. Analysts must draw out this uncanny foreign object from the analysand's ordinary acts and utterances and will only be able to do so by aptly managing the *semblant* during transference. From a Brechtian standpoint, the analyst should offer the analysand a sort of interpretation or performance in which the object can be recognised as something unnatural beyond conventional meaning and even beyond the realm of meaning itself. As the

German playwright says, what is as stake is an "unusual thing," or "something strange".

The effect of strangeness is described through the concept of *mise-en-scène*, a performance inherent in the analytic act and setting that somehow reproduces Freudian *Unheimlich* ("*The Uncanny*"). The *mise-in-scéne* during the analytic act is *per se* quite uncanny because the presentation of the *semblant* by the analyst is a sort of disguise that enables analysands to unveil their surplus-jouissance. The *semblant* is the only way to catch the Real. Thus, analysts, each with their own style and approach, potentially embody some freaky figure such as the riddle, the sphinx, the oracle, to put on stage the gaze and the voice as *objects a*.

Theatrical interpretation

Art has much to teach us about the *semblant* during the analytical act. Drama shows us the art of make-believe, poetry the expression of our equivocations and jokes of *Lalangue* as we are going to see in 3.3. The analyst as actor lends the *semblant* a body and a physical presence. The actor enacts that *semblant* before the analysand-viewer, not for the latter to sit back (or lie down) and take in the show but rather to reveal in full colour the disruptive essence embodied in the *semblant* performance.

Here we should ask what does the *semblant* performance of *object a* mean? *Object a* is not a character envisaged by playwright. In strict Lacanian terms, *object a* is a place to be occupied, a *locus* to be temporarily filled until the end of analysis. As a *semblant, object a* could generically represent all possible characters since any may appear in the truth of unconscious knowledge shaping the *semblant* itself. Both psychoanalysis and drama deal with an act, a *semblant* and a truth, albeit not the same truth. While the actor's truth is based on his or her unconscious, that of the analyst's is firmly entrenched in the AD, in which specific kinds of knowledge (K1, K2 and K3 examined previously) occupy the place of this social bond's truth. The make-believe, theatrical performance and *semblant* support the analyst-actor, not according to his or her personal wishes or whims, but through the strategy of *plus-de-jouir* and surplus jouissance and the politics we outlined earlier.

Lacan would claim he could make words mean anything he liked. Meanings transcend mere words because the former depend on how the latter are said, like the actor's interpretation of the text of a pay. Try reading your lines aloud and you will see just what interpretation is. Speech in general is already interpretation since words can come to mean even the exact opposite of what is being said. I can even say "I love you" so it comes across as "I hate you". Is this theatre? No, just a characteristic of speaking beings when they talk: when we talk we are always performing a text.

Lacan gives us two examples of the "saying-only-half-the-thing" concerning interpretation: riddles and quotes. Riddles correspond to a form of utterance, whereas quotes correspond to extractions from the text provided by the analysand's own plot. Thus, like a grand slam in tennis, the analyst whacks back at the analysand, his or her own words. In this sense, the analysand can be confounded by his or her own utterances that turn into riddles or enigmas. The analysand's inflections, facial expressions, gestures, silences, and intonations say much more than the actual words and can provide the analyst with helpful hints to construct the analyst's own *semblant*. The strangeness extracted from discourse is, in fact, the very cause of the discourse itself (*object a*), as actors interpret their lines, the analyst performs likewise with the analysand's text by acting it out. The analyst attributes the literal effect of the text to the theatrical essence of the *semblant*.

As contemporary French playwright Valère Novarina (b. 1947) states, theatre is the place of living poetry. A closed book of verse is poetry's tomb; poetry is only brought to life when it is spoken and heard. Analysts are the interpreters who resurrect *lalangue* through the *poiesis* of their utterances. Albeit absent as subjects, analysts hand themselves over to the *semblant* performed in the analytic setting. They step on to the Other's stage and encroach on the analysand's unconscious. Through strategy and tactics, the analyst highlights the analysand's signifier representations and strips them down, one-by-one, until all that is left is a hollow core which the patient perceives.

Der Anderer Schauplatz: the Other Scene. The German word literally brings to mind the public square (*Platz*) of the gaze (*Schau*). The analytic scene becomes the Other's scene, that stage featuring big-time stars such as the Other's gaze and the Other's voice. Gaze and voice are two modalities of *object a* far beyond the realm of love demands, but they are sly and tricky operators because they can cause love and desire. This is the theatre of transference love.

During analysis, style is what analysts convey to the analysand since each analyst will interact uniquely with the *semblant*. An actor usually lends his characters something of his own even if he fails to relate to the role. The actor's unique style belongs to him alone and it is something he cannot fail to lend to his role: it is unavoidably included in the performance and makes the performance unique.

Regarding ancient Greek tragedy, *object a* represents the goat or Dionysus as a dismembered god, the god of the theatre who represents the *Semblant* of *semblants*. According to Freud, the Greek theatre is a "treatment through dramatisation" wherein psychoanalysis first appeared as a "cathartic treatment". We all know how analysands bring up the most hideous parts of their life on the couch where they often break down in tears. Just like an actor who lends part of his unconscious knowledge to his character to catalyse catharsis in the audience, analysts lend their presence and unique style to draw out the Real. Analysis brings to the setting/stage the subject's destiny and alienation dictated and shaped by the big Other, which the analyst should counter through the analytical act. However, analysis is neither a gruesome horror flick nor a play for the Theatre of the Oppressed.[3] Like the effect of performing a tragedy for an audience, the analyst must take the analysand to the point of enthusiasm. This is the sensation analysands should experience at the end of the process in which they emerge as analysts. As Lacan says about enthusiasm, "[…] without such a feeling we can say that there has been an analysis, but certainly not an analyst!" (Lacan, 2001, p. 309).

Enthusiasm originally meant in Greek that overwhelming feeling that possessed people and drove them out of their mind as they fused with a divine power (*entheos*). Enthusiasm is that state of being out of one's mind and one with a god. Which god? For the Greeks, artists during the act of creation or performance, just like enthusiastic people, were possessed by Dionysus. Enthusiasm is the state of "ecstasy of the inspired poet"—a Dionysian state of mind precisely related to the creative act of *poiesis*. Although analytic theatre is referred to as tragedy since it deals with the worst and the most critical episodes of the analysand's life story, it can also inspire the patient with a real new-found enthusiasm and motivate him or her to get off the "I-feel-miserable-express" and hop on that streetcar named desire.

Interpretation and *lalangue*

L acan revolutionised psychoanalytical interpretation by shifting it from hermeneutics to inciting analysands to find their own answers and meanings. There are no ready-made answers and formulas and analysts provide no solutions for the analysand's hang-ups. Throughout his teaching, Lacan provides us with some technical guidelines for the tactics of interpretation and the handling of transference strategy during treatment. Interpretation always goes hand-in-hand with transference and targets the lack gaps and incompleteness inherent in the speaking beings. Specifically, analytical interpretation addresses the absence of the Other and the presence of *object a* (desire's cause).

What is the exact structure of interpretation and transference? Analysts cannot actually occupy the place of the big Other: they can only interpret it through the strategy of *semblant* because the Other is lacking and vacuous. The Other—as a treasure trove of signifiers—lacks completeness: $S(\cancel{A})$ represents the hollowness of the signifier that points to and highlights this lack, a lack that cannot be signified in any shape or form. The Other guarantees nothing, and certainly not happiness or meaning. The analyst that takes the place of the Other (in some way as a loving, wise, knowledgeable mentor who knows exactly what the analysand needs) is a phony. Analysis cannot be a self-help therapy that makes big promises to give meaning to the patient's entire life.

In short, if analysts make believe they are the Other, they will occupy the command post and act as the commander-in-chief representing the empty guarantee of this Other. This is a great fallacy and one that must be addressed. Since analysts are liable to be lined up for this position in the game, they run the risk of supporting the analysand's endless and idolising signifiers and demands. And clinical practitioners who take on this role surrender themselves to trivial registers of communication and command. To distinguish themselves from other social-bond agents, such as in MD or UD, the analyst should not give patients "What-you-are-saying-is-that" answers but instead make them talk and bring on the unconscious. In analysis, the true interpreter who answers the questions "What's it all about?" and "What shall I do?" is the analysand's own free association. The analyst's interpretation is not really an answer but a finger pointing elsewhere.

The uniqueness of the analyst's answer is not in the statement uttered but the very utterance itself through which the analyst's desire is expressed as an enigma that spotlights the enigma of the Other's desire.

Lacan borrows the concept of utterance from Benveniste who separates the utterance from the statement, the way the text is said. In theatre this is called interpretation. There are countless ways of interpreting the text, and you can even convey a text wordlessly or using gestures and acting. Here we set linguistics aside to enter the Real of the act that is beyond verbal utterance. Body language can utter without any words. This is exactly what Lacan starts to stress and use in his own clinical practice during the 1970s through the act and the wordless-discourse concept that posit that the agent of discourse is the *semblant*. Since analysts stand in lieu of *object a*'s *semblant* in the AD, they make believe they are *object a* (*Ils font semblant d'objet a*) for the analysand. Interpretation is always performed within this conceptual framework of the analytic act. Analytic interpretation is a performance with words and silences for the analysand to perceive the hollow shell of his or her desires. An "act" in analysis, such as the cut, is wordless.

Linguists such as J. L. Austin hold that certain words are explicitly performative, i.e., "action words" or imperatives such as: "Fire!", "Go!", "Come!". Words that, once uttered, imply immediate actions. How do analysts avoid having their words misconstrued as imperatives, advice or guidance? Lacan says that the analyst must use language's capacity and artistic talent for creating the equivocal. But what does he mean? He stresses that the listener provides the meanings rather than the speaker. Concurrently, analysts must be on guard not to conduct analysis as though they were putting on a show or a stage performance: they should never forget that the core of analysis is to reach the analysand's jouissance and that all acts during analysis are based on analytical knowledge. Nonetheless, Lacan hardly highlights the silent performative capacity of the analytical act. I, however, am strongly convinced it is there staring us in the face throughout his teaching, from the initial reference (*Seminar* I) during the 1950s to Zen Buddhism and wordless discourse to the theory (1970s) of the social bonds and the *semblant* in the analytic act. Certainly, we have videos of Lacan on YouTube that clearly show how he performs during his seminars and fills them with all kinds of facial expressions, silences, weird grimaces, as well as gestures. What analysts say within the strategy of the *semblant* to analysands must be raised to the level of an act in order to be properly called interpretation.

Neither oracle nor delusion

What are the conditions for the analyst's answer, namely, the analyst's interpretation? Lacan is somewhat embarrassed about using the term "interpretation" to describe the analyst's speech, because it evokes to "[…] such diverse fields as the oracle and the outside discourse of psychosis" (Lacan, 2001, p. 490). Let us now briefly address interpretation in these two different fields.

The delusional interpretation in psychosis is a kind of answer full of meaning. Paranoia stuffs the void of meaning with a delusion-dictated postulate (i.e., "someone is after me") possessing its own logic and sense. Everything is granted a meaning and there is no place for chance in psychosis: the Other's every gesture, as well as words and things that happen in the world all have meaning for the psychotic. So, if paranoids see even a small leaf falling from a tree, they will attribute a meaning to it to shape their own experience: "This falling leaf is somehow about me." They may not even know what this means, but the meaning is always there, consciously or unconsciously. Interpretation based on meaning is paranoid insofar as it is based on to some previous semantic default setting. This is diametrically opposed to psychoanalytic ethics that guide us toward detaching the analysand from pre-established signifiers and pointing towards the absence of sense.

THE ART OF THE ANALYST   147

Oracular interpretation is not prophecy but rather a sign. Lacan started evoking the oracle in 1958 as an example of analytical interpretation. "As an interpreter of what is presented to me in words and deeds, I choose my own oracle and articulate it as I please, sole master on my ship after God" (Lacan, 1966, pp. 587–588). Later on he evokes Heraclitus: the oracle, like the analyst, neither reveals nor conceals; he sends a signal. In Greek, the word "oracle" (*khrēsmoi/ορχρησμοί*) means "obscure word" or "enigma"—which is precisely what analytical interpretation as cryptic half-saying (*mi-dire*) should be. But when analysts play the role of the oracle as prophets, they run the risk of being understood as soothsayers who are leading their analysands to read their destiny in oracularly enunciated utterances. True oracles in ancient Greece always presented their sayings as enigmas or riddles to be deciphered by the listener. These seers of old were master equivocators in all ways.

So, how can we avoid this conundrum and sidestep the risk of being gurus, prophets or fortune tellers? Freud shows us: the analyst should follow in the artist's footsteps. Take the word *interpretation* as the interpretation a musician offers of a musical score or that of an actor of the lines in a play. Whereas the musician interprets a work on an instrument, the actor interprets an author's text. The analyst's art consists of interpreting the analysand's speech in this same way. We will see what these forms of artistic interpretation can teach the analyst.

The "x" of the enunciation

In "Proposition of October 9 on the Psychoanalyst and the School", Lacan says: "The analyst's desire is his or her utterance, which can only operate if analysts position themselves as "x" (Lacan, 2001, p. 251). The analyst's desire upholds the x as a question: analysts enact the x that the analysand must deal with when he or she comes face-to-face with the Other's desire. In effective analysis, analysands will question, revise, interrupt and try to outdo the prior and various replies they have already given to the *Che-vuoi* proposition and ask themselves instead, "What do I want?" The analyst's enigmatic desire calls into question the analysand's responses to the Other's enigmatic desire such as the ego, symptoms and the fantasy (*Cf.* the Graph of Desire), while the analyst's intervention should always be supported by enigmatic or even equivocal utterance rather than straightforward statements.

Analysts use the logical tool Lacan called the analyst's desire as an enigma to perform analysis and lead subjects to ask themselves about the analyst "What did he or she mean?", "What does he or she want?" or "What does he or she want me to do or say?" Like the Brechtian actor, the analyst is detached while sounding out the Other's desire during transference. Furthermore, the analyst's enigmatically enunciated desire brings into play an unknown element in the equation and leaves it up to the analysand to decipher it.

Interpretation should preserve its "allusive virtue", as Lacan commented on the famous Leonardo Da Vinci painting in which John the Baptist is pointing upwards towards the heavens. The analyst, like the figure in the painting, should point to "the uninhabited horizon of being" (Lacan, 1966, p. 641). Analysts should point towards S(Ⱥ): lack of the Other, lack of completeness, lack of a final answer, solution or a theory of everything, lack of meaning … lack, and more lack. The only meaning of meaning is that it is leaky, like the barrel in the myth of the Danaides. And so if the lack is leaky and hollow, then the same leakiness and hollowness permeates everything that tries to signify it. This is the analyst's slippery terrain where interpretation aims at undoing libido's knots of meaning.

What is stated might establish different social bonds depending on its utterance—a way enacting it. Thus, if the statement merely replicates the MD and is understood as an order or suggestion, analysis turns into mesmerism and hypnosis. And if the statement is another carbon copy of the UD, then the analyst is just another clone of the pompous professor spewing out an impressive array of erudition. Everything depends on the way and the place from which something is said. If interpretation is shaped by the MD or UD or is the expression of the analyst's own personality or subjectivity, he/she is still a far cry from the AD. In none of these cases are the analysts are the analysand's *object a* because they are acting as S_1 in MD or as S_2 in UD.

Analysts are never the subjects in analysis, not even as a *semblant* as in the HD. That there is only one unconscious subject—the one who speaks and acts "in" the analysand—should be absolutely clear. Analysts do not treat analysands as objects (UD), slaves (MD) or masters (HD) but only as subjects of the unconscious (AD).

Riddles and quotations

In *Seminar* XVII—"The Other Side of Psychoanalysis"—Lacan proposes two forms of interpretation as half-saying (*mi-dire*): riddles and quotations. He equates utterance with the riddle the analyst poses and quotation with a part of the analysand's ongoing plot and text. Through utterance the analyst "enigmatises" what is stated and brings out the uncanny element that, albeit beyond discourse, nevertheless engenders discourse. This performing act resembles the actor who, having learned a script by heart, interprets it on stage: likewise the analyst brings out the enigma through the analysand's words. This kind of interpretation is exactly what the musician does with the score, interpreting the composer's intentions with dynamics, timbre, coloratura, tempos, etc. Both riddle utterance and the extraction of quotation are verbal forms of interpreting the enigma of the Other's desire for the analysand; both fully engage the analyst's entire body and intonation. The analyst's desire is an enigma in action.

Utterance not only implies speech but also gestures, movements, silences and context for its *mise en scène*. Using words (with their accompanying gestures), the utterance of the interpretation can evoke in the analysand the remembrance and contexts of past traumas. All those factors that make up and shape the situation come into play as in Joyce's childhood scene in *The Portrait of the Artist as a Young Man* I will examine later.

Lacan often avoids the term "interpretation", because it has manifold meanings and the semantic function comes to mind before the propositional one, i.e., that a sentence can transcend the words which make up its meaning. Lacan discards the semantic side and divests interpretation of any attempt at meaning. He differentiates the saying (*le dire*) from the said (*le dit*). Whereas saying corresponds to utterance, the said is aligned with repeatable enunciated statements. The sayings can also correspond to a context where some specific words were said.

As the curtain was closing on his final days of teaching, Lacan often equated interpretation with equivocation, pointing out that equivocation is the only weapon against the symptom. And, furthermore, he indicates that in interpretation: "The equivocations written next to an utterance are concentrated in three nodal points," which are homophony, grammar and logic (Lacan, 2001, p. 491). Lacan's text offers an essential demonstration: "[…] the fact that we are saying remains forgotten in what is said behind what is heard" (ibid, 2001, p. 449). The words are not forgotten but the fact that they are utterances eclipses the way they are uttered. When we speak, we tend to focus on what we say (statement) rather than on the act of speaking to a listener who is hearing. Thus, in conversation, we foreground the statement while the utterance remains in the background. Of all that is heard, something remains forgotten, which is more related to what I am uttering than to the supposed content of what I am saying.

Geometrically speaking, interpretation as equivocation is always à-côté, located on a tangent or slant, on the side, occurring diagonally or peripherally. But where exactly? In the analysand's commonplace everyday utterances. Interpretation does not tell the analysand "what you mean to say is this", but rather touches an off-side tangent (à-coté), that is to say, a *locus* alongside the signifying chain where *object a* slips away like a fish. It is worth stressing here that the *how* is more important than the *what*, since utterance and the statement are conveyed on different planes of communication. As a rule of thumb, analysts should always remember that utterance is the soul of analytical interpretation. Nowadays, I have ascertained from personal experience that analysis in many cases targets primarily the statement, which only shows the prevalent misreadings of Lacan. The analysand's utterances must come into play rather than any dissection or scrutinising of their content or meaning. Although Lacan provides no examples of utterance—something quite difficult to describe—he offers myriad examples of equivocation that shape utterances as well as examples of enunciative equivocation. As a form or inflection of verbal communication, enunciation is a style of verbal communication that always compounds the utterance. The words themselves are secondary to the way they are spoken: in analysis, a gesture of giving is really the gift itself.

You can insult someone with the most inoffensive word (signifier) just from your tone of voice as Freud's "Rat Man" deftly illustrates. During childhood, whenever the Rat Man got angry at his father, he would yell "You napkin!", "You plate!", "You lamp!" since as a child he lacked more colourful words to convey his anger. This is a perfect example of utterance making words say one thing but meaning another.

The speech act is the key to psychoanalytical interpretation. Analysts must never forget they speak from a vantage point and what they say is perceived from that point. But it is precisely the utterance that is forgotten in speech, because we haplessly chase the illusion of meaning and are unaware that the utterance is conveying meaning beyond our words. Consequently, utterances can have a causal function as we see in "Irma's Injection", a paradigmatic example. What brought on Freud's dream was the tone used by his colleague when they met on the street: "Irma, your former patient, is not well!" (Freud, 1900a, p. 106). Freud perceived criticism of himself as a doctor in his colleague's remark: an utterance that transcended mere words and triggered a disturbing dream for Freud.

Modes of equivocation

In "L'Étourdit", Lacan equates interpretation and equivocations and presents an analytical tool that has three (3) modes: homophony, grammar, and logic. Starting with the Sophists and then highlighting Lacan's discoursiveness, Barbara Cassin further develops this tool using a term she calls logology, evoking the equivocal nature of *lalangue* and the performative nature of discourse (Badiou, & Cassin, 2010). Cassin affirms that Lacan, in his threefold structure (homophony-grammar-logic) of equivocation, updates and mirrors the *Organon* of Aristotle who proposes a similar structure for equivocal use of words, sentences and reasoning: (ibid, 2010).

Lacan	*Aristotle*
Homophony	Words
Grammar	Sentence
Logic	Reasoning

Regarding homophonic equivocations, Lacan says "[…] I'd venture to say that any move goes here since anyone is capable of doing so without realizing that they are playing us" (Lacan, 2001, p. 491).

We constantly deal with puns and word plays. According to the definition of the unconscious as knowledge of *lalangue* (which we will see further ahead), the subject is a plaything of such homophonic equivocations. But "[…] the poets calculate such equivocations and psychoanalysts use them at their own will" (Lacan, 2001, p. 491). Lacan thus merges interpretation and poetry. What poets calculate, psychoanalysts use. Years later, Lacan openly states that analysts should follow in the footsteps of poets to interpret. But what does that mean? That words play us like an instrument (rather than the other way around) and interpretation must be thought out in the same way as poets construct their poetry. As analysts, our own thoughts, reflections, familiarity with psychoanalytical literature, and training are compounded by the knowledge gained from each of our clinical cases. Thus, as accomplished poets create their poetry based on their wide reading and life experiences, analysts develop and craft their interpretation based on both theoretical and analytical knowledge and mastery of the language in which the analysis is being conducted. I cannot stress enough the need for us analysts to become close readers—as Freud and Lacan were—of poetry and literature.

During his teaching career, Lacan had always freely danced between mathemes and poetry. The mathemes I have examined are a theoretical attempt to give psychoanalytical concepts a logical and communicable structure in something resembling mathematical terms in order to sidestep any possible equivocations. They appeal to the scientific and mathematical mindset that wants things expressed in the most pristine and precise form.

Poetry, on the other hand, is what brings the knowing (since it knows and is embedded in *lalangue*) of the unconscious into play. While mathemes reflect the scientific and empirical spirit of our age, poetry was first reflected in Lacan's teaching through his initial contact with the surrealists and finally, towards the end of his life, through his reading of James Joyce. Mathemes and poetry thus enjoy a perfect marriage in Lacan's theoretical framework.

In interpretation through homophony, all the chips that language allows are on the table because the very sounds of language always run the risk of getting mixed up: "I love you" may be grasped as gibberish such as "I love view", or "I loft you". This is how the unconscious works: nonsense beyond sense, sound beyond meaning. To avoid transforming analysis into a mere language game, puns, jokes and malapropisms must be calculated on the basis of knowledge (S_2) in the place of truth in this social bond, as the AD matheme (see 1.2) shows. Freud's *Jokes and their Relation to the Unconscious* shows us eleven (11) different types of technique for differentiating jokes, which could also correspond to analytical interpretation based on *lalangue*. One of the most important types highlighted by Freud is precisely the equivocal or double meaning.

Regarding grammatical equivocation: there are several possibilities such as commas, ellipsis and punctuation in general. Punctuating a sentence differently can totally change its meaning and create an equivocal statement (i.e., "I need to help you get a job", "I need to help you. Get a job"). This is a way of using equivocation through grammar.

Word omission also provides us with an example, such as Freud's interpretation in "Negation" in which the patient says: "You ask who this person in the dream can be. It's *not* my mother." What does Freud do? He takes out the "not" and separates it from the rest of the sentence and says, "So it is your mother" (Freud, 1925h, p. 235). Examples of equivocal statement abound, but suffice to say, Lacan formalises and expands Freud's teaching.

Regarding equivocation in logic, Lacan cites the paradox as an example. Paradox shows there is no contradiction in the unconscious: a thing can simultaneously be and not be. The paradox entails two simultaneously opposing propositions, such as the classic self-contradictory paradox of the liar (i.e., "Everything I say is a lie"). Is this statement true or false? It is both true and false. Like this example, the unconscious also holds simultaneously opposing propositions, as Freud demonstrates. Thus, there are no "either-this-or-that" but rather "this-and-that" propositions in which both elements are concomitantly true and false. The unconscious excludes nothing, including contradictions. The figure of speech known as the oxymoron is another kind of paradox that provides us with a further example. We find various examples of it in *Romeo and Juliet* used to mean love. Actually, there is nothing more paradoxical than love. According to Shakespeare's Romeo in Act 1, Scene 2:

> [...] o loving hate,
> O anything of nothing first create;
> O heavy lightness, serious vanity
> Misshapen Chaos of well-seeming forms,
> Feather of lead, bright smoke, cold fire, sick health,
> Still-waking sleep, that is not what it is!
> This love feel I, that feel no love in this.

An analytical reading here shows the paradoxical nature of the unconscious itself, which allows Romeo to perceive the ultimate "ab-sense" (lack of sense). *Romeo and Juliet* is a treatise on the non-existent sexual relationship and equivocation between men and women. Romeo also performs a splendid interpretation of the paradox of logic.

As an analyst, Romeo sidesteps the issue: this represents the same ethics of psychoanalysis. The analyst is aware of a commanding power he or she holds over every enunciated utterance but it is the enunciation that expresses the analyst's desire—never to be confused with any desire for or towards the analysand. The goal of the desire of the analyst is to push analysands forward in exploring and unveiling the workings of their own unconscious.

La-la-la-langue

In his twilight years, Lacan stressed that interpretation must be poetic to be effective; he himself complained he was still not enough of a poet. This strikes a contemporary note and matches perfectly the definition of the unconscious as knowledge about *lalangue*. The capacity of analytical interpretation as equivocation should bring into play ambiguities, homonyms, rhymes, puns, musicality, and other features of *Lalangue*. Lacan defines *lalangue* as a language that is: "[...] among others, nothing more than the whole set of the equivocations its history has perpetuated and preserved over time" (Lacan, 2001, p. 490).

In *The Interpretation of Dreams*—actually a major treatise on psychoanalytical interpretation—Freud stresses the importance of words in which the dream occurs and how they make every side of the crystal of language shine uniquely in different tongues such as English, German, Spanish, etc. In fact, French and other Romance languages have two different terms—*le langage* and *la langue*—English lacks. The first is the linguistic structure—whose laws are metaphor and metonymy—which defines and shapes every human as a speaking being. The second is any specific language (tongue) with its own possibilities for sounds, rhymes, puns, equivocal statements, etc.

Dreams make full use of language; although untranslatable, they are not unexplainable. Dreams show us that the unconscious is structured as a language (*langage*) and that it also is a knowledge of *lalangue*. Lacan raises *lalangue* to the category of a concept: *lalangue* spelled as one word. Whereas language refers to signifiers and semantic relationships shaped by the unique unconscious of each subject, *lalangue* takes us further back to the time, before meaning and signifiers, of baby talk and lallation. *Lalangue* describes the pre-semantic and pre-signifier effect of language—devoid of meaning—on the subject. Accordingly, *lalangue* has no theoretical existence, it intervenes in the form of the spoken tongue:

> According to how *lalangue* was spoken and also heard by this or that subject in its uniqueness, that is how it will come out in his/her dreams, with all kinds of equivocations, all kinds of speech. That is the materialism wherein dwells the apprehension of the unconscious.[4]

The universal rules and laws of language are the same for every speaking being, and every subject is subjected to both signifiers manifested in conscious speech and the free flow of the unconscious in dreams, lapses, humorous puns, equivocal utterances, and also neurotic symp-toms. *Lalangue* stems from the subject's mother tongue and, although it encompasses a specific language such as English, French or Portuguese, it is also much more. *Lalangue* belongs to you and me and our relation-ship with our native language spoken and heard where we were born and raised.

Lalangue is what we receive from our mother tongue. Like a downpour or hail storm of our native language, its signifiers drench us with mani-fold sonorities, ambiguities, mistakes, malapropisms, equivocations, meanings, and nonsense. It is "the deposit, the silt, the petrification left as a mark of the group unconscious experience".[5] This is the linguistic and family group. Every language has its own potential and features for equivocation, ambiguities, rhymes, phonemic associations, and puns and each subject of the group is prone to them both consciously and uncon-sciously. Furthermore, every language has its own asemantic musicality with words that sound more or less alike, regardless of their meaning. This is also part of what makes certain features of a language untranslat-able. When I switch from Portuguese to English, it is like going from *bossa nova* to jazz, from one music and beat to another, and thus while certain associations are lost (in translation) others are gained. Translators know this, especially when facing the daunting task of translating poetry.

Lalangue is also a Lacanian pun that merges "langue" and "lalla-tion" or the baby talk new parents are likely to hear when their child is approximately between the ages of one to two-and-a-half years. Lal-lation is the baby talk invented by infants before acquiring a specific language for meaningful utterances: before grammar and metaphors. Baby talk is also the infant's "trans-lallation" of *lalangue* or the most primitive and primeval form of language heard in the earliest years of the child's development.

During their development as speaking beings, the specific language of a place rains down on children. Baby talk, gibberish or lallation are unique creations with their own rhythms, cadences, intonations, sharps, and flats that allow the child to express desires and demands—from hunger to mommy or daddy's attention—to emotions—from joy to hatred, sadness to excitement.

Lacanian *lalangue* redefines the unconscious: "[…] the Unconscious is knowledge registered in *lalangue*", or "[…] knowing how to deal (*savoir-faire*) with *lalangue*". When analysts interpret, they give patients the chance to decipher the unconscious by confronting the *lalangue*-induced enigmas that affect the speaking subject.

An epiphanic trauma

Joyce tells us about the effects—which he named "epiphanies"—of this rain of language where sound prevailing over the meaning of words branded him as a writer. He would receive the words and phrases like raindrops on his head and group them together regardless of their meaning. He was aware that the sound of words had their own musicality, which he also incidentally found in poetry.

According to Lacan, *lalangue* does not belong solely to the order of language. It stems from jouissance and is the source of the enigmatic affects. As *lalangue* itself is quite an enigma and mystery, psychoanalytical interpretation should allow analysands to hear their equivocations and ambiguities because, like neurotics, the certainties and illusions that cause their pain tend to dampen their awareness and deafen their ears.

There is jouissance contained in *lalangue* with its torrential effects that leave grooves, marks, and berths in the human being. Each being is carried away and traumatised by the overwhelming sound shower of *lalangue* enigmas. The Lacanian trauma, insofar as it is the first encounter with the jouissance of *lalangue*, goes hand in hand with the Freudian sexual trauma.

On page one of *A Portrait of the Artist as a Young Man*, Joyce describes his own traumatic childhood experience with *lalangue* through the character of Stephen Dedalus as a young boy. The novel begins with his father telling him a story about a meeting of a "moocow" and a little boy named "Baby Tuckoo". Dedalus Sr turns the little word game into a song and sings: "O, the wild rose blossoms/On the little green place." This is followed by the mother's song: young Stephen hears his father's voice replaced by his mother's as she hammers away a lively hornpipe and bids him to dance: "Tralalalala/Tralalatralaladdy/Tralalalala/Tralalalala." While mother sings, the boy dances: he is a singing and dancing body. The music takes place in his body—the voice and *lalangue*, or as Lacan punningly puts it, *Lalanglaise*. This initial scene gives way to the next one where Uncle Charles and Dante clap. Young Stephen tells them when he grows up he is going to marry Eileen. Soon afterwards, he hides under the table. His mother asks him to apologise and Dante (the pious fire-and-brimstone Catholic governess of the children) threatens him: "O, if not the eagles will come and pull out his eyes." Here Stephen has his childhood epiphany as he hears the voice of the superego through Dante's fire-and-brimstone admonition: "Pull out his eyes/Apologise/Apologise/Pull out his eyes" (Joyce, 1991, p. 4).

Through the young Dedalus, we can examine Joyce's original contact with *lalangue*; the first name (Baby Tuckoo) from his father enchants the boy and storytelling quickly gives way to his mother's chant. The father's silly story is joined to the mother's chant that gets young Dedalus dancing and lets his body feel the music. But just as the fun was beginning for Young Stephen and he reveals his desire for a girl he wants to marry, the threat of danger, castration and physical punishment appear as a traumatic form of *lalangue*: the epiphany chant: "Pull out his eyes! Apologise." This example shows that both pleasure and pain, delight and horror—the twofold features of jouissance—are associated with *lalangue*. Here a classic of literature (like Sophocles and Shakespeare for Freud) provides a solid bedrock for analytical concepts.

The music of language

In his text on Joyce, Lacan redefines the symptom as an event of the body and states that this body is linked to what is sung in language: "l'on l'a, l'on l'a de l'air, l'on l'aire, de l'on l'a" (Lacan, 2001, p. 569). These are nonsensical French words from a childhood song. As Lacan puts *lalangue* on centre stage by referring directly to lallation, he included a *lalangue* tune popular among French youngsters. Joyce's "tra-la-la-la-la-la"—gibberish which means nothing—shows that Joyce as an artist and poet intuitively understood *a priori* the *lalangue* concept. *Lalangue* is composed of signifiers in the mother tongue + the music with which they are uttered and heard.

The baby's lallated language stems from the link between the mother tongue as it is spoken and the way it is heard. When we distinguish what is enunciated from its enunciation, the latter takes the form of music as it is perceived by the subject.

The unconscious as "lucubration on *lalangue*" (Lacan) is the musical unconscious. If the unconscious pre-empts the nonsense potential in the words of any language, it is because it invests in the musicality and sound effects that touch the subject as a being-towards-art and make the body a singing and dancing one. Poetic analytical interpretation, therefore, takes into account *lalangue's* musicality where the poetry of sound prevails over meaning.

If Lacan is correct in finding inspiration in Joyce as a way of dealing with *lalangue* and targeting the unconscious with the psychoanalyst's poetic interpretation, it is because as an analyst-artist, like Joyce, he too chose the sound of words over their meaning.

The series of epiphanies that inspire Dedalus to dedicate his life to art starts with a consoling verse he recites while heading to the Irish Sea: "A day of dappled seaborne clouds. The phrase, the day and the scene harmonised in a chord" (Joyce, 1991, p. 208). Asking himself if these colours account for the harmony, he soon realises that his mood is due to the stableness and balance of the words he has uttered. And that surprising realisation is his epiphany: "Did he then love the rhythmic rise and fall of words better than their associations of legend and colour?" (ibid, 1991, p. 208).

The sea waves following the balance of the words of the en-chanted poetry are like the treble clefs of *lalangue*. This is emotional and swinging melopoeia prevailing over rational and rigid logopoeia.

> He heard a confused music within him as of memories and names which he was almost conscious of but could not capture even for an instant; then the music seemed to recede, to recede, to recede: and from each receding trail of nebulous music there fell always one longdrawn calling note, piercing like a star the dusk of silence. (ibid, 1991, p. 209)

Would the analyst's interpretation be able to rise to the poetic efficacy of this star-note in the horizon of its silence?

"The paradox of the pulsing rhythm is that of making a timing be heard ..."—it is a movement in the musical sense, such as *allegro ma non troppo, agitato, adagio*, or even more aptly stated by Alain Didier-Weil, "[...] a swing whose repetitive characteristic is never experienced as a monotonous repetition" (Didier-Weill, 2007, pp. 33–34).

Fort! Da!

Musical rhythm—the procession of the notes organised accompanying silences over time—exists in *lalangue* during the child's lallation period, before acquiring standard speaking skills. A regular rhythm can be found in Freud's "*Fort!*" and "*Da!*" game as he watched his toddler grandson in the cradle playing with a wooden reel tied to a string. The baby would grab the string, fling out the spool and utter some descending "ooo" sounds, followed by silence, and then as he pulled in the reel, he would make ascending "aaa" sounds. Freud equated the German words *fort* (gone) with the baby's "ooo", and *da* (there) with "aaa". It is the hide-and-seek game in which the adult asks the baby: "Where are you?" "You found me!" Freud shows how the baby plays this game to represent the comings and goings, presence and absence of its mother. Lacan adds that it is also a symbolic act in which the game is the starting point for the child to metaphorically represent the mother and be able to separate from her, since, after all, it is just a game. For me personally, what is at stake is a creative act which entails a performance and utterances resembling musical rhythm. This baby's lallation is not aimed at communication, but rather pure jouissance—*Genuss*—which can also tragically be represented through *lalangue* as the disappearance of the Other. But as pure fun and games, the signifying opposition (ooo—aaa) sounds uncannily like the "uuh-yeah!" you hear when people are rock and rolling.

The analyst's interpretation

In light of this discussion, one important issue still remains: what should we say and how should we say it to our analysands if we want them to become the analysts of their own experience of the unconscious and find the signifiers of their *lalangue* where their dramas and symptoms are hiding. Rather than searching for or supplying meanings, analysands must focus on the associative musical chains of their utterances. And analysts must avoid persuasion or ordering their patients at any level of speech and focus rather on those features of *lalangue* that engender equivocations. Analytical interpretation finds support in *lalangue's* real unconscious that plays not only with equivocal signifiers, but also with the musicality, i.e., the rhythm and organisation of silence, sounds, pitch, intensity, inflection, and changing tone inherent in every voice. Tone tells me if a sound comes from a violin, an airplane, a thunder clap or a mother with her child. Analysts changing the tone of their voice when repeating the analysand's signifiers (the interpretation as "quoting") produce a different effect even while the enunciated remains the same. Everything partakes of enunciation, which is the equivalent of the analyst's desire.

I sound, therefore I am

Analytical interpretation performs its job not only through its text, but also through its delivery. Given the enormous possibilities of uttering, any sentence (e.g., the "Rat Man" cursing his father), it should not surprise us that Lacan boasts of his ability to convey any meaning he wants. Our way of addressing another person conveys something beyond the simple effect of the signifiers that make up the utterances.

The enunciated element varies according to the enunciative mode: interrogative, elliptical, imperative, bland, energetic, etc … Actually, any enunciation of a text is already an interpretation. In that sense, speaking is on-going performance and interpretation. We act, therefore we are. Life is a stage, we are the actors and we are living texts. We most certainly can equate analytical interpretation with a theatrical mode in which the analyst strongly resembles the actor performing a text. As analysts, we are performing the analysand's text to them. Each session is a unique and single staging just for that moment. The analytical act is an ephemeral affair. Through enunciation, pauses, intonations, and musicality of the text, analysts have much leeway for creating different meanings and even the opposite of what their utterances literally mean. The analyst's office is indeed a stage where living poetry can take place. Like the bards of old, the analyst brings poetry alive through the spoken word. The music of speech with its tone, timing, pauses, etc., are like the musician's *crescendos*, *diminuendos*, *ritardandos*, *piano* and *forte* that breathe life into the score performed on a musical instrument.

As Paul Valéry put it, "Poetry—that long hesitation between sound and sense" (Valéry, 1960, p. 636). This sound of poetry can be found in *lalangue's* music, as we find in the *Robert Dictionaire* of the French language which defines poetry as the "[…] art of language that aims at expressing or suggesting something through rhythm, harmony and image". Rhythm and harmony are integral parts of music. In 1953, Lacan said: "It is enough to listen to poetry […] for one to understand its polyphony and align all discourse as if it were written on the various staves of the musical score" (Lacan, 1966, p. 503). Likewise, the unconscious as *lalangue* knowledge is polyphonic—written by several voices that echo in speech, in thought and in the body of the speaking subject. Henri Michaux's words are also a timely reminder for us analysts: "*Je suis gong, ouate e chant neigeux: je le dis et j'en suis sûr*" (I am gong, cotton and snow songs; I said it and I am sure of it) (Michaux, 2001, p. 505). This chant sums up our humanity: musical, vibrant, percussive, gong-cotton-, wool- or silk–like. Speech is an act of musical performance that affirms the existence of beings shaped by language who breathe its air in their conscious and unconscious life.

The Real lacks a sense, but it is sound and fury. It bursts forth in the resonance and musicality of *lalangue*. There where sense vanishes, a new cogitation is revealed for the speaking being and the dancing body: I sound, therefore, I am.

NOTES

Prelude to the afternoon of an analyst

1. I will begin using mathemes in Chapter 1.2 and throughout the book where their meaning is explaining in more detail. Here $\bar{S}$ = the split subject, a = the lost object and $\lozenge$ = all the possible relations between the two.

I

1. In English, the expression has been rendered as surplus (or even left-over) jouissance which is the term I will use henceforward. Lacan bases this concept on the Marxist concept of surplus value.
2. According to Lacan, the *agalma*—that precious thing Alcibiades wanted from Socrates in Plato's *The Symposium*—is that mysterious thing/object which causes desire for an object.
3. A better pun on the word is in French (*di-amant*) or other Romance languages such as Portuguese, Spanish or Italian (*di-amante*) which is translated as "pertaining to or of the lover", the prefix "di" meaning possession and the word "amante" from its Latin root, *amoris*, or love or lover.

4. *"Le surmoi, c'est l'impératif de la jouissance—Jouis!"* (Lacan, 1972–1973, p. 10).

II

1. Translated by Gaylord E. Smith. Available at: http://smitty.home. montereybay.com/episodes.html
2. The French *étourdit* allows a pun since suffix *-dit* is the same as to the word *dit* which means utterance in French.
3. Or the place where "[…] signified and signifier are knotted together" (Lacan, 1993, p. 268).
4. The scene can be viewed at: https://www.youtube.com/watch? v=g__ANxxwKIk

III

1. *The Oxford English Dictionary* gives the following definitions: 1. An outward or token appearance. 2. A representation; a copy. 3. The barest trace.
2. The term was first coined by Russian literary critic Viktor Shklovsky (1893–1984) in "Art as Technique", in which he analyses examples of the technique in Russian literature (Tolstoy, Pushkin, Gorky, etc.) Available at: www.vahidnab.com/defam.htmdfsdfsdf
3. *O Teatro do Oprimido*, or Theatre of the Oppressed (I think the nomenclature needs no explanation) was a popular stage form in Brazil during the 1960s (military dictatorship) envisioned by Brazilian playwright and director Augusto Boal (1931–2005).
4. This statement is from The Third, a lecture Lacan gave on November 1st 1974 in Rome. As the lecture is unpublished, I have made use of the materials available at: http://www.valas.fr/Lalingua-nos-seminarios-conferencias-e-escritos-de-Jacques-Lacan-Dominique-Fingermann-e-Conrado-Ramos-Orgs.

REFERENCES

All references marked by an asterisk (*) are my own translations from the originals in French and Portuguese.

*Badiou, A. (2002). Pequeno manual de inestética. Marina Appenzeller (Trans.) São Paulo: Estação Liberdade.
*Badiou, A., & Cassin, B. (2010). *Il n'y a pas de rapport sexuel. Deux leçons sur "L'Etourdit" de Lacan.* Paris: Fayard.
Bloom, H. (1994). *The Western Canon: The Books and School of the Ages.* New York: Harcourt Brace.
*Bornheim, G. (1992). *Brecht: a estética do teatro.* Rio de Janeiro: Graal.
Brecht, B. (1961). On Chinese Acting. *Tulane Drama Review,* 6(1): 130–136.
Clausewitz, Carl von (1918). *On War.* Col. J. J. Graham (Trans.). London: Kegan.
*Didier-Weill, A., & Safouan, M. (2007). *Travailler avec Lacan.* Paris: Aubier.
*Donnet, J.-L. (1988). La psychanalyse et la Société Psychanalytique de Paris en 1988—Présentation à l'usage d'um lecteur profane. In: *Revue Française de Psychanalyse, n° III.* Paris: PUF.
*Fenichel, O. (1951). Problèmes de technique psychanalytique. In: *Revue Française de Psychanalyse.* Paris.
Freud, S. (1893–1895). *Case Histories. S. E., 02.* London: Hogarth.
Freud, S. (1900a). *The Interpretation of Dreams. S. E., 4.* London: Hogarth.

Freud, S. (1901b). *The Psychopathology of Everyday Life. S. E., 6.* London: Hogarth.
Freud, S. (1905d). *Three Essays on Sexuality. S. E., 7.* London: Hogarth.
Freud, S. (1908e [1907]). *Creative Writers and Day-dreaming. S. E., 09.* London: Hogarth.
Freud, S. (1909d). *Notes Upon a Case of Obsessional Neurosis. S. E., 10.* London: Hogarth.
Freud, S. (1912b). *The Dynamic of Transference. S. E., 12.* London: Hogarth.
Freud, S. (1913c). *On Beginning the Treatment. S. E., 12.* London: Hogarth.
Freud, S. (1913–1914). *Totem and Taboo. S. E., 13.* London: Hogarth.
Freud, S. (1914c). *On Narcissism: An Introduction. S. E., 14.* London: Hogarth.
Freud, S. (1920g). *Beyond the Pleasure Principle. S. E., 18.* London: Hogarth.
Freud, S. (1923b). *The Ego and the ID. S. E., 19.* London: Hogarth.
Freud, S. (1925h). *Negation. S. E., 19.* London: Hogarth.
Freud, S. (1927e). *On Fetishism. S. E., 21.* London: Hogarth.
Freud, S. (1930a [1929]). *Civilization and its Discontents. S. E., 21.* London: Hogarth.
Freud, S. (1937c). *Analysis Terminable and Interminable. S. E., 23.* London: Hogarth.
Freud, S. (1940a [1938]). *An Outline of Psycho-analysis. S. E., 23.* London: Hogarth.
Freud, S. (1950a [1895]). Project for a Scientific Psychology. *S. E., 1.* London: Hogarth.
*Freud, S. (1981). "Conseil aux médecins sur le tratement analytique", *La technique psychanalytique.* Paris: PUF.
*Gernet, L. (1968). *Anthropologie de la Grece Antique.* Paris: Maspero.
Halliwell, S., & Aristotle. (1998). *Aristotle's Poetics.* Chicago: University of Chicago Press.
Hawthorne, N. (1991). *The Scarlet Letter.* New York: Courage Books.
*Held, R. (1963). Rapport clinique sur les psychotherapies d'inspiration psychanalytique freudienne. In: *Revue Française de Psychanalyse.* Paris.
*Jakobson, R. (1973). La dominante. In: *Questions de poétique.* Paris: Seuil.
Joyce, J. (1991). *A Portrait of The Artist as a Young Man.* London: Everyman's Library.
Kafka, F. (1973). *The Great Wall of China and Other Works.* Malcom Pasley (Trans.). London: Penguin Books.
*Lacan, J. (1966). *Écrits.* Paris: Seuil.
*Lacan, J. (1968). La méprise du sujet supposé savoir. In: *Scilicet n. 1.* Paris: Seuil.
*Lacan, J. (1970). Radiophonie. In: *Scilicet n. 2/3.* Paris: Seuil.
*Lacan, J. (1971–1972). *Le savoir du psychanalyste.* Paris: Seuil.
*Lacan, J. (1973). *Le Séminaire 11, Les quatre concepts fondamentaux de la psychoanalyse* (1964). Paris: Seuil.

*Lacan, J. (1975a). *Le Séminaire 1, Les ecrits techniques de Freud* (1953–1954). Paris: Seuil.

*Lacan, J. (1975b). *Le Séminaire 20, Encore* (1972–1973). Paris: Seuil.

*Lacan, J. (1976). Conférences et entretiens dans les universités nord-américanes. In: *Scilicet n. 6/7*. Paris: Seuil.

*Lacan, J. (1977). *Ouverture de la section clinique, ornicar? nº 9*. Paris: Lyse.

*Lacan, J. (1981). *Le Séminaire 3, Les psychoses* (1955–1956). Paris: Seuil.

*Lacan, J. (1984). Comptes rendus d'enseignements—l'Acte psychanalytique. In: *Ornicar? nº 29*. Paris: Navarin.

*Lacan, J. (1991a). *Le Séminaire 8, Le transfer* (1960–1961). Paris: Seuil.

*Lacan, J. (1991b). *Le Séminaire 17, L'envers de la psychoanalyse* (1969–1970). Paris: Seuil.

Lacan, J. (1993). *The Seminar, Book 3. The Psychoses* (1955–1956). Russell Grigg (Trans.). London: Routledge.

*Lacan, J. (2001). *Autres écrits*. Paris: Seuil.

*Lacan, J. (2006). *Le Séminaire 16, D'un Autre à l'autre* (1968–1969). Paris: Seuil.

*Lacan, J. (2011). *Le Séminaire 19, … ou pire* (1971–1972). Paris: Seuil.

*Letarte, P. (1989) *Voir ou ne pas voir … De la diversité des techniques de l'analyste dans l'entretien individual*. Comunicação prévia para o Congresso dos Psicanalistas de Língua Francesa dos Países Românicos. Paris.

*Lévi-Strauss, C. (1958/1974). Le sorcier et sa magie. In: *Anthropologie Structurale*. Paris: Plon.

*Marx, K. (1969). *Le Capital, livro I*. Paris: Garnier/Flammarion.

*Marx, K. (1984). Le Capital. In: *Argent et psychanalyse*. Pierre Martin. Navarin.

*Michaux, H. (2001). Mes Propriétés. *Œuvres complètes, I*. Paris: Gallimard.

*Naveau, P. (1988). Marx e o sinthoma. In *Falo n. 3*. Salvador: Revista Brasileira do Campo Freudiano.

Plato (1951). *The Symposium*. Walter Hamilton (Trans.). London: Penguin Books.

Quinet, A. (1991). *As 4+1 Condições de Análise*. Rio de Janeiro: Jorge Zahar Editor.

Quinet, A. (2003). *Le plus de regard*. Paris: Editions du Champ Lacanien.

*Regnault, F. (2001). *Em torno do vazio: a arte à luz da psicanálise*. Rio de Janeiro: Contra Capa.

Ribson (1600). *Great Dictionary of Precious* or *The Key Language of the Streets*.

Soros, G. (1998). *The Crisis of Global Capitalism: Open Society Endangered*. New York: PublicAffairs.

Suzuki, D. T. (1949). *The Zen Doctrine of Non-mind*. London: Buddhist Society.

*Valéry, P. (1960). Rhumbs. *Œuvres complètes, II*. Paris: Gallimard.

Watts, A. (1994). *The Spirit of Zen*. New York: Grove Press.

INDEX

For Product Safety Concerns and Information please contact our EU
representative GPSR@taylorandfrancis.com
Taylor & Francis Verlag GmbH, Kaufingerstraße 24, 80331 München, Germany